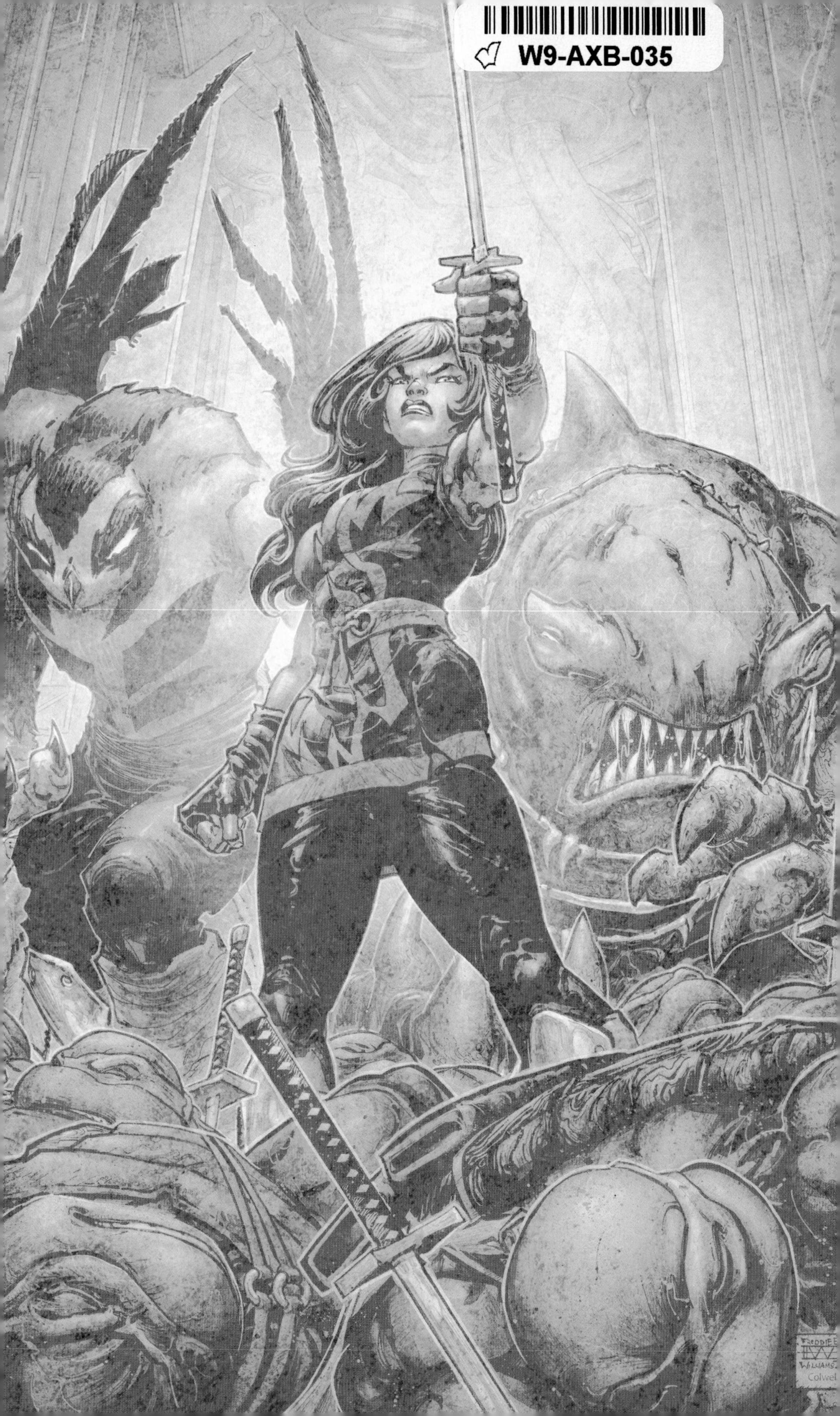

Facebook: **facebook.com/idwpublishing**
Twitter: **@idwpublishing**
YouTube: **youtube.com/idwpublishing**
Tumblr: **tumblr.idwpublishing.com**
Instagram: **instagram.com/idwpublishing**

COVER ART BY
SOPHIE CAMPBELL

COLLECTION EDITS BY
JUSTIN EISINGER
AND ALONZO SIMON

COLLECTION DESIGN BY
JEFF POWELL

PUBLISHER
TED ADAMS

ISBN: 978-1-63140-146-5   21 20 19 18   1 2 3 4

Originally published as TEENAGE MUTANT NINJA TURTLES UNIVERSE issues #11–15.

Ted Adams, CEO & Publisher
Greg Goldstein, President & COO
Robbie Robbins, EVP/Sr. Graphic Artist
Chris Ryall, Chief Creative Officer
David Hedgecock, Editor-in-Chief
Laurie Windrow, Senior VP of Sales & Marketing
Matthew Ruzicka, CPA, Chief Financial Officer
Lorelei Bunjes, VP of Digital Services
Jerry Bennington, VP of New Product Development

Special thanks to Joan Hilty & Linda Lee for their invaluable assistance.

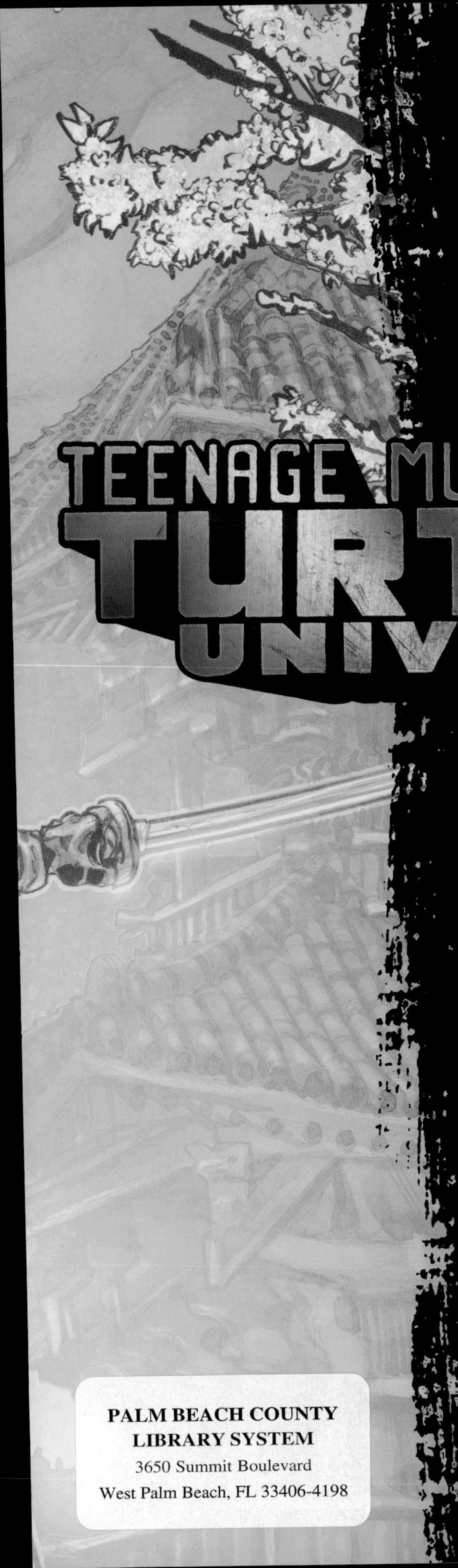

TEENAGE MUTANT NINJA TURTLES UNIVERSE

THE JERSEY DEVIL

WRITTEN BY **RICH DOUEK**
ART BY **AARON CONLEY**
COLORS BY **TRIONA FARRELL**

KARAI'S PATH

WRITTEN BY **ERIK BURNHAM**
WITH **SOPHIE CAMPBELL**
ART BY **SOPHIE CAMPBELL**
COLORS BY **BRITTANY PEER**

PREY

STORY, ART, & LETTERS BY
SOPHIE CAMPBELL

LETTERS BY **SHAWN LEE**
SERIES EDITS BY **BOBBY CURNOW**

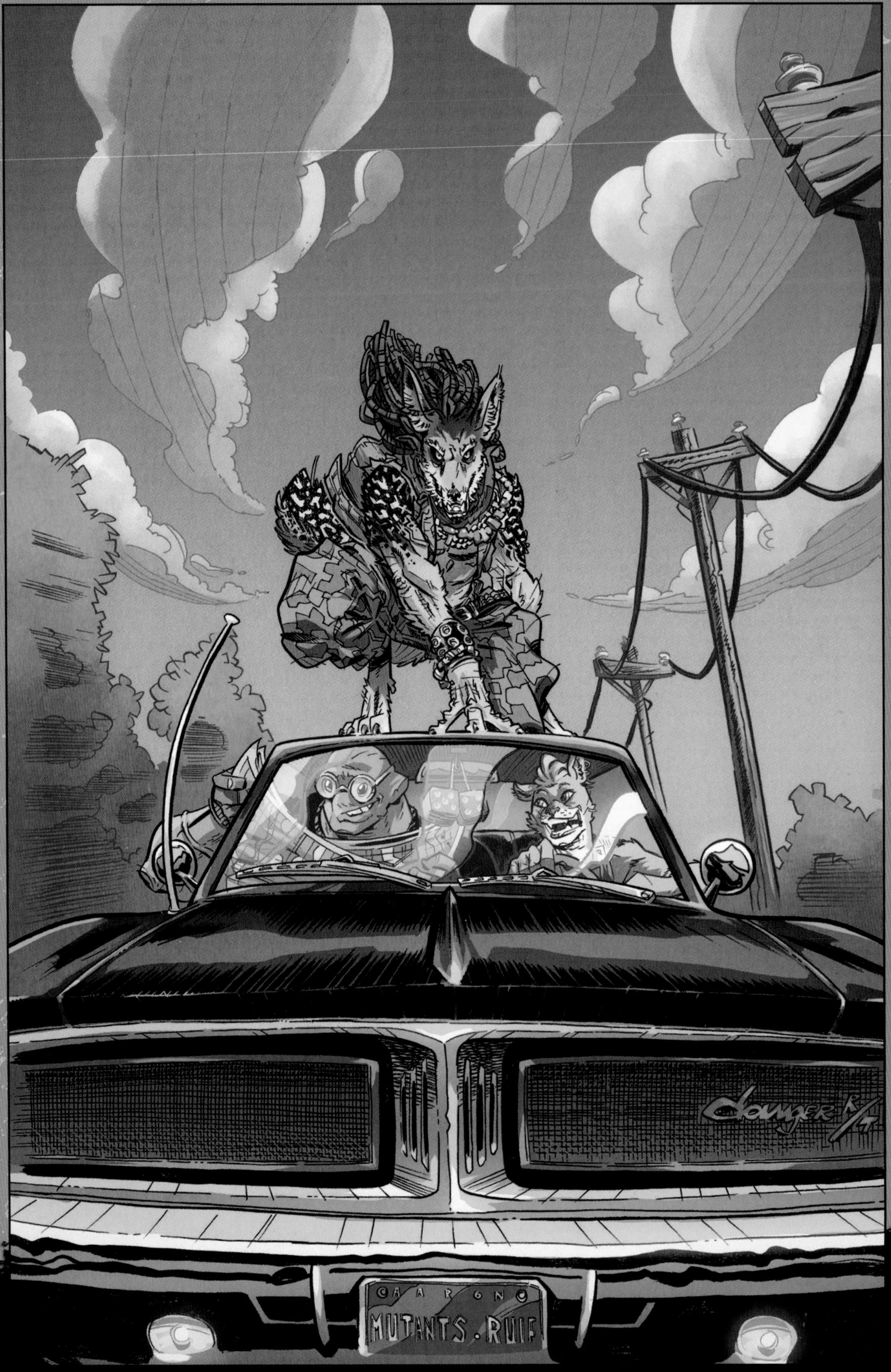

ART BY **AARON CONLEY**
COLORS BY **JEAN-FRANCOIS BEAULIEU**

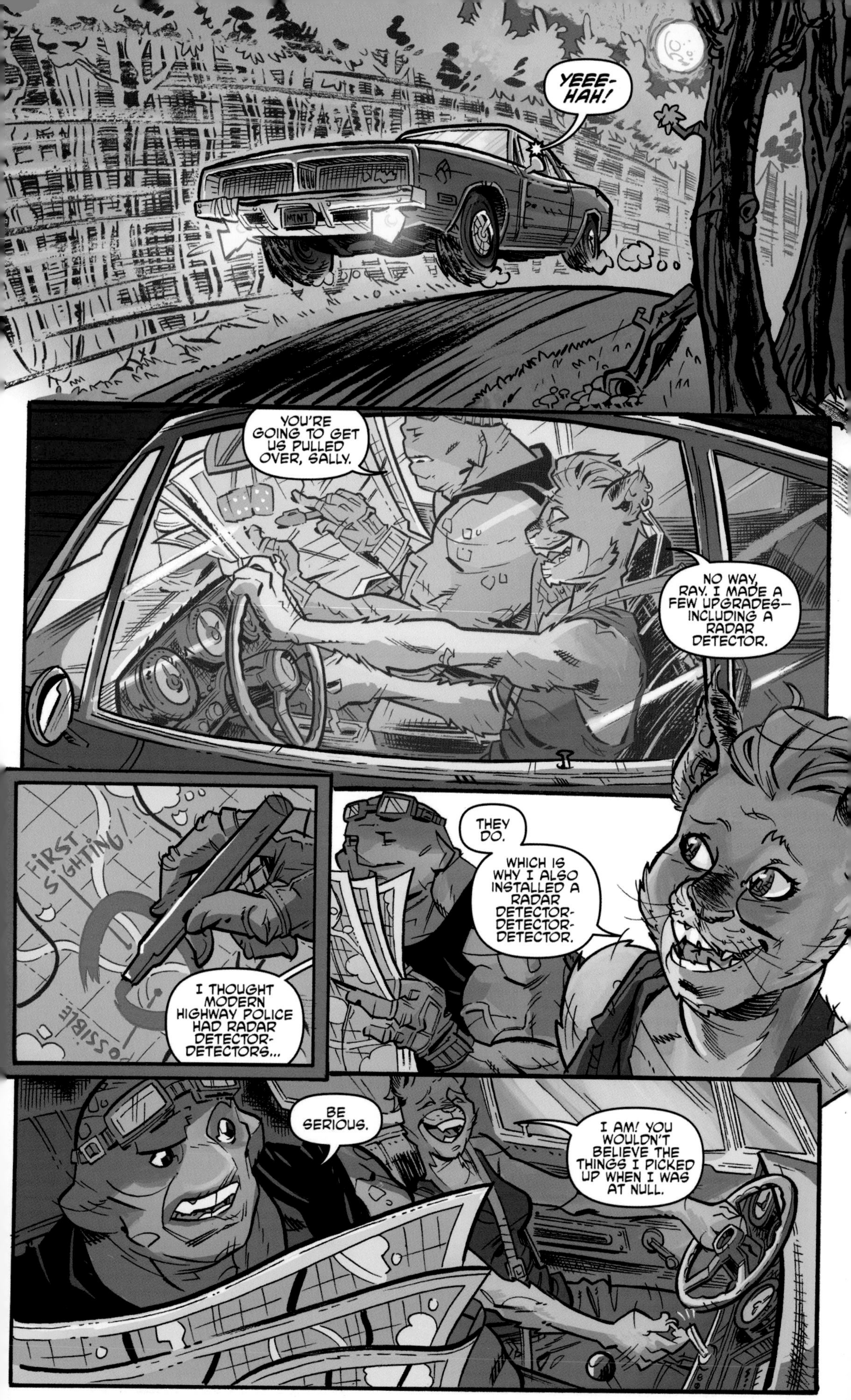
YEEE-HAH!
MTNT
YOU'RE GOING TO GET US PULLED OVER, SALLY.
NO WAY, RAY. I MADE A FEW UPGRADES— INCLUDING A RADAR DETECTOR.
FIRST SIGHTING!
POSSIBLE
I THOUGHT MODERN HIGHWAY POLICE HAD RADAR DETECTOR-DETECTORS...
THEY DO.
WHICH IS WHY I ALSO INSTALLED A RADAR DETECTOR-DETECTOR-DETECTOR.
BE SERIOUS.
I AM! YOU WOULDN'T BELIEVE THE THINGS I PICKED UP WHEN I WAS AT NULL.

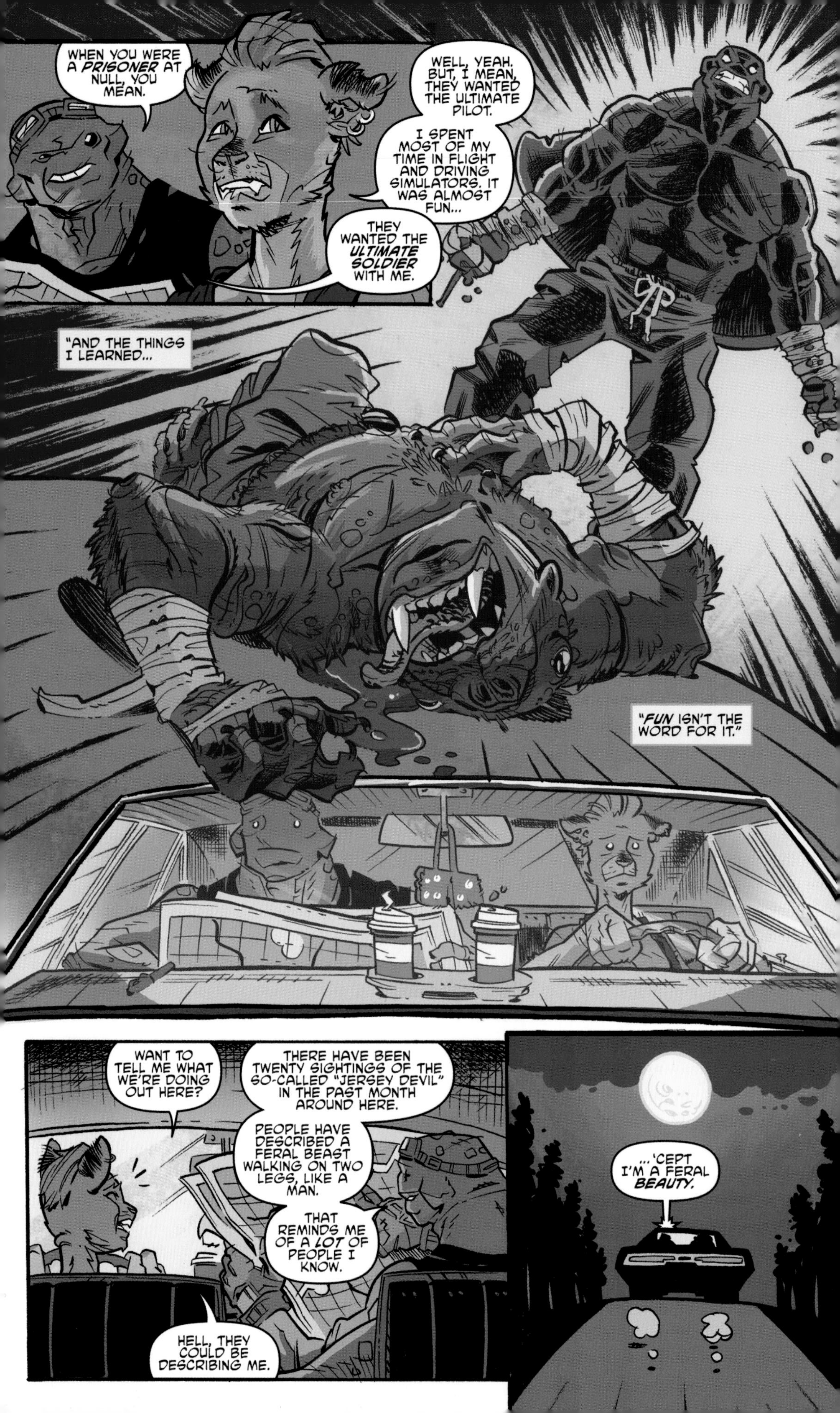
WHEN YOU WERE A PRISONER AT NULL, YOU MEAN.
WELL, YEAH. BUT, I MEAN, THEY WANTED THE ULTIMATE PILOT.
I SPENT MOST OF MY TIME IN FLIGHT AND DRIVING SIMULATORS. IT WAS ALMOST FUN...
THEY WANTED THE ULTIMATE SOLDIER WITH ME.
"AND THE THINGS I LEARNED...
"FUN ISN'T THE WORD FOR IT."
WANT TO TELL ME WHAT WE'RE DOING OUT HERE?
THERE HAVE BEEN TWENTY SIGHTINGS OF THE SO-CALLED "JERSEY DEVIL" IN THE PAST MONTH AROUND HERE.
PEOPLE HAVE DESCRIBED A FERAL BEAST WALKING ON TWO LEGS, LIKE A MAN.
THAT REMINDS ME OF A LOT OF PEOPLE I KNOW.
HELL, THEY COULD BE DESCRIBING ME.
...'CEPT I'M A FERAL BEAUTY.

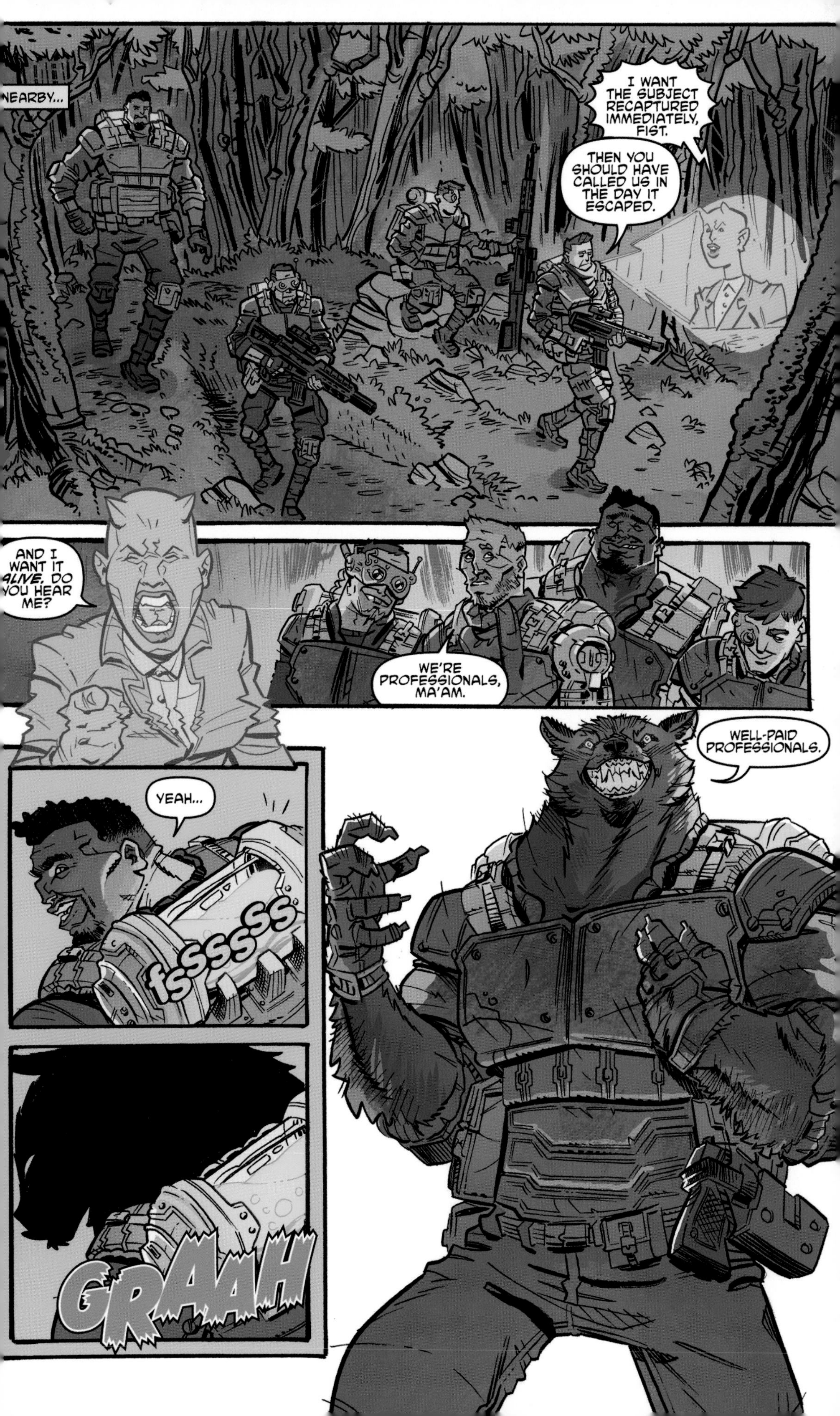
NEARBY...
I WANT THE SUBJECT RECAPTURED IMMEDIATELY, FIST.
THEN YOU SHOULD HAVE CALLED US IN THE DAY IT ESCAPED.
AND I WANT IT ALIVE. DO YOU HEAR ME?
WE'RE PROFESSIONALS, MA'AM.
WELL-PAID PROFESSIONALS.
YEAH...
fsSSSSS
GRAAH

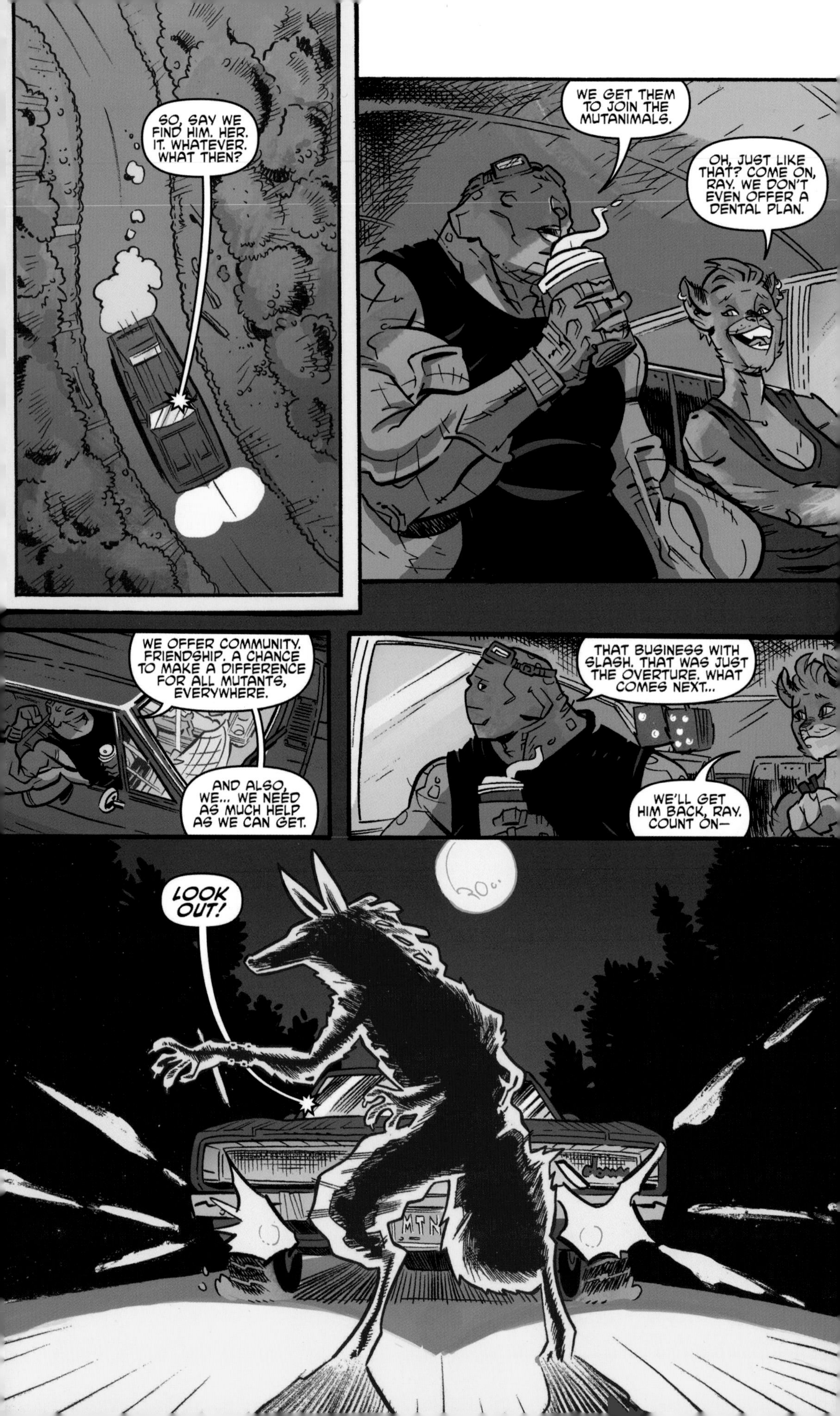
SO, SAY WE FIND HIM. HER. IT. WHATEVER. WHAT THEN?
WE GET THEM TO JOIN THE MUTANIMALS.
OH, JUST LIKE THAT? COME ON, RAY. WE DON'T EVEN OFFER A DENTAL PLAN.
WE OFFER COMMUNITY. FRIENDSHIP. A CHANCE TO MAKE A DIFFERENCE FOR ALL MUTANTS, EVERYWHERE.
AND ALSO, WE... WE NEED AS MUCH HELP AS WE CAN GET.
THAT BUSINESS WITH SLASH. THAT WAS JUST THE OVERTURE. WHAT COMES NEXT...
WE'LL GET HIM BACK, RAY. COUNT ON—
LOOK OUT!
MTN

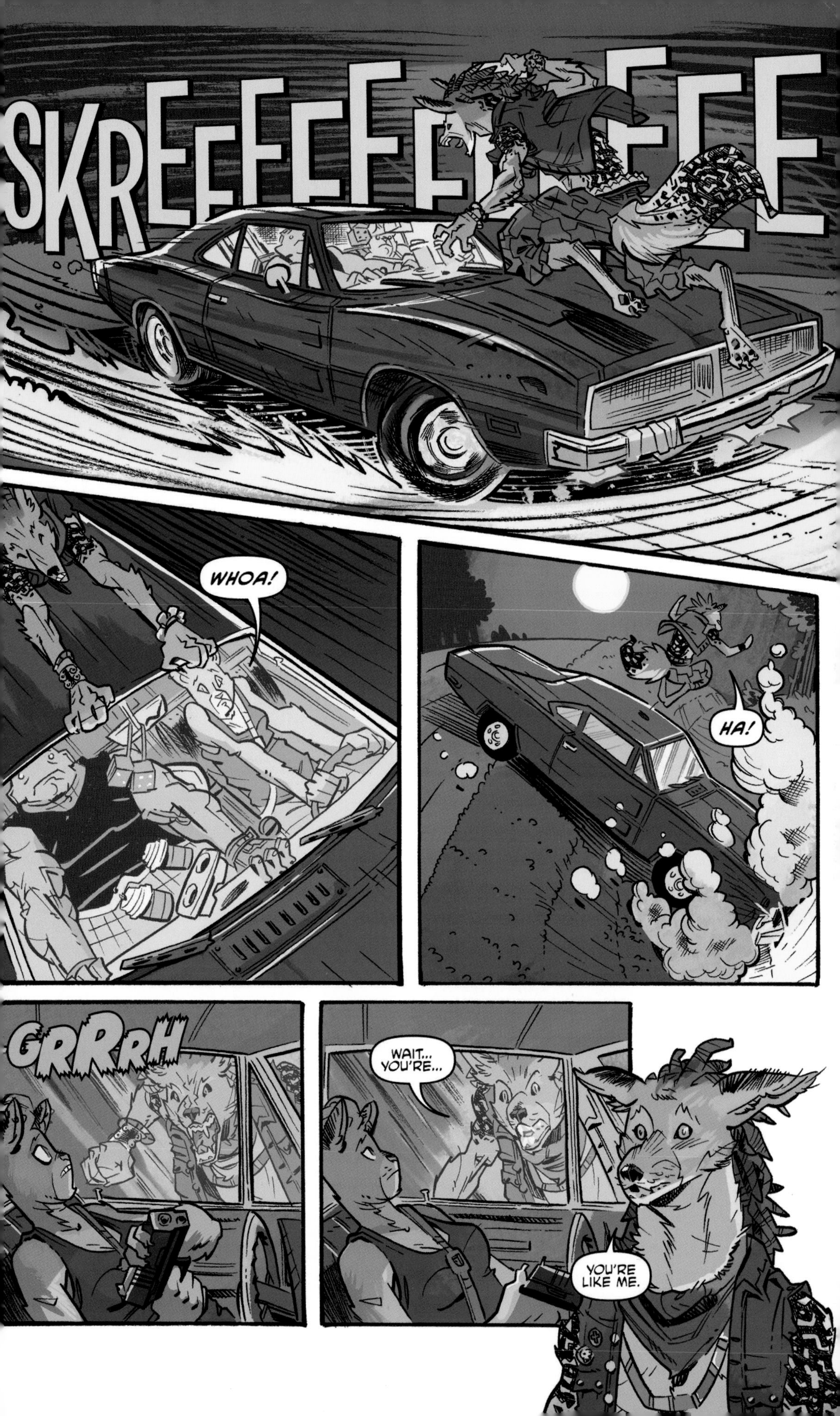
SKREEEEEEEEE
WHOA!
HA!
GRRRH
WAIT... YOU'RE...
YOU'RE LIKE ME.

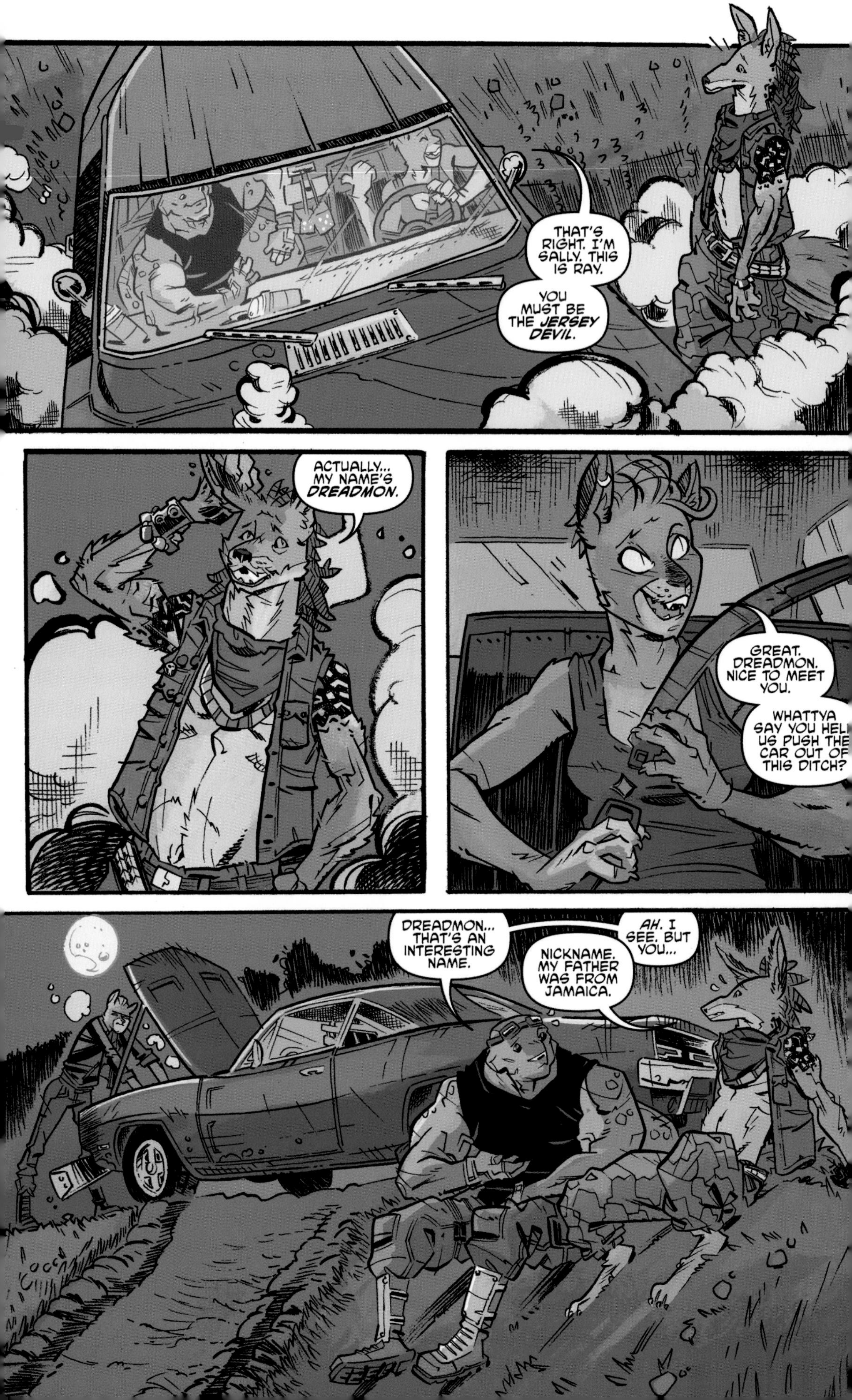
THAT'S RIGHT. I'M SALLY. THIS IS RAY.
YOU MUST BE THE *JERSEY DEVIL*.
ACTUALLY... MY NAME'S *DREADMON*.
GREAT. DREADMON. NICE TO MEET YOU.
WHATTYA SAY YOU HEL US PUSH THE CAR OUT OF THIS DITCH?
DREADMON... THAT'S AN INTERESTING NAME.
NICKNAME. MY FATHER WAS FROM JAMAICA.
AH. I SEE. BUT YOU...

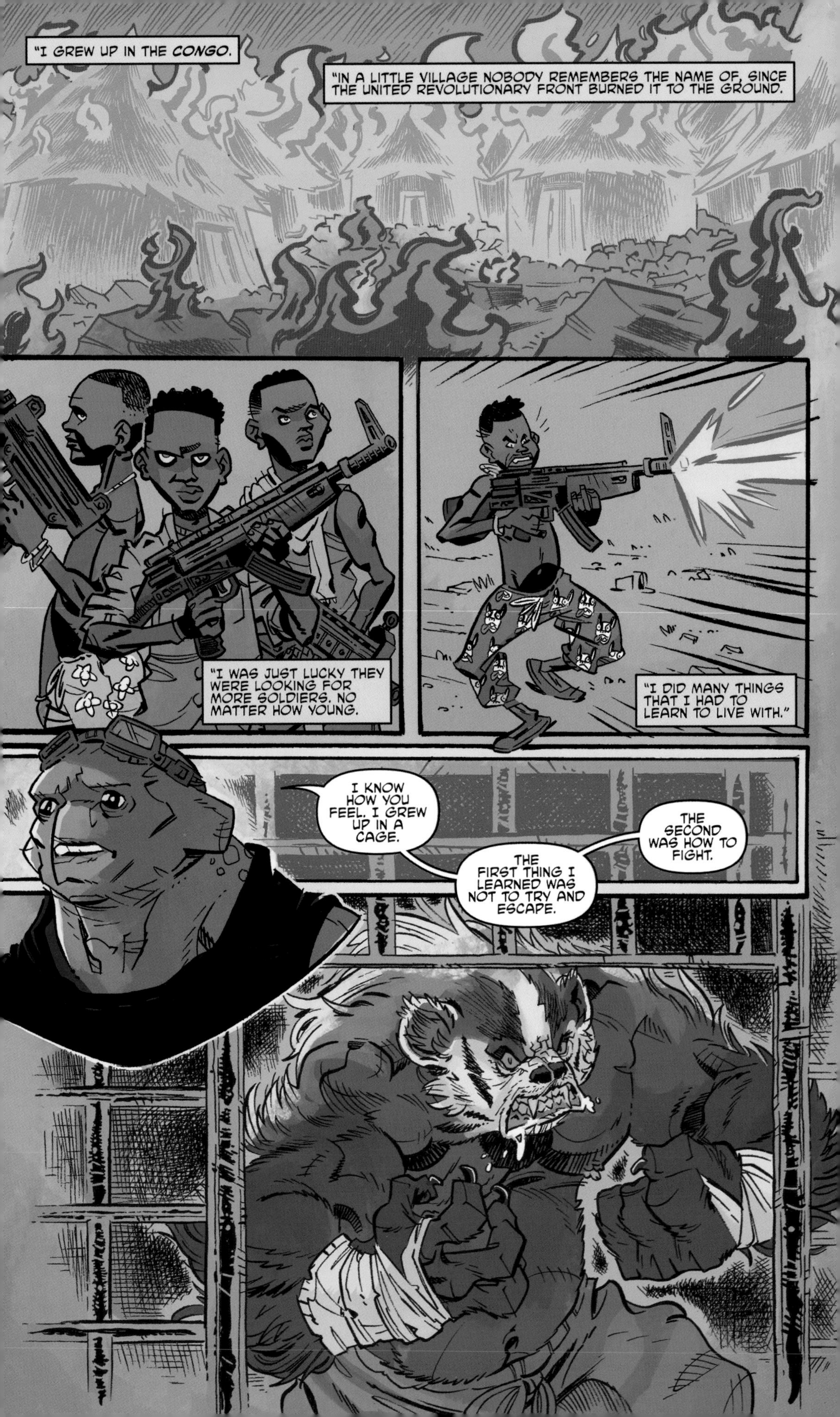
"I GREW UP IN THE CONGO.
"IN A LITTLE VILLAGE NOBODY REMEMBERS THE NAME OF, SINCE THE UNITED REVOLUTIONARY FRONT BURNED IT TO THE GROUND.
"I WAS JUST LUCKY THEY WERE LOOKING FOR MORE SOLDIERS. NO MATTER HOW YOUNG.
"I DID MANY THINGS THAT I HAD TO LEARN TO LIVE WITH."
I KNOW HOW YOU FEEL. I GREW UP IN A CAGE.
THE FIRST THING I LEARNED WAS NOT TO TRY AND ESCAPE.
THE SECOND WAS HOW TO FIGHT.

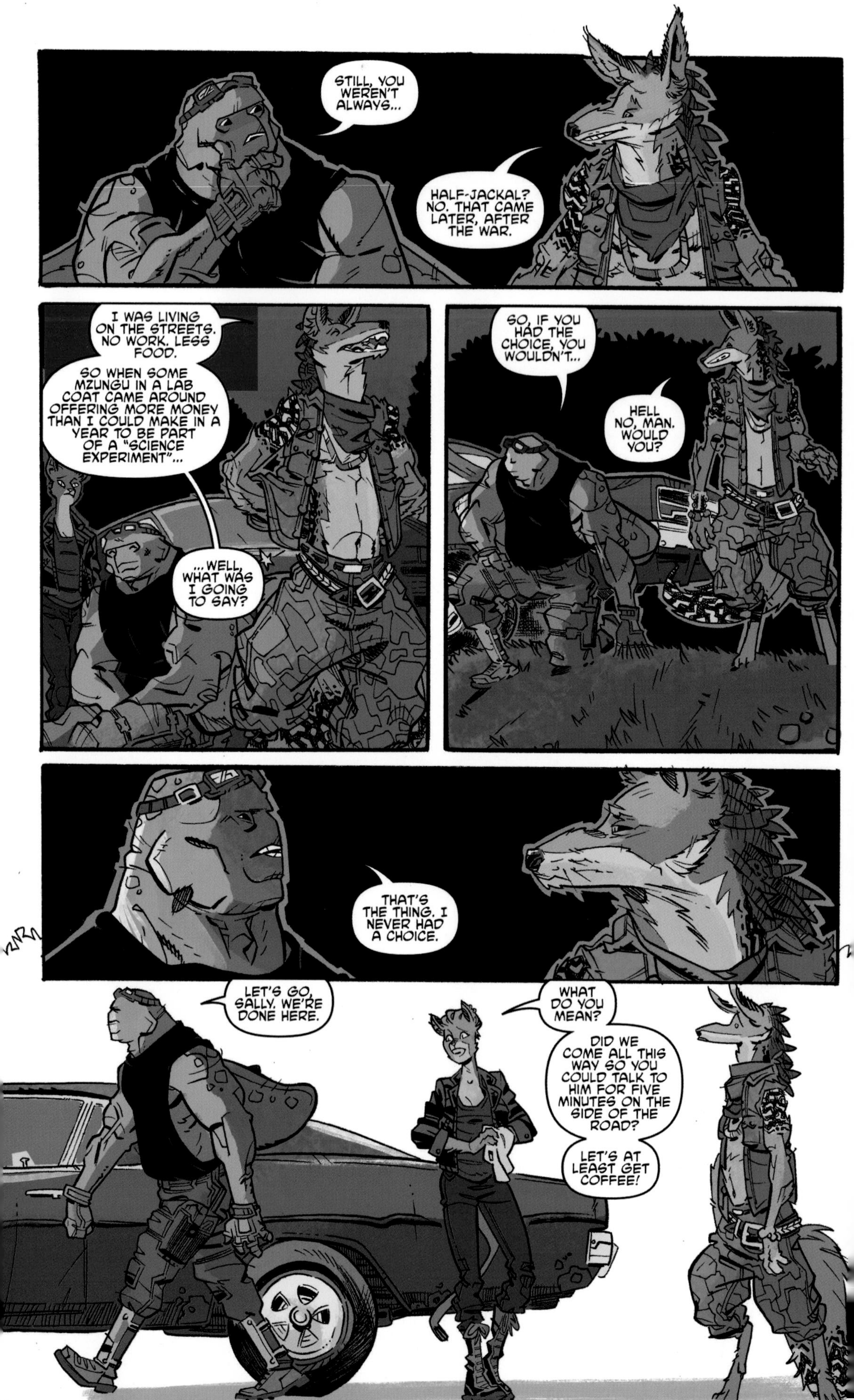
STILL, YOU WEREN'T ALWAYS...
HALF-JACKAL? NO. THAT CAME LATER, AFTER THE WAR.
I WAS LIVING ON THE STREETS. NO WORK. LESS FOOD.
SO WHEN SOME MZUNGU IN A LAB COAT CAME AROUND OFFERING MORE MONEY THAN I COULD MAKE IN A YEAR TO BE PART OF A "SCIENCE EXPERIMENT"...
...WELL, WHAT WAS I GOING TO SAY?
SO, IF YOU HAD THE CHOICE, YOU WOULDN'T...
HELL NO, MAN. WOULD YOU?
THAT'S THE THING. I NEVER HAD A CHOICE.
LET'S GO, SALLY. WE'RE DONE HERE.
WHAT DO YOU MEAN?
DID WE COME ALL THIS WAY SO YOU COULD TALK TO HIM FOR FIVE MINUTES ON THE SIDE OF THE ROAD?
LET'S AT LEAST GET COFFEE!

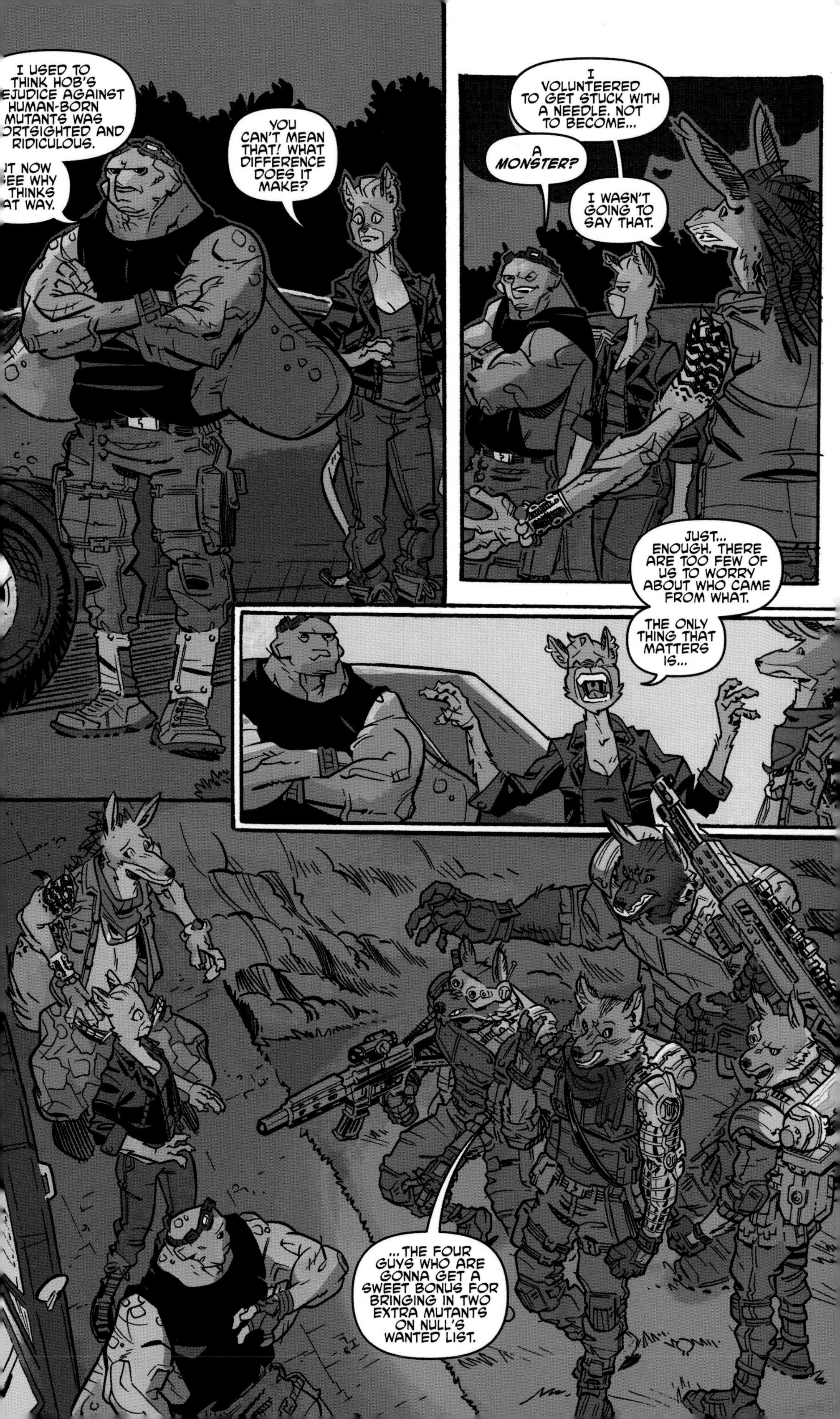
I USED TO THINK HOB'S EJUDICE AGAINST HUMAN-BORN MUTANTS WAS ORTSIGHTED AND RIDICULOUS.
IT NOW EE WHY THINKS AT WAY.
YOU CAN'T MEAN THAT! WHAT DIFFERENCE DOES IT MAKE?
I VOLUNTEERED TO GET STUCK WITH A NEEDLE. NOT TO BECOME...
A *MONSTER?*
I WASN'T GOING TO SAY THAT.
JUST... ENOUGH. THERE ARE TOO FEW OF US TO WORRY ABOUT WHO CAME FROM WHAT.
THE ONLY THING THAT MATTERS IS...
...THE FOUR GUYS WHO ARE GONNA GET A SWEET BONUS FOR BRINGING IN TWO EXTRA MUTANTS ON NULL'S WANTED LIST.

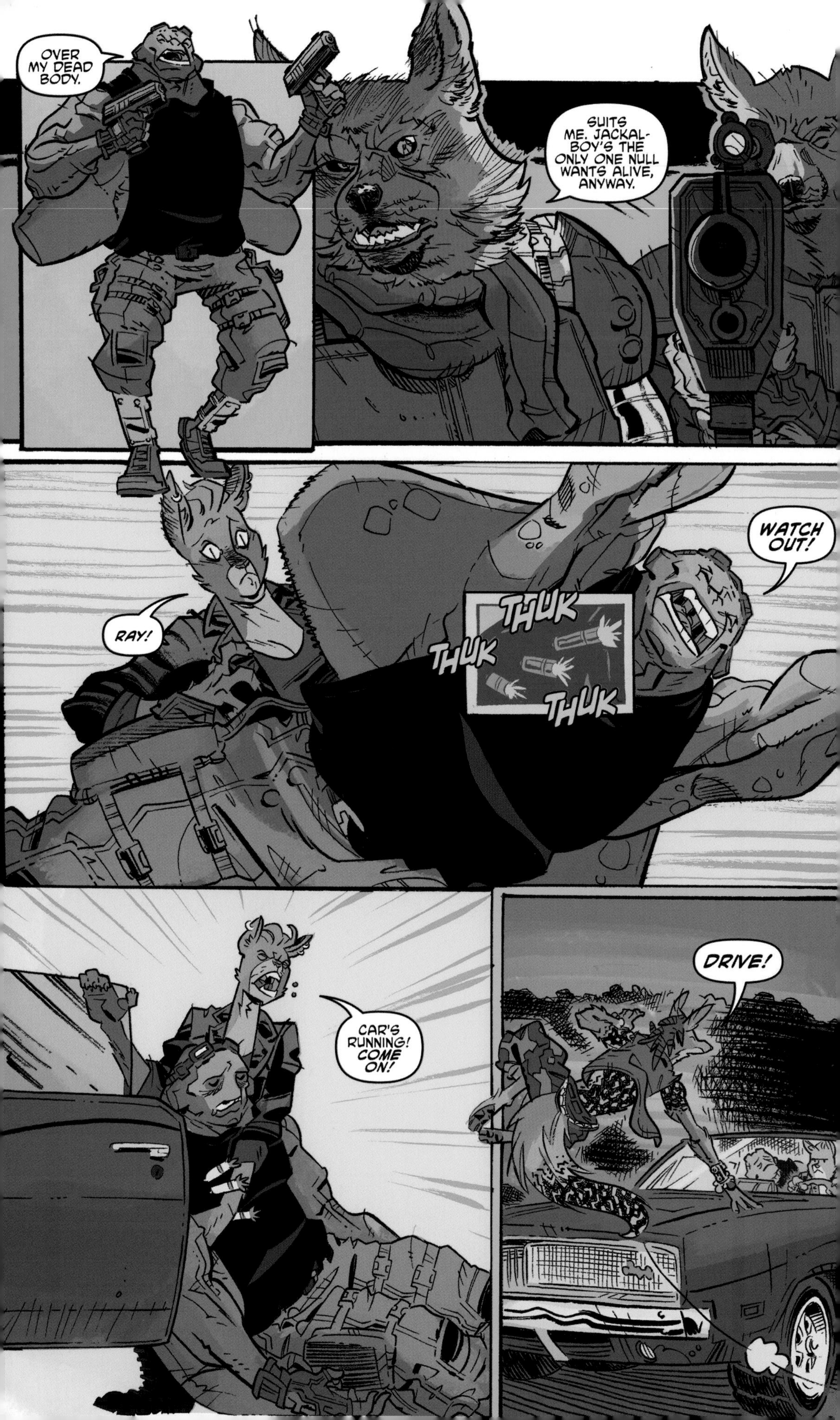
OVER MY DEAD BODY.
SUITS ME. JACKAL-BOY'S THE ONLY ONE NULL WANTS ALIVE, ANYWAY.
WATCH OUT!
RAY!
THUK
THUK
THUK
CAR'S RUNNING! COME ON!
DRIVE!

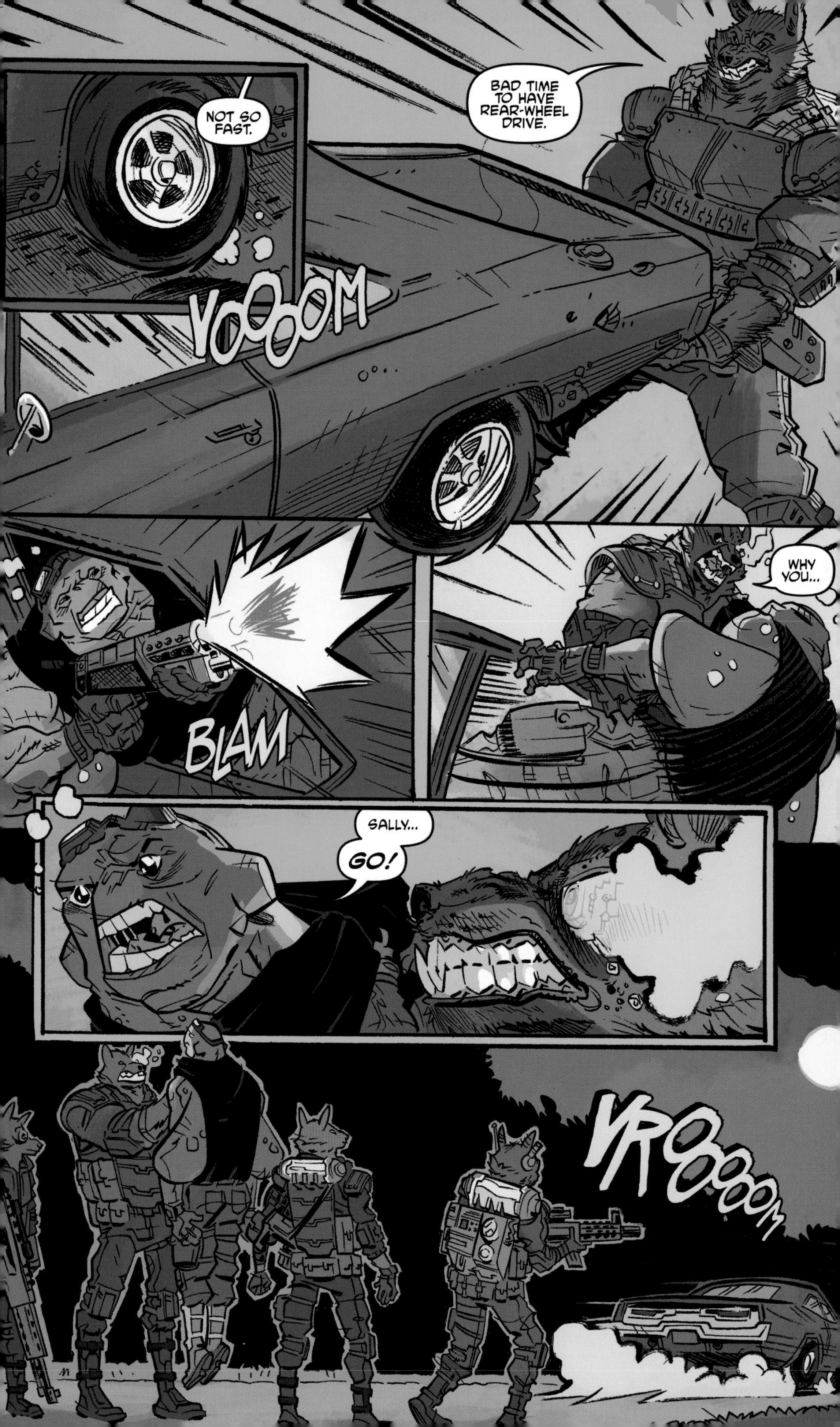
NOT SO FAST.
BAD TIME TO HAVE REAR-WHEEL DRIVE.
VOOOOOM
BLAM
WHY YOU...
SALLY...
GO!
VROOOOOOM

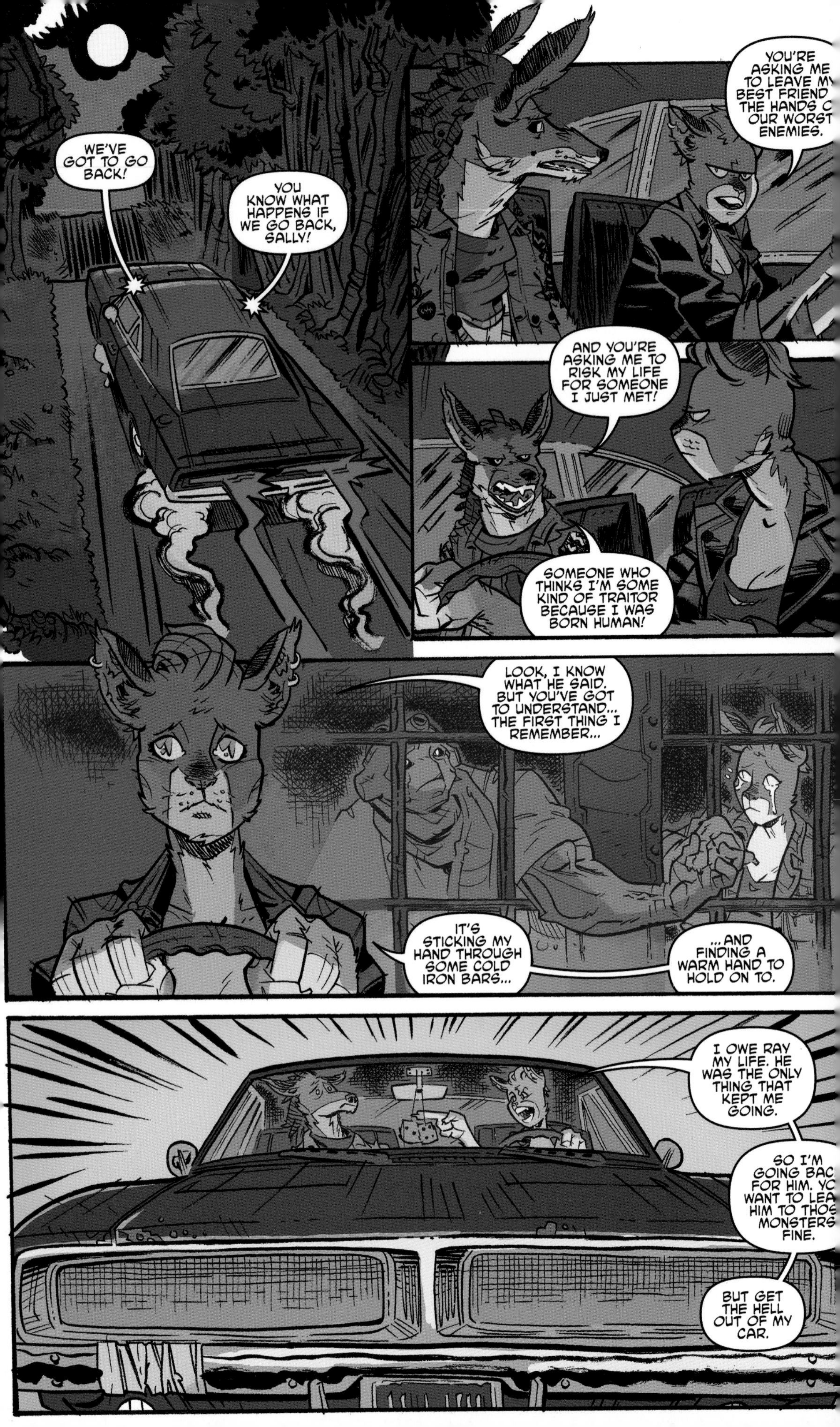
WE'VE GOT TO GO BACK!
YOU KNOW WHAT HAPPENS IF WE GO BACK, SALLY!
YOU'RE ASKING ME TO LEAVE MY BEST FRIEND THE HANDS O OUR WORST ENEMIES.
AND YOU'RE ASKING ME TO RISK MY LIFE FOR SOMEONE I JUST MET!
SOMEONE WHO THINKS I'M SOME KIND OF TRAITOR BECAUSE I WAS BORN HUMAN!
LOOK, I KNOW WHAT HE SAID. BUT YOU'VE GOT TO UNDERSTAND... THE FIRST THING I REMEMBER...
IT'S STICKING MY HAND THROUGH SOME COLD IRON BARS...
...AND FINDING A WARM HAND TO HOLD ON TO.
I OWE RAY MY LIFE. HE WAS THE ONLY THING THAT KEPT ME GOING.
SO I'M GOING BAC FOR HIM. YO WANT TO LEA HIM TO THOS MONSTERS FINE.
BUT GET THE HELL OUT OF MY CAR.

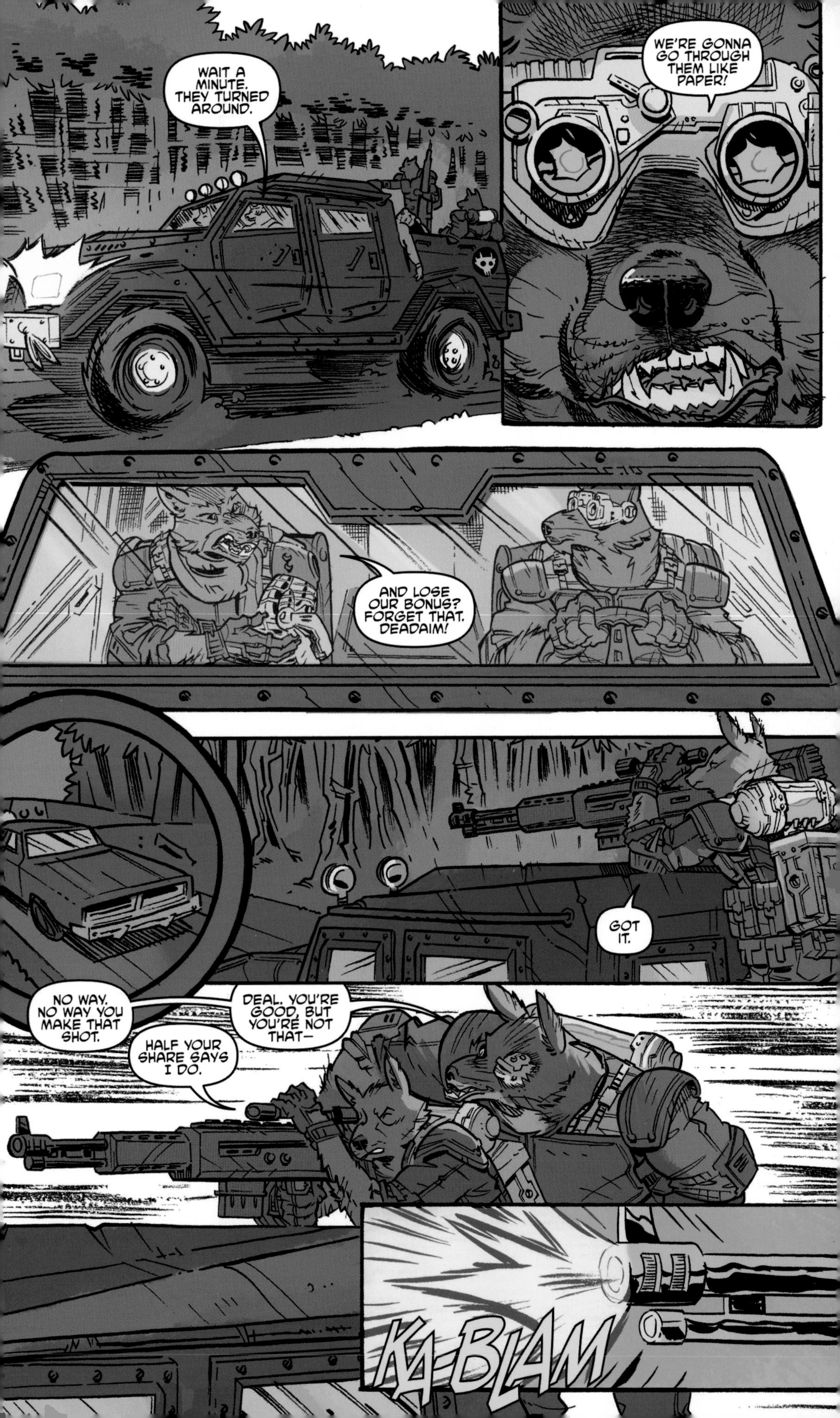
WAIT A MINUTE. THEY TURNED AROUND.
WE'RE GONNA GO THROUGH THEM LIKE PAPER!
AND LOSE OUR BONUS? FORGET THAT. DEADAIM!
GOT IT.
NO WAY. NO WAY YOU MAKE THAT SHOT.
HALF YOUR SHARE SAYS I DO.
DEAL. YOU'RE GOOD, BUT YOU'RE NOT THAT–
KA-BLAM

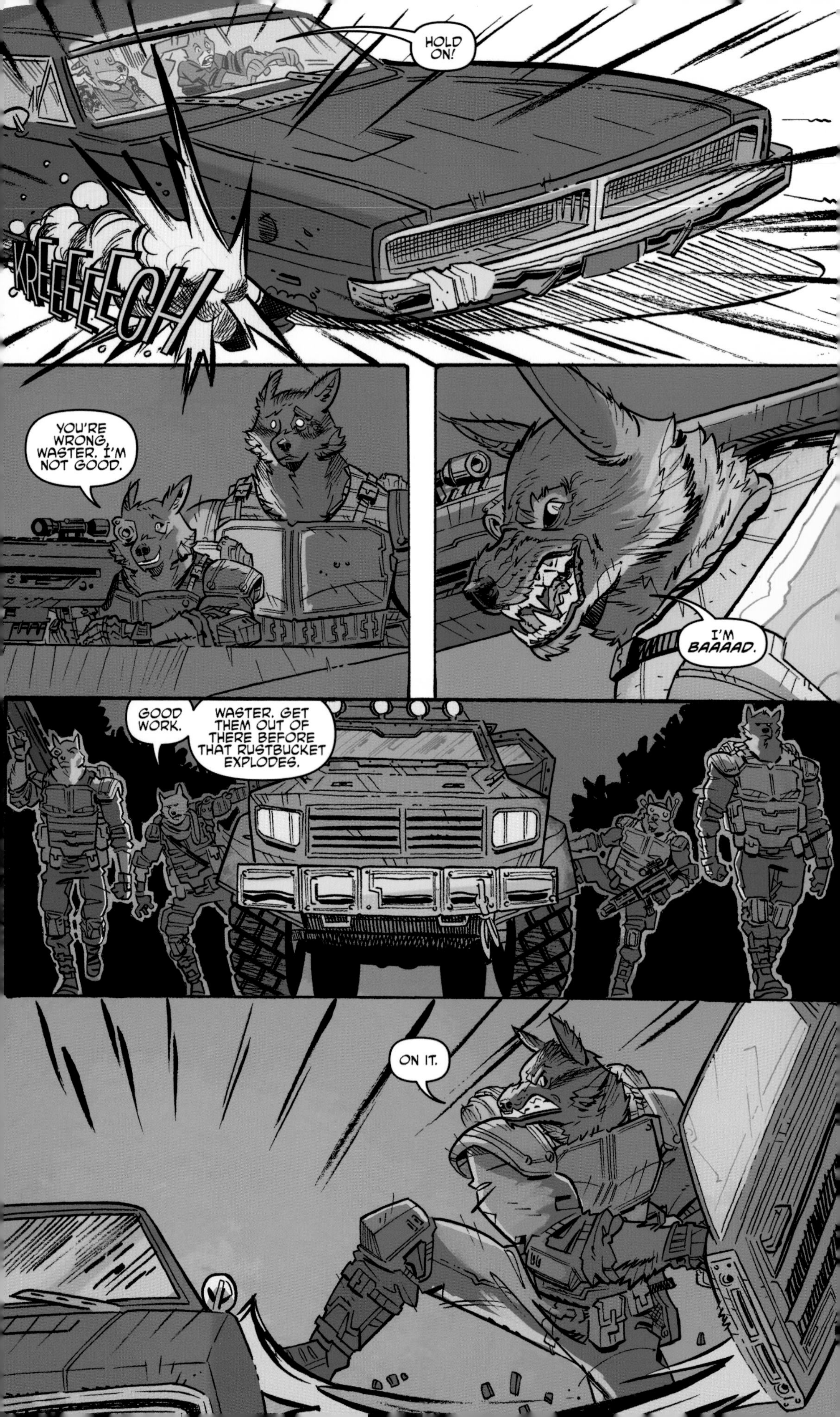
HOLD ON!
KREEEEEECH
YOU'RE WRONG, WASTER. I'M NOT GOOD.
I'M BAAAAD.
GOOD WORK.
WASTER. GET THEM OUT OF THERE BEFORE THAT RUSTBUCKET EXPLODES.
ON IT.

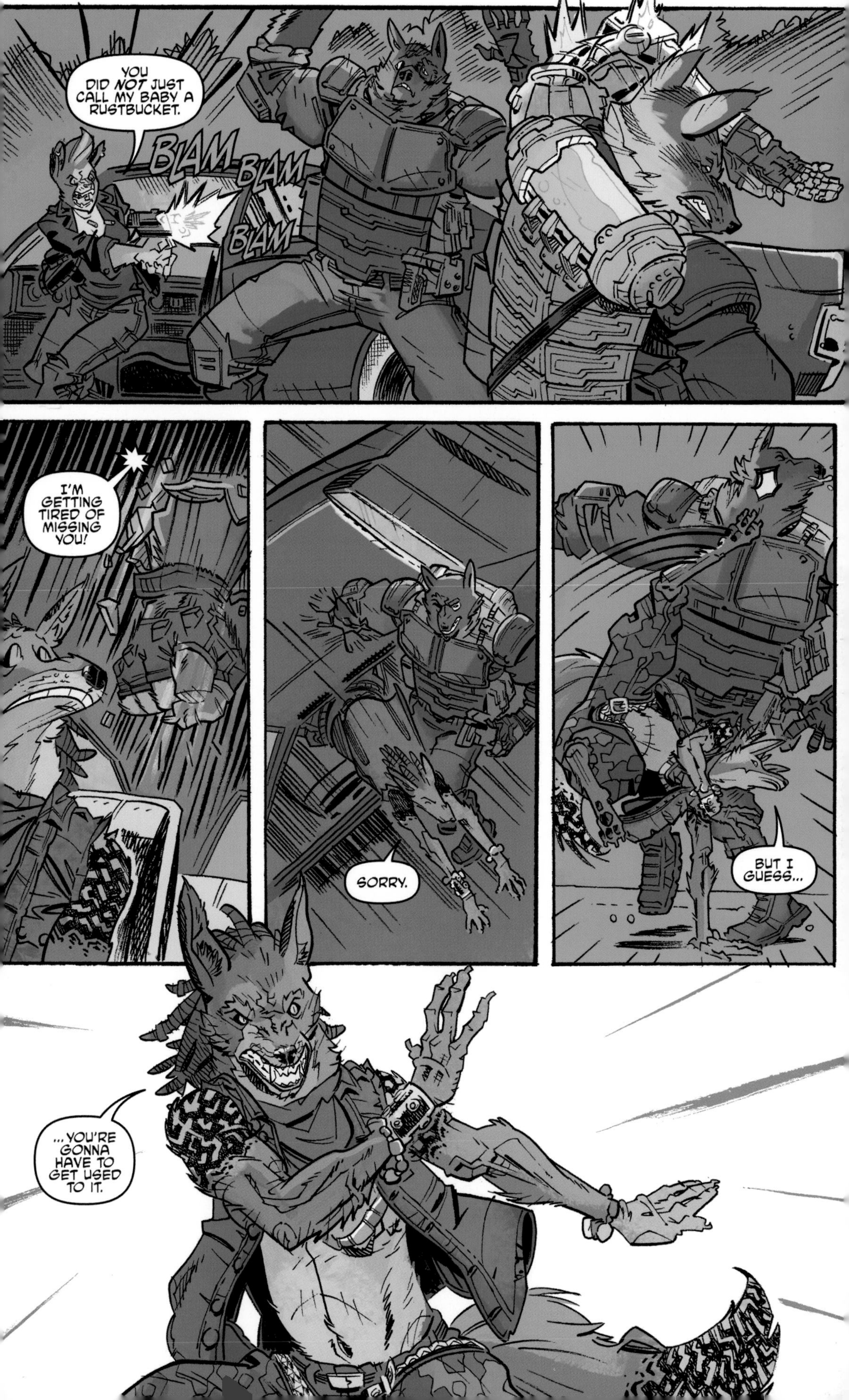
YOU DID NOT JUST CALL MY BABY A RUSTBUCKET.
BLAM
BLAM
BLAM
I'M GETTING TIRED OF MISSING YOU!
SORRY.
BUT I GUESS...
...YOU'RE GONNA HAVE TO GET USED TO IT.

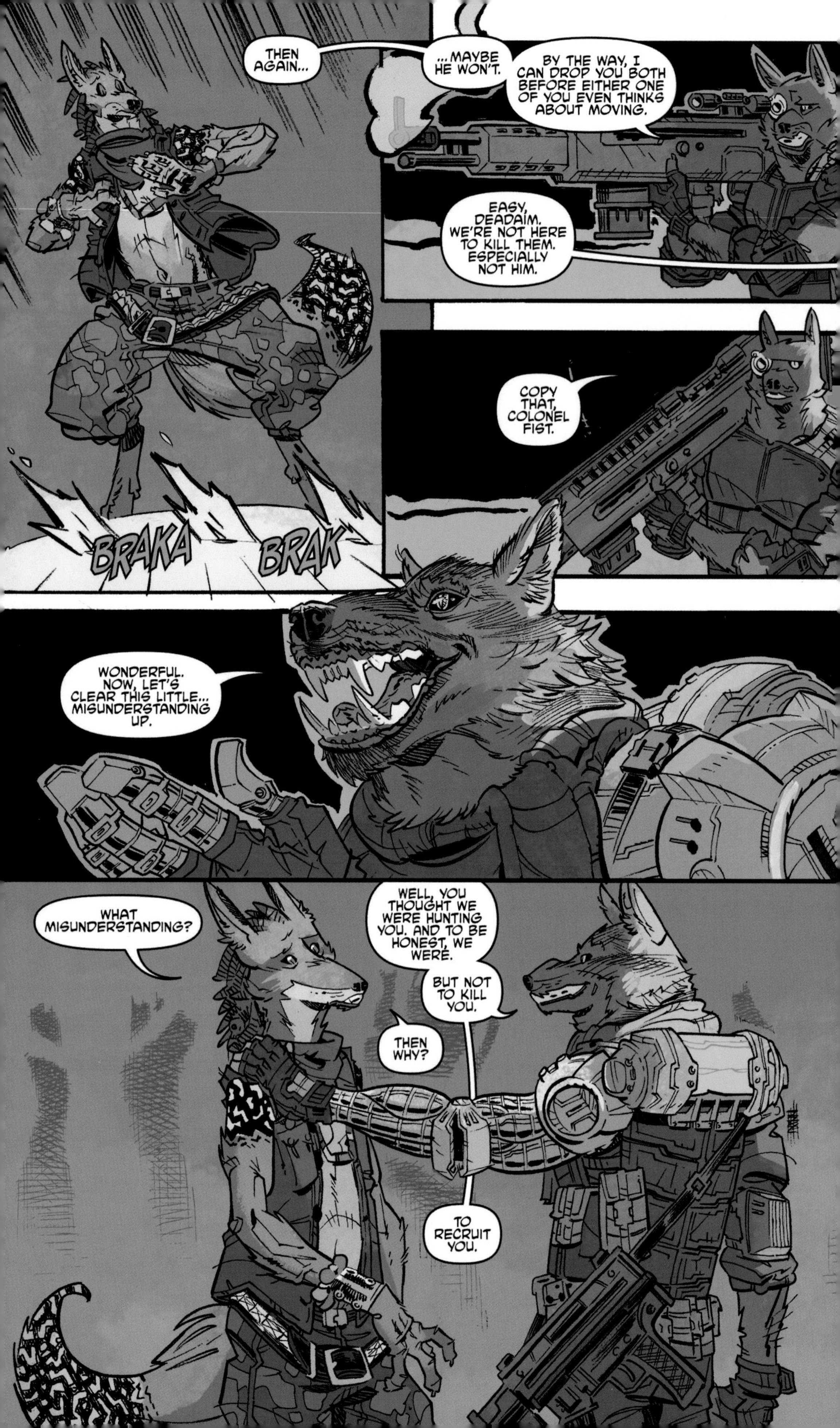
THEN AGAIN...
...MAYBE HE WON'T.
BY THE WAY, I CAN DROP YOU BOTH BEFORE EITHER ONE OF YOU EVEN THINKS ABOUT MOVING.
EASY, DEADAIM. WE'RE NOT HERE TO KILL THEM. ESPECIALLY NOT HIM.
BRAKA BRAK
COPY THAT, COLONEL FIST.
WONDERFUL. NOW, LET'S CLEAR THIS LITTLE... MISUNDERSTANDING UP.
WHAT MISUNDERSTANDING?
WELL, YOU THOUGHT WE WERE HUNTING YOU. AND TO BE HONEST, WE WERE.
BUT NOT TO KILL YOU.
THEN WHY?
TO RECRUIT YOU.

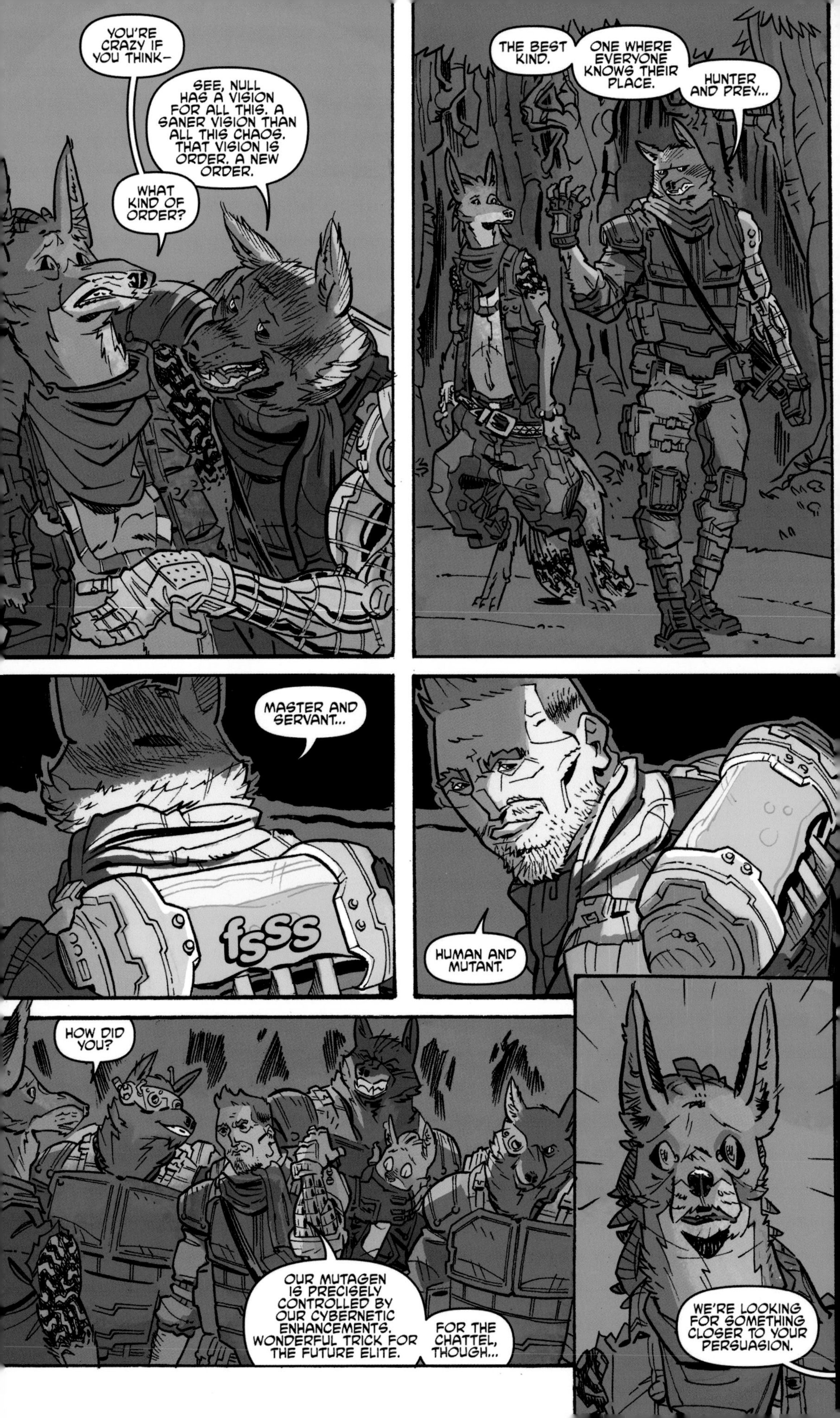
YOU'RE CRAZY IF YOU THINK–
SEE, NULL HAS A VISION FOR ALL THIS. A SANER VISION THAN ALL THIS CHAOS. THAT VISION IS ORDER. A NEW ORDER.
WHAT KIND OF ORDER?
THE BEST KIND.
ONE WHERE EVERYONE KNOWS THEIR PLACE.
HUNTER AND PREY...
MASTER AND SERVANT...
fsss
HUMAN AND MUTANT.
HOW DID YOU?
OUR MUTAGEN IS PRECISELY CONTROLLED BY OUR CYBERNETIC ENHANCEMENTS. WONDERFUL TRICK FOR THE FUTURE ELITE.
FOR THE CHATTEL, THOUGH...
WE'RE LOOKING FOR SOMETHING CLOSER TO YOUR PERSUASION.

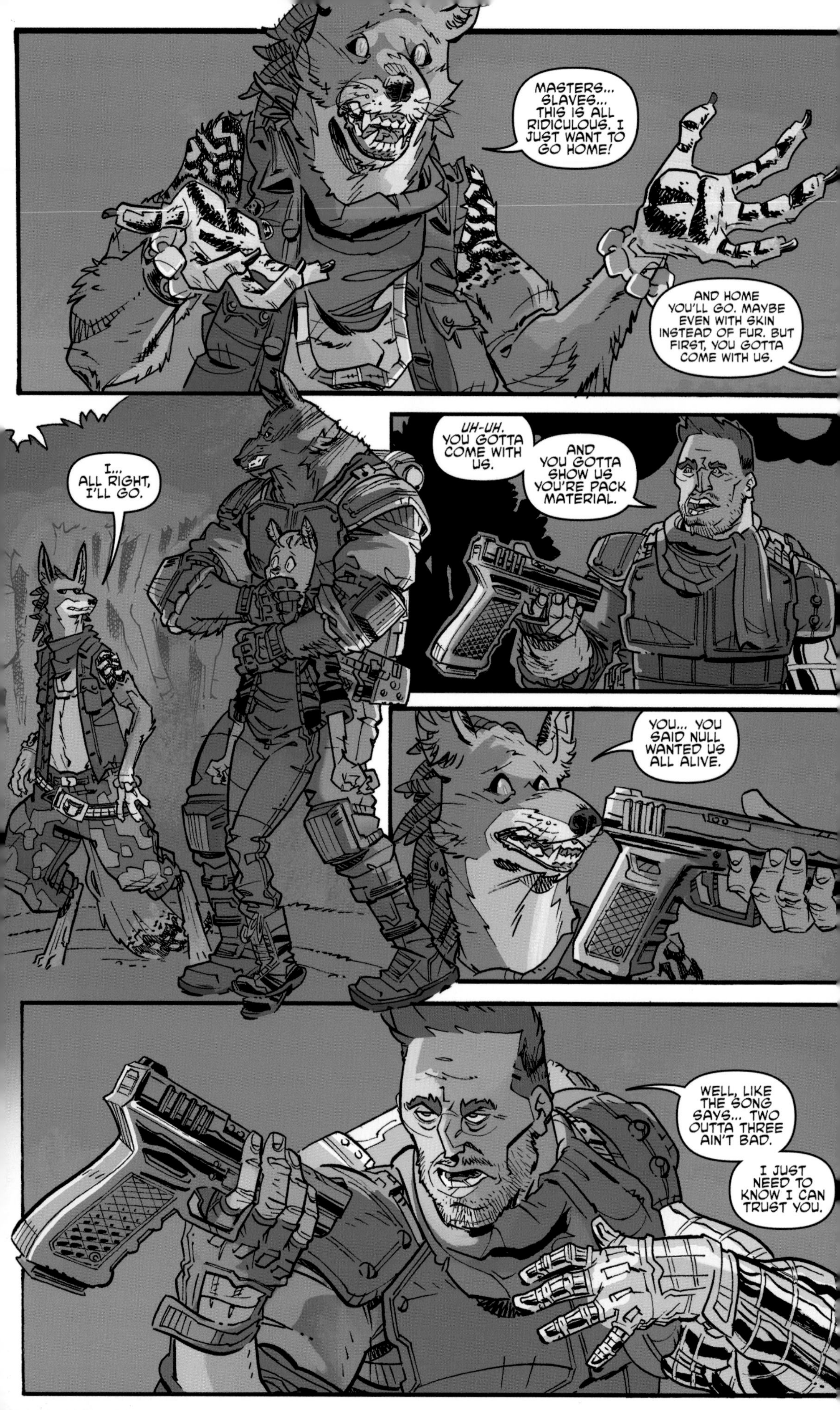
MASTERS... SLAVES... THIS IS ALL RIDICULOUS. I JUST WANT TO GO HOME!
AND HOME YOU'LL GO. MAYBE EVEN WITH SKIN INSTEAD OF FUR. BUT FIRST, YOU GOTTA COME WITH US.
I... ALL RIGHT, I'LL GO.
UH-UH. YOU GOTTA COME WITH US.
AND YOU GOTTA SHOW US YOU'RE PACK MATERIAL.
YOU... YOU SAID NULL WANTED US ALL ALIVE.
WELL, LIKE THE SONG SAYS... TWO OUTTA THREE AIN'T BAD.
I JUST NEED TO KNOW I CAN TRUST YOU.

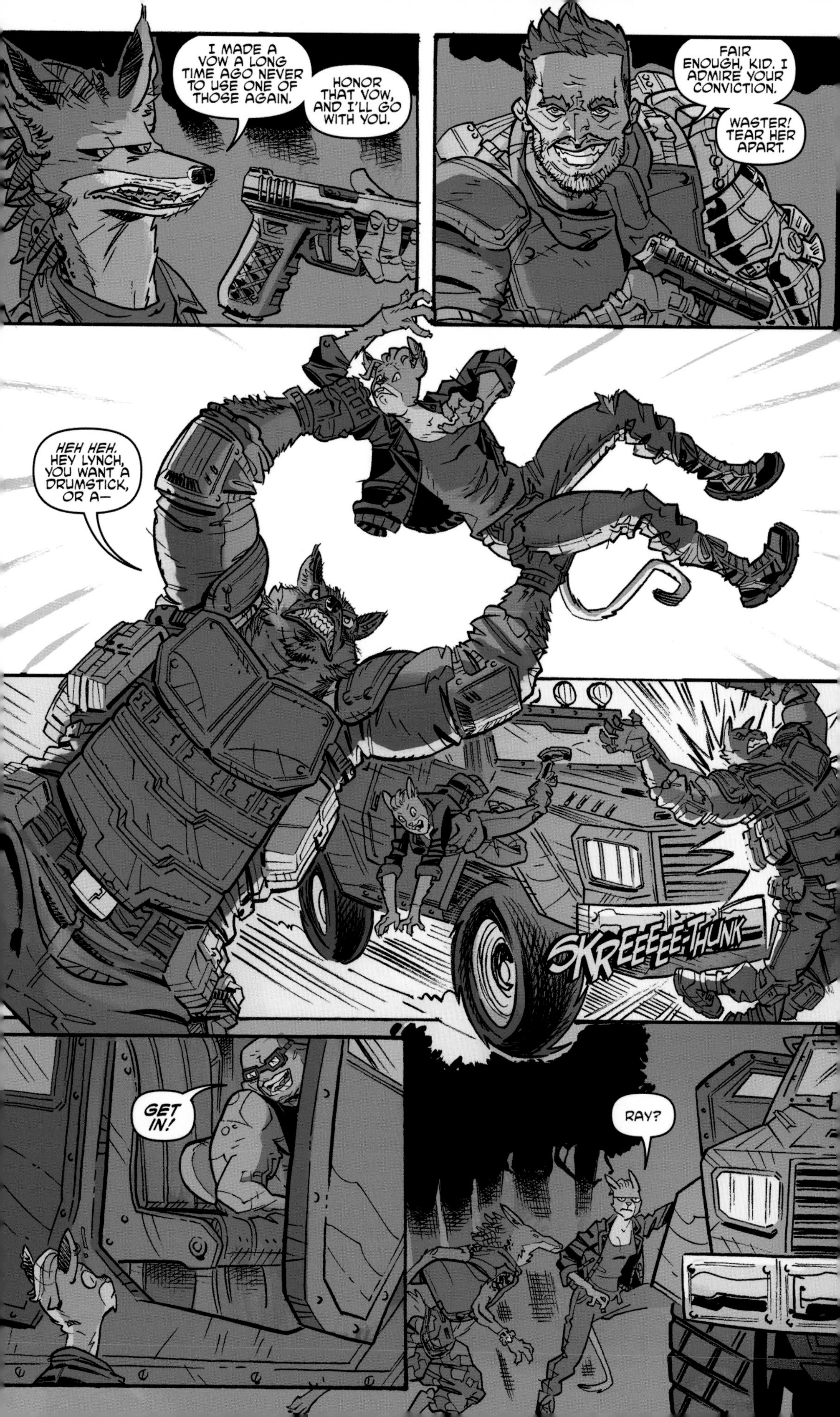
I MADE A VOW A LONG TIME AGO NEVER TO USE ONE OF THOSE AGAIN.
HONOR THAT VOW, AND I'LL GO WITH YOU.
FAIR ENOUGH, KID. I ADMIRE YOUR CONVICTION.
WASTER! TEAR HER APART.
HEH HEH. HEY LYNCH, YOU WANT A DRUMSTICK, OR A—
SKREEEEE-THUNK
GET IN!
RAY?

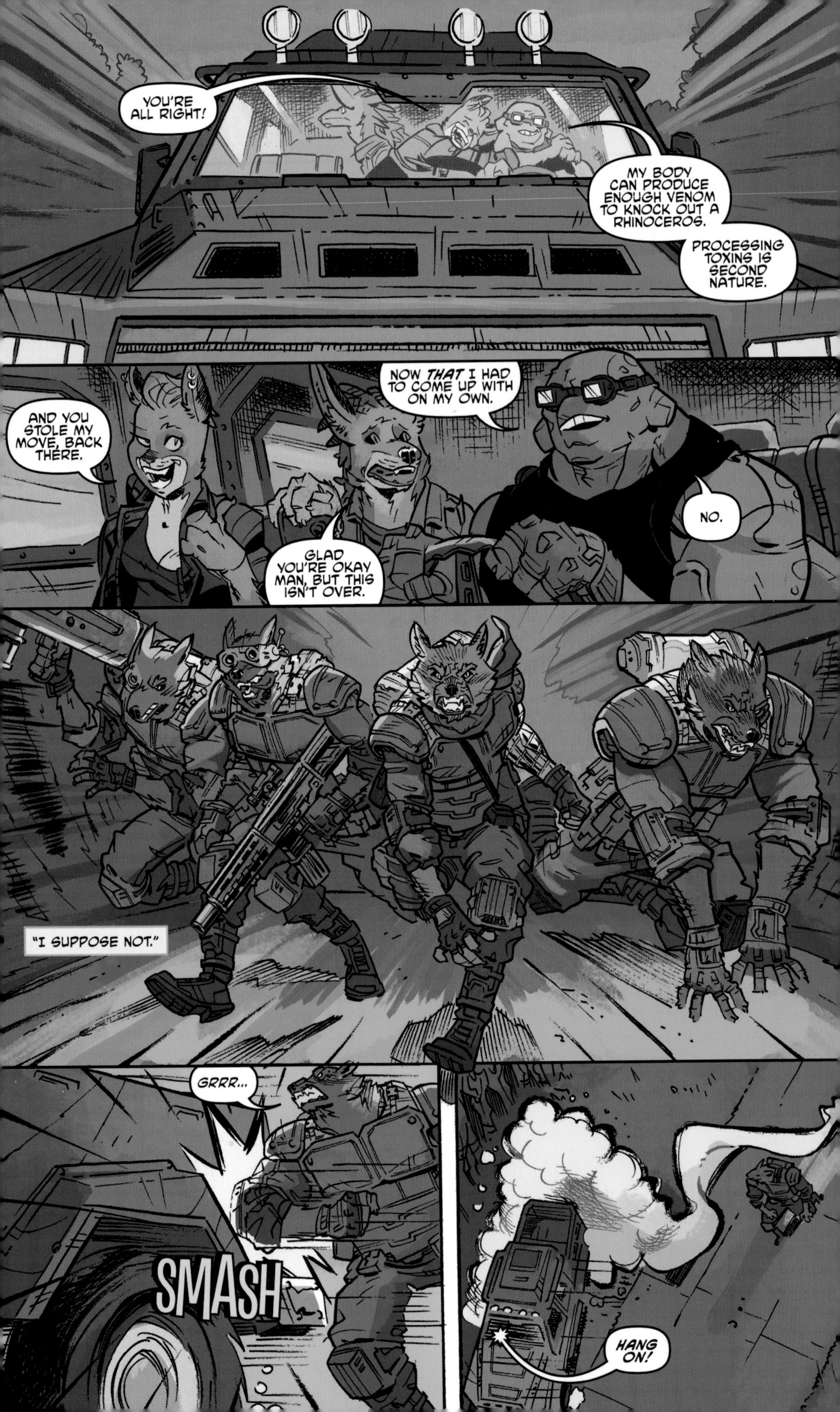

YOU'RE ALL RIGHT!
MY BODY CAN PRODUCE ENOUGH VENOM TO KNOCK OUT A RHINOCEROS.
PROCESSING TOXINS IS SECOND NATURE.
AND YOU STOLE MY MOVE, BACK THERE.
NOW THAT I HAD TO COME UP WITH ON MY OWN.
NO.
GLAD YOU'RE OKAY MAN, BUT THIS ISN'T OVER.
"I SUPPOSE NOT."
GRRR...
SMASH
HANG ON!

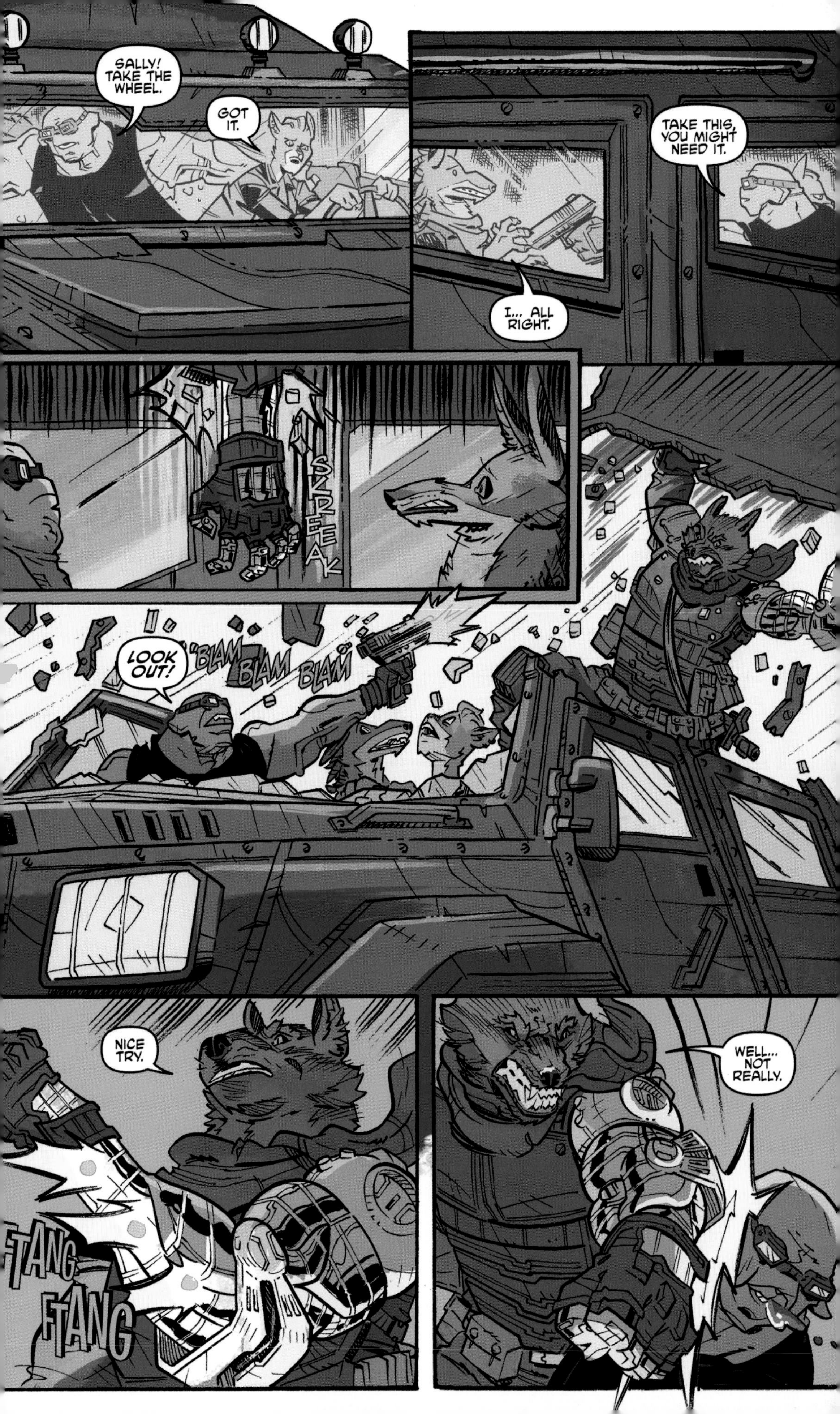
SALLY! TAKE THE WHEEL.
GOT IT.
TAKE THIS, YOU MIGHT NEED IT.
I... ALL RIGHT.
SKREEEAK
LOOK OUT!
BLAM BLAM BLAM
NICE TRY.
FTANG FTANG
WELL... NOT REALLY.

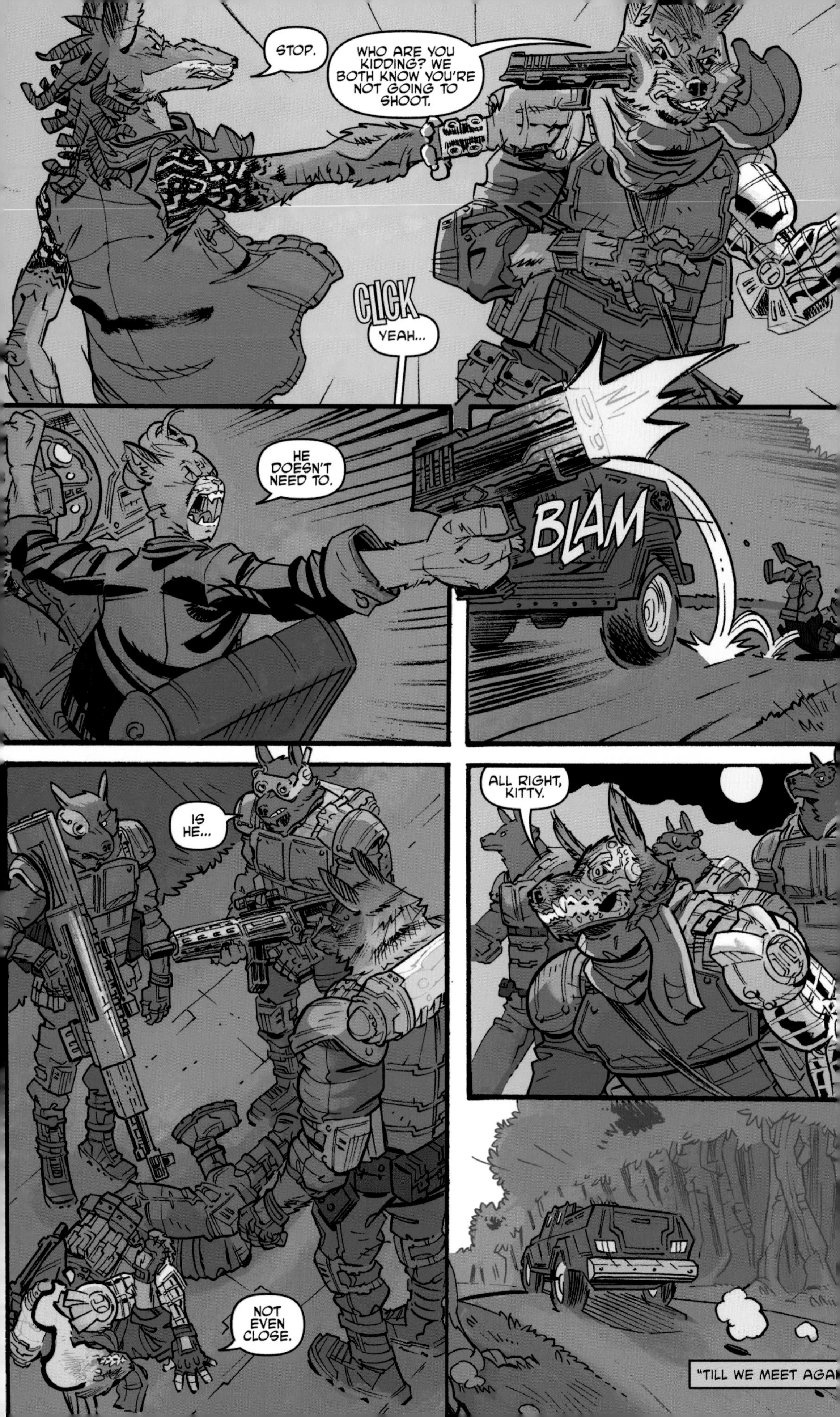
STOP.
WHO ARE YOU KIDDING? WE BOTH KNOW YOU'RE NOT GOING TO SHOOT.
CLICK
YEAH...
HE DOESN'T NEED TO.
BLAM
IS HE...
NOT EVEN CLOSE.
ALL RIGHT, KITTY.
"TILL WE MEET AGA

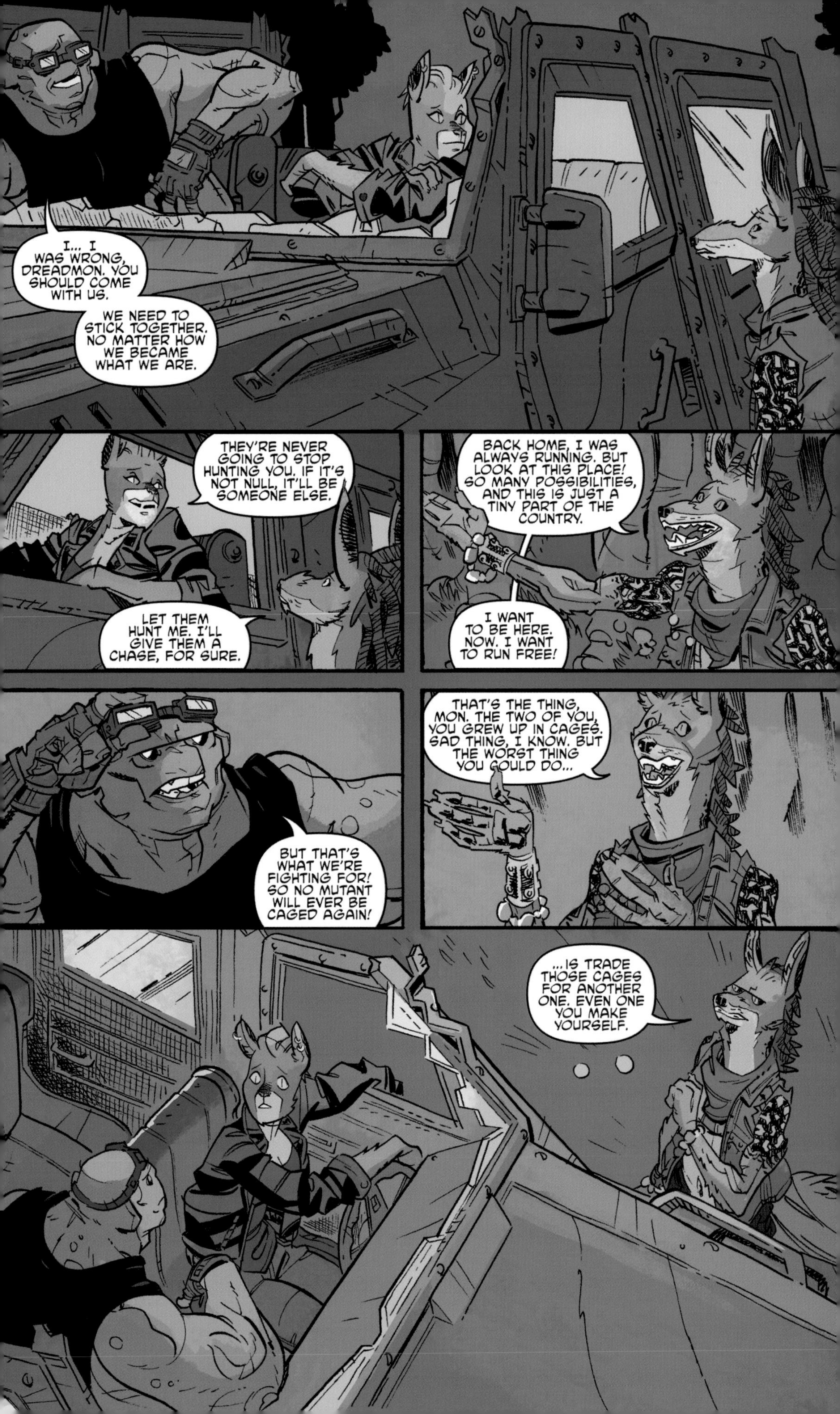
I... I WAS WRONG, DREADMON. YOU SHOULD COME WITH US.
WE NEED TO STICK TOGETHER. NO MATTER HOW WE BECAME WHAT WE ARE.
THEY'RE NEVER GOING TO STOP HUNTING YOU. IF IT'S NOT NULL, IT'LL BE SOMEONE ELSE.
LET THEM HUNT ME. I'LL GIVE THEM A CHASE, FOR SURE.
BACK HOME, I WAS ALWAYS RUNNING. BUT LOOK AT THIS PLACE! SO MANY POSSIBILITIES, AND THIS IS JUST A TINY PART OF THE COUNTRY.
I WANT TO BE HERE. NOW. I WANT TO RUN FREE!
BUT THAT'S WHAT WE'RE FIGHTING FOR! SO NO MUTANT WILL EVER BE CAGED AGAIN!
THAT'S THE THING, MON. THE TWO OF YOU, YOU GREW UP IN CAGES. SAD THING, I KNOW. BUT THE WORST THING YOU COULD DO...
...IS TRADE THOSE CAGES FOR ANOTHER ONE. EVEN ONE YOU MAKE YOURSELF.

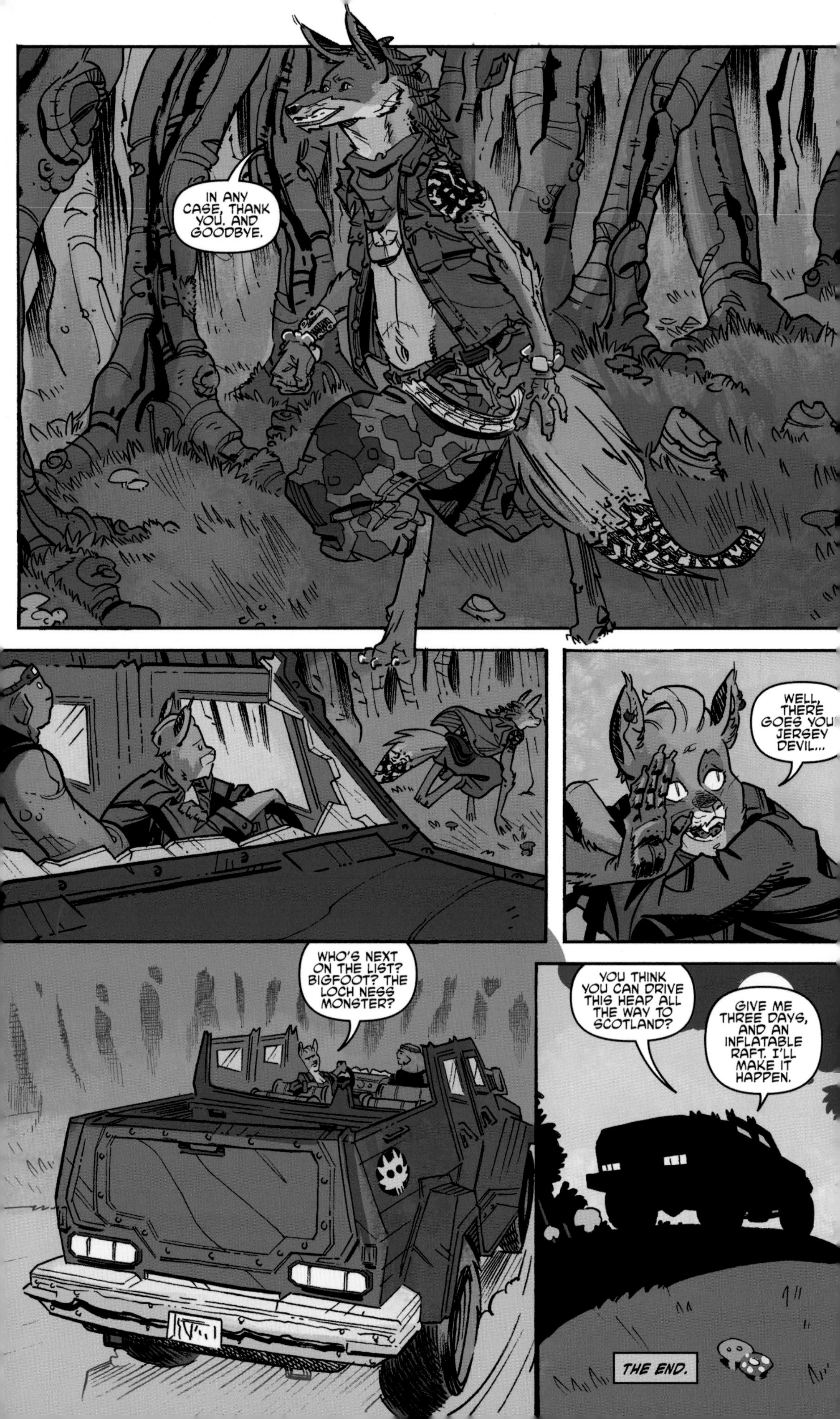

IN ANY CASE, THANK YOU. AND GOODBYE.
WELL, THERE GOES YOU JERSEY DEVIL...
WHO'S NEXT ON THE LIST? BIGFOOT? THE LOCH NESS MONSTER?
YOU THINK YOU CAN DRIVE THIS HEAP ALL THE WAY TO SCOTLAND?
GIVE ME THREE DAYS, AND AN INFLATABLE RAFT. I'LL MAKE IT HAPPEN.
THE END.

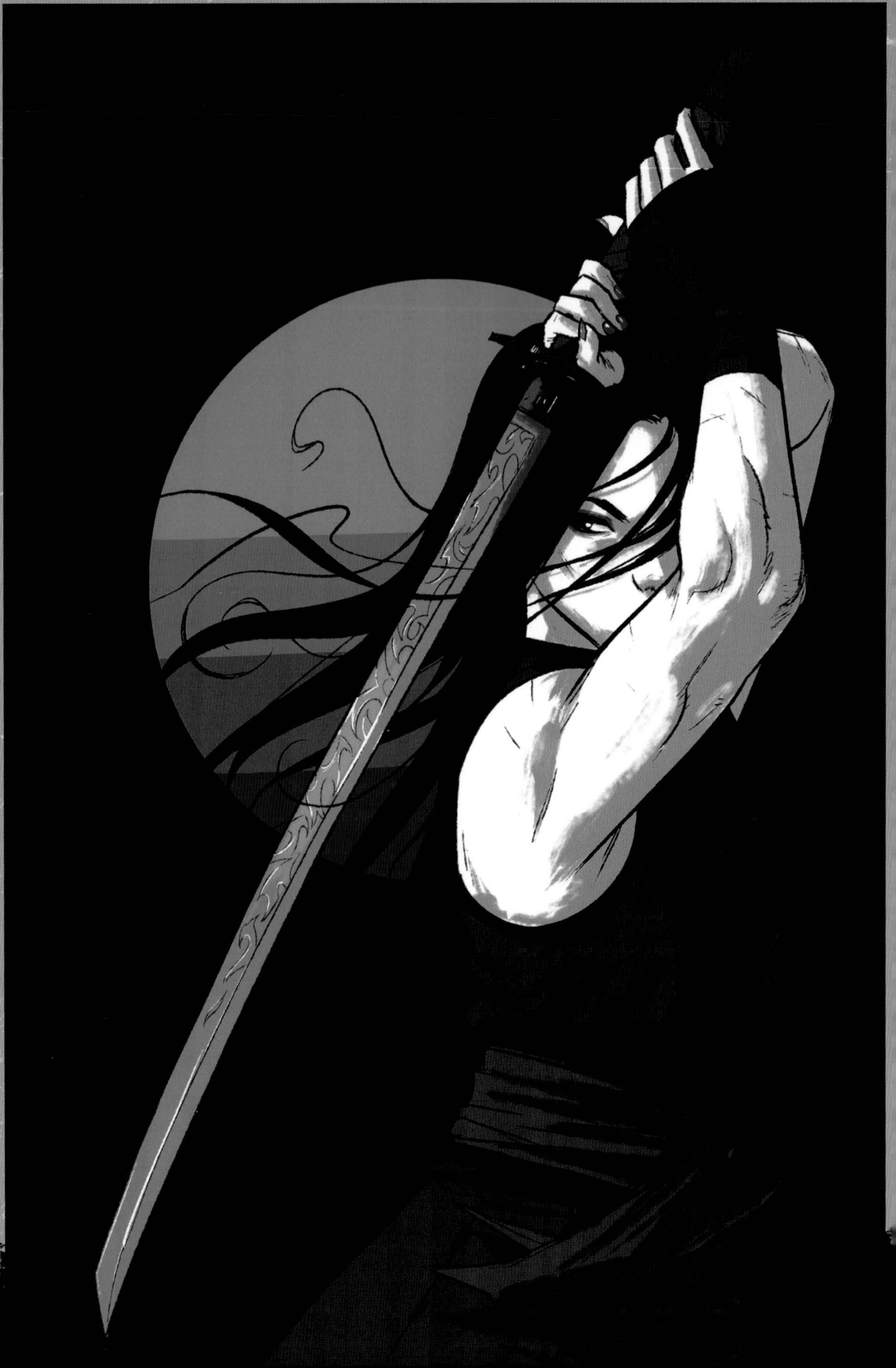

ART BY SOPHIE CAMPBELL

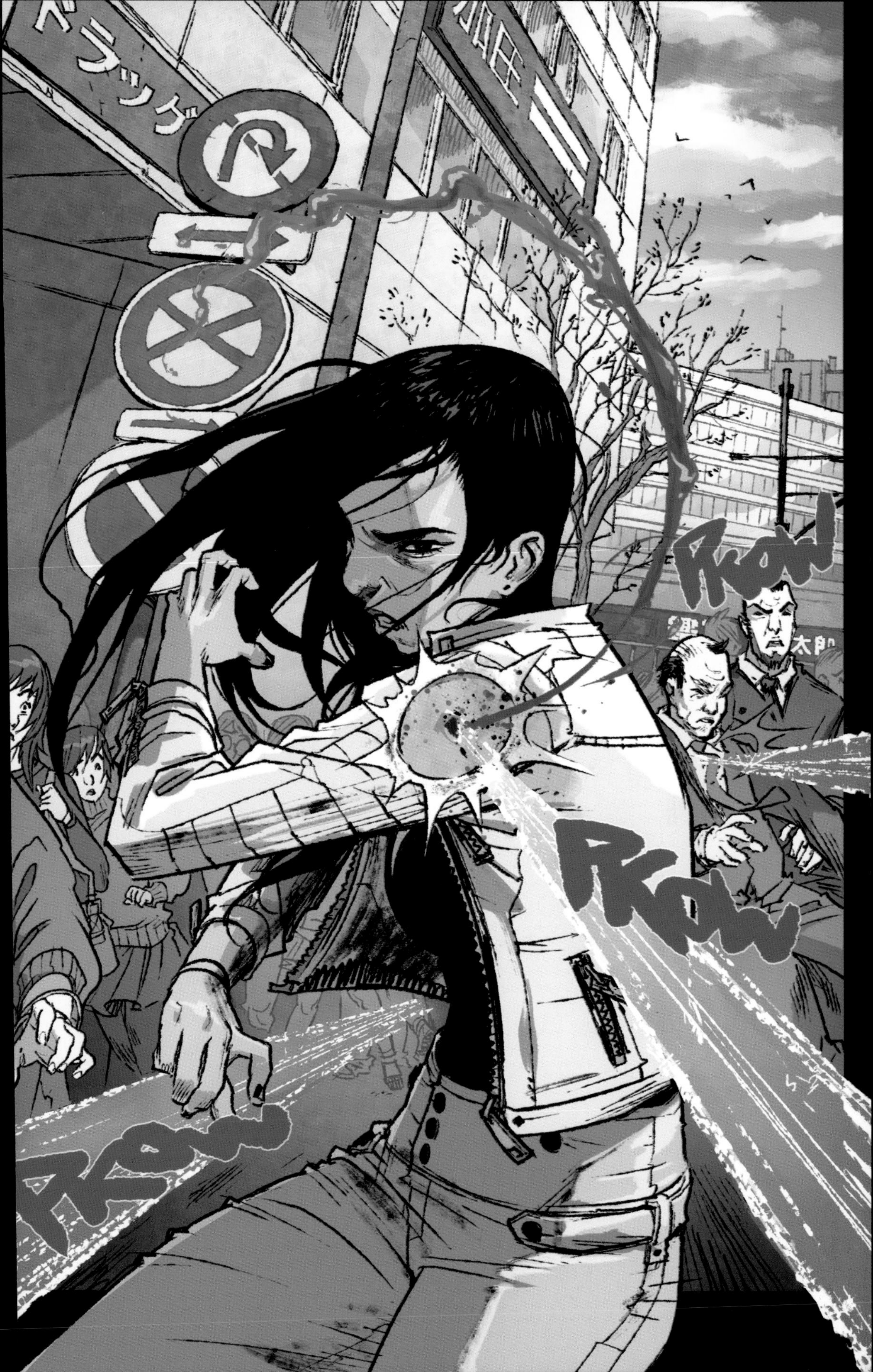
ドラッグ
PKOW
PKOW

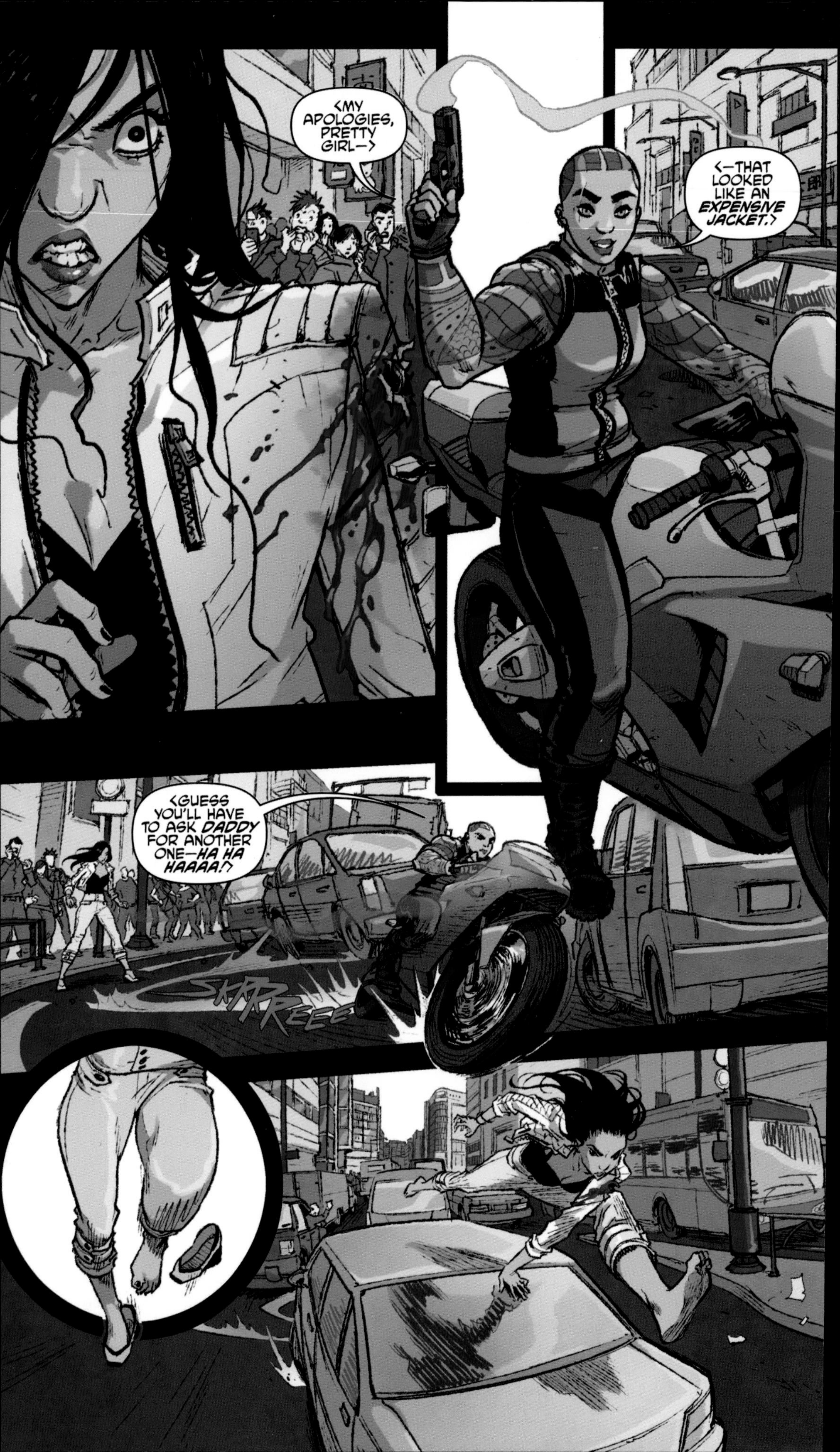
<MY APOLOGIES, PRETTY GIRL—>
<—THAT LOOKED LIKE AN *EXPENSIVE JACKET.*>
<GUESS YOU'LL HAVE TO ASK *DADDY* FOR ANOTHER ONE—*HA HA HAAAA!*>
SKRRREEEE

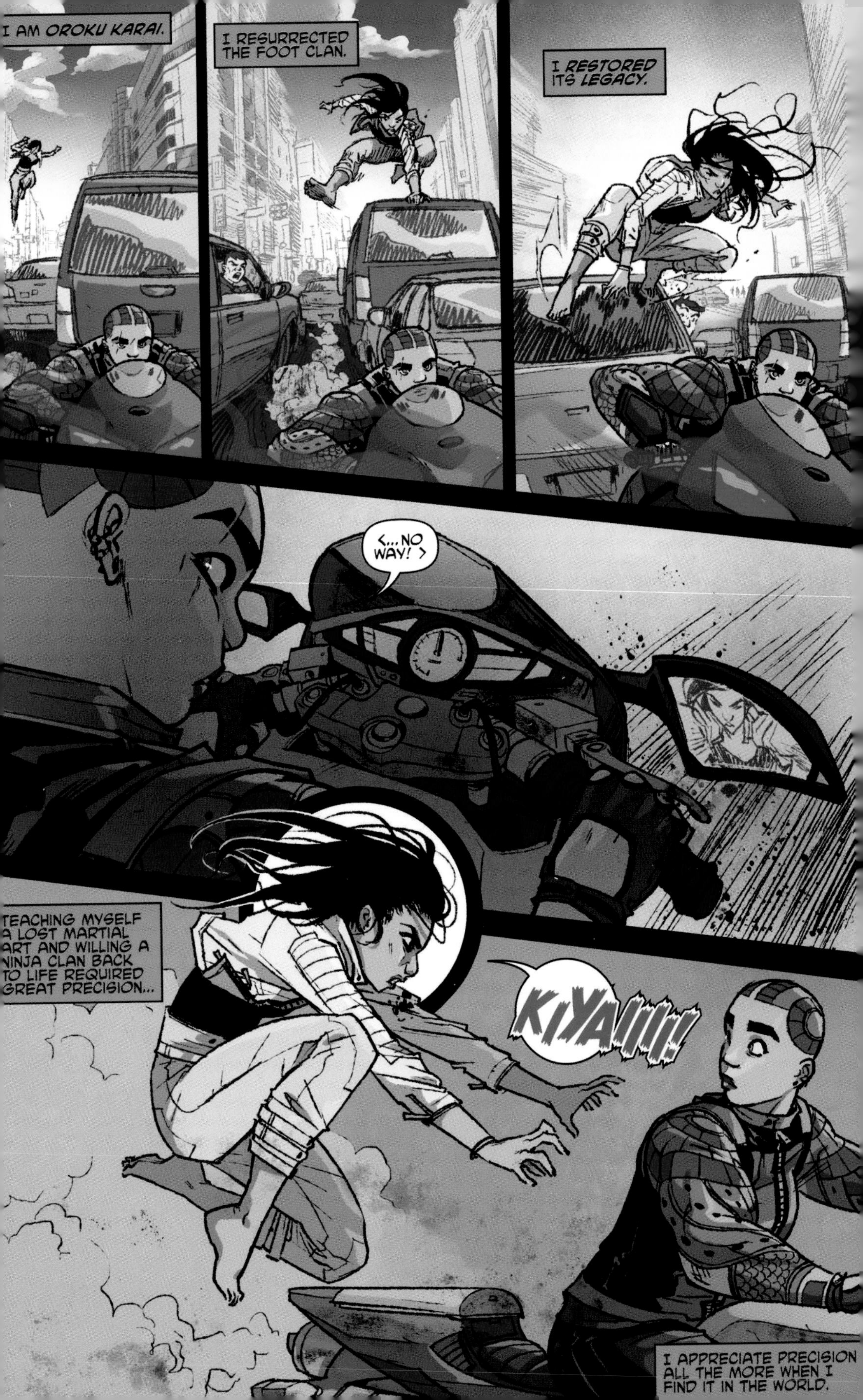
I AM OROKU KARAI.
I RESURRECTED THE FOOT CLAN.
I RESTORED ITS LEGACY.
<...NO WAY! >
TEACHING MYSELF A LOST MARTIAL ART AND WILLING A NINJA CLAN BACK TO LIFE REQUIRED GREAT PRECISION...
KIYAIIII!
I APPRECIATE PRECISION ALL THE MORE WHEN I FIND IT IN THE WORLD.

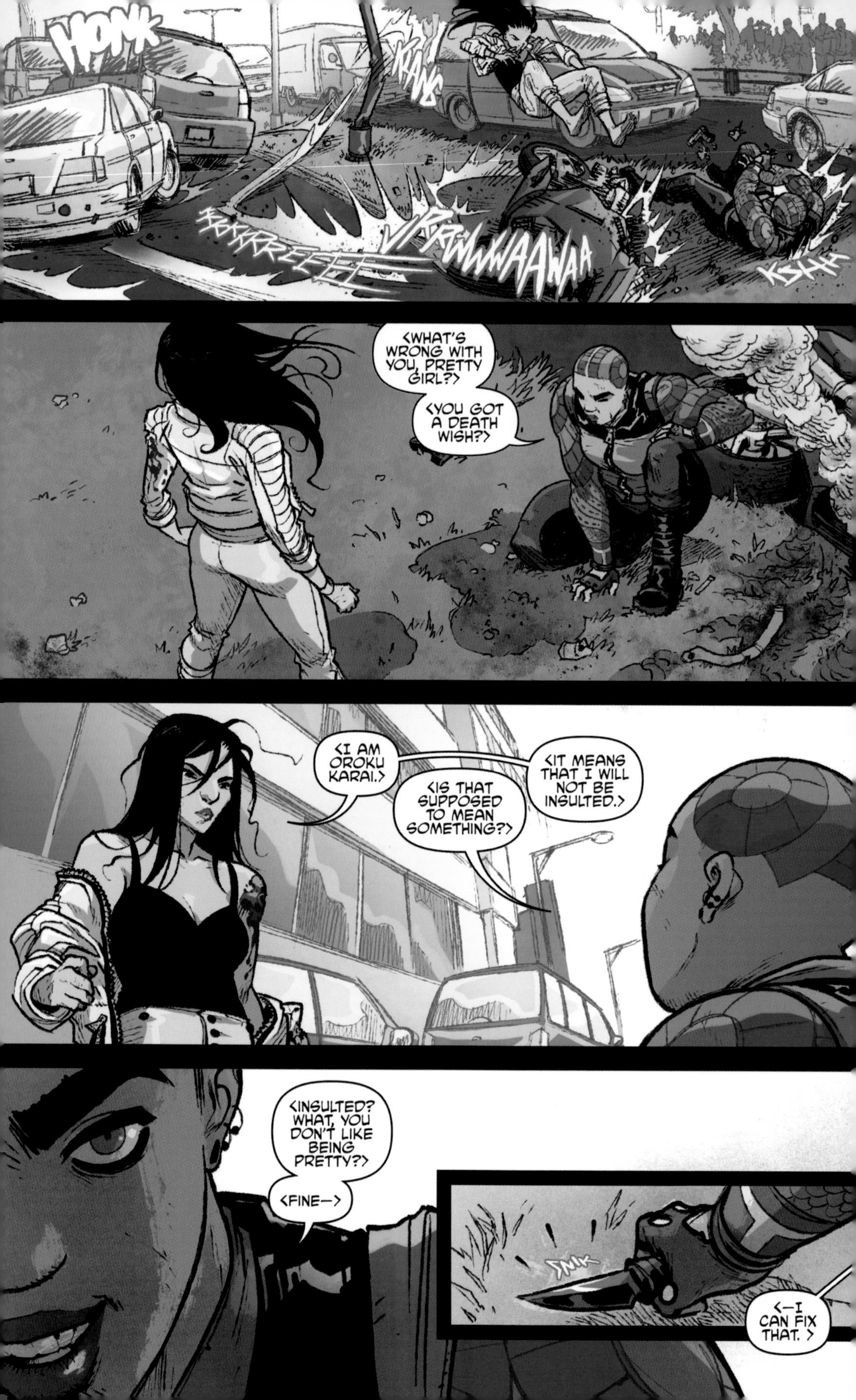
HONK
KLANG
SKKKRREEEEEE
VRRWWWAAWAA
KSHH
<WHAT'S WRONG WITH YOU, PRETTY GIRL?>
<YOU GOT A DEATH WISH?>
<I AM OROKU KARAI.>
<IS THAT SUPPOSED TO MEAN SOMETHING?>
<IT MEANS THAT I WILL NOT BE INSULTED.>
<INSULTED? WHAT, YOU DON'T LIKE BEING PRETTY?>
<FINE—>
SNIK
<—I CAN FIX THAT.>

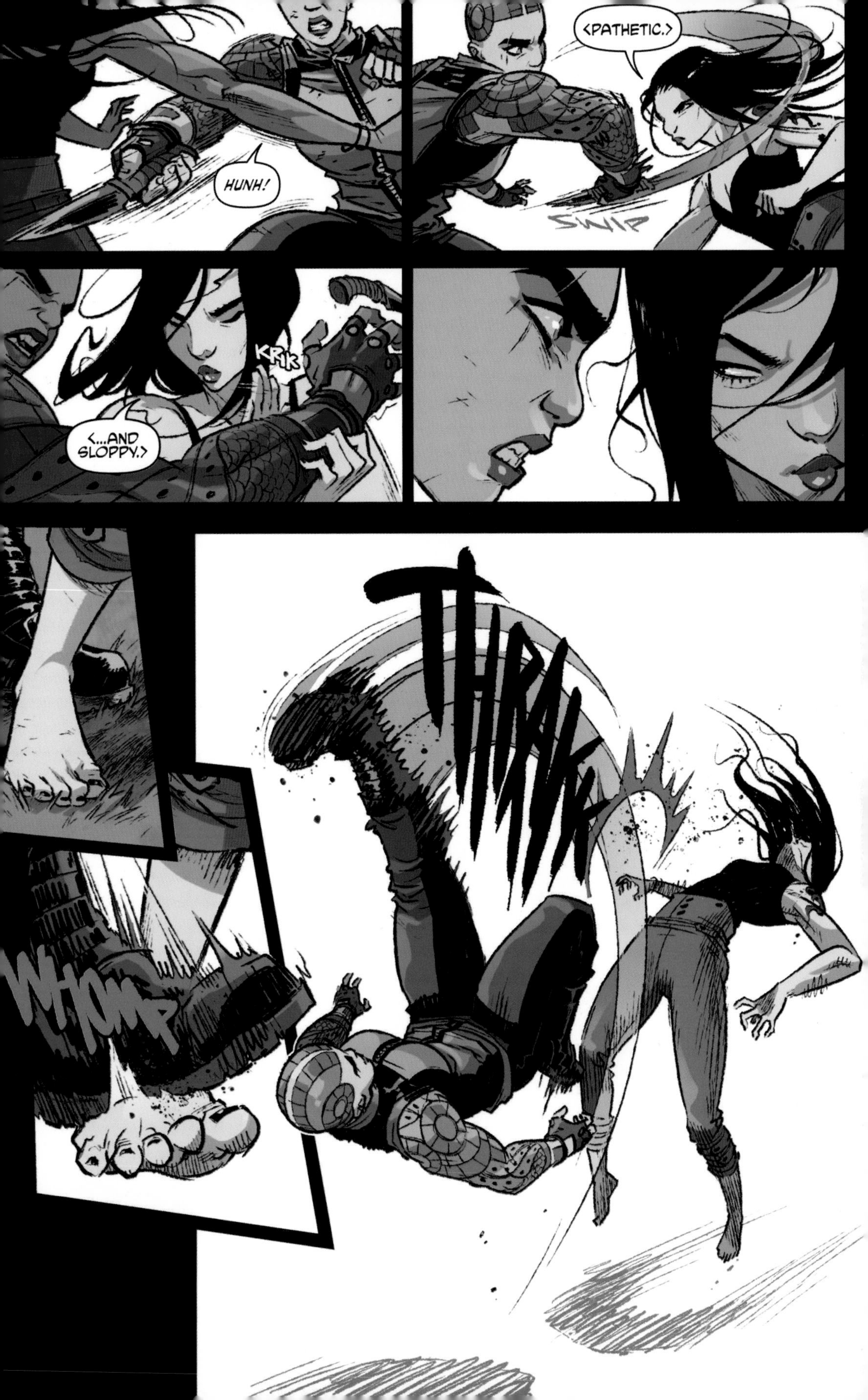
HUNH!
<PATHETIC.>
SWIP
KRIK
<...AND SLOPPY.>
WHOMP

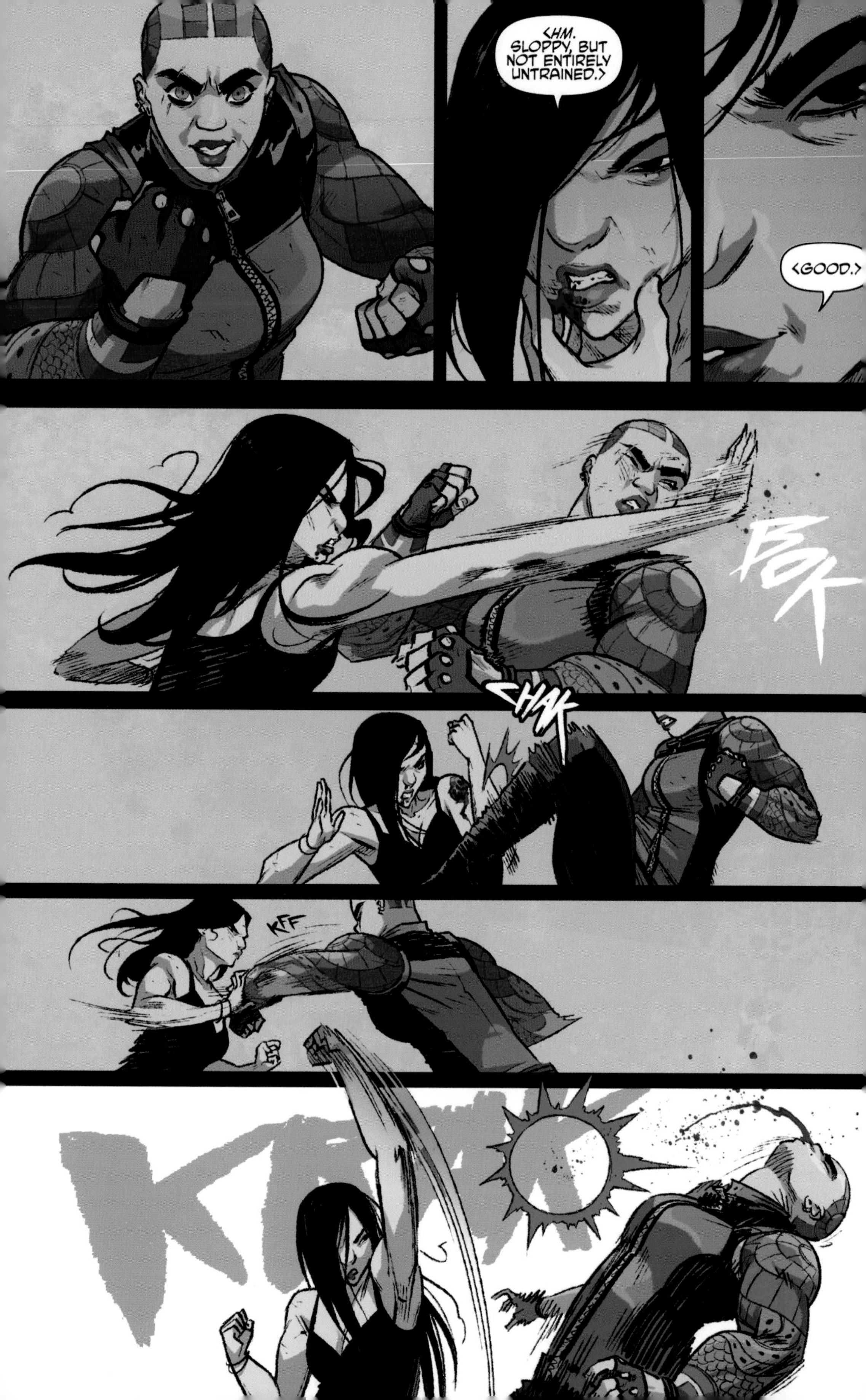
<HM. SLOPPY, BUT NOT ENTIRELY UNTRAINED.>
<GOOD.>
BOK
CHAK
KFF

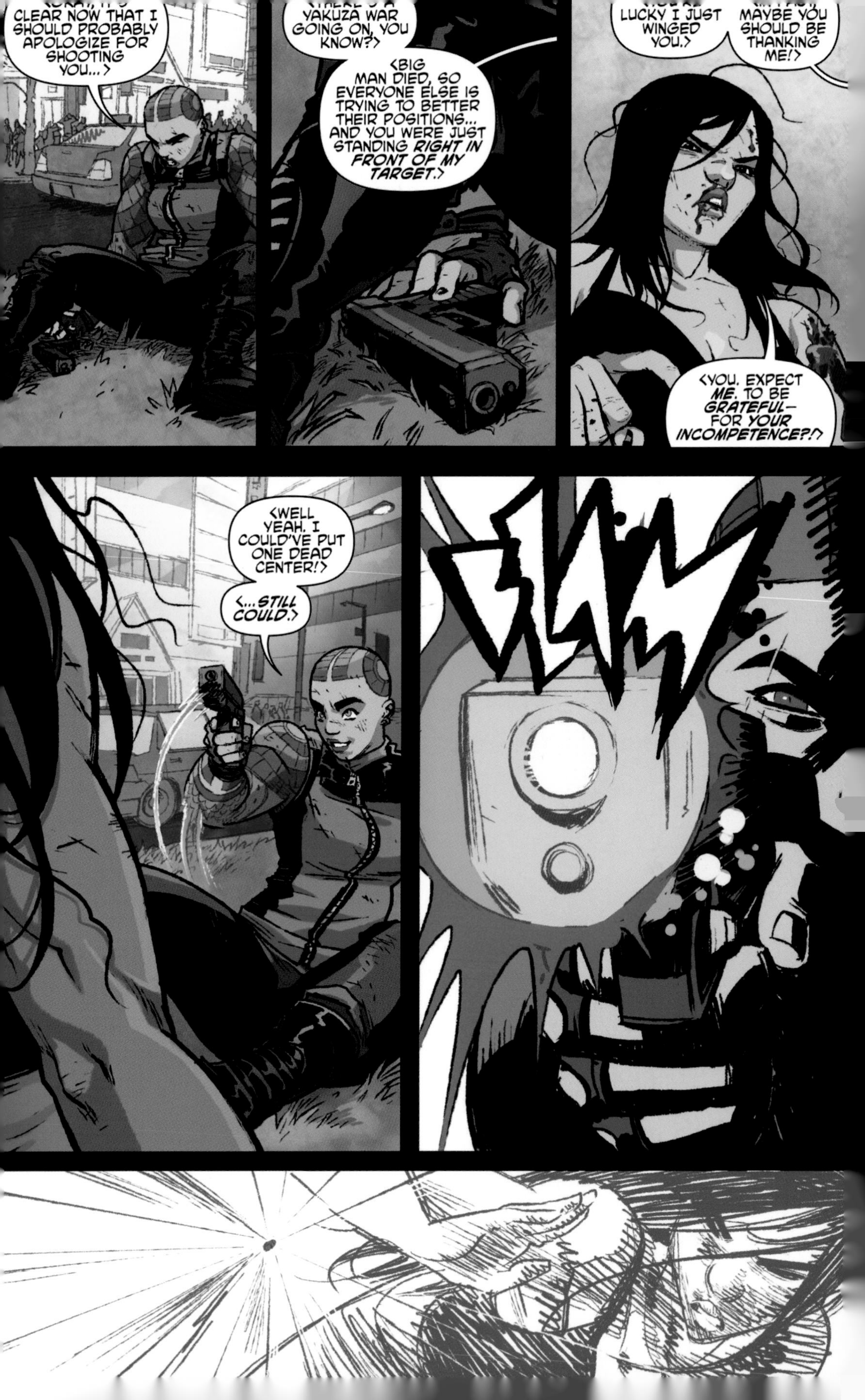
CLEAR NOW THAT I SHOULD PROBABLY APOLOGIZE FOR SHOOTING YOU...>
YAKUZA WAR GOING ON, YOU KNOW?>
<BIG MAN DIED, SO EVERYONE ELSE IS TRYING TO BETTER THEIR POSITIONS... AND YOU WERE JUST STANDING *RIGHT IN FRONT OF MY TARGET.*>
LUCKY I JUST WINGED YOU.>
MAYBE YOU SHOULD BE THANKING ME!>
<YOU. EXPECT *ME.* TO BE *GRATEFUL*— FOR *YOUR INCOMPETENCE?!*>
<WELL YEAH. I COULD'VE PUT ONE DEAD CENTER!>
<*...STILL COULD.*>

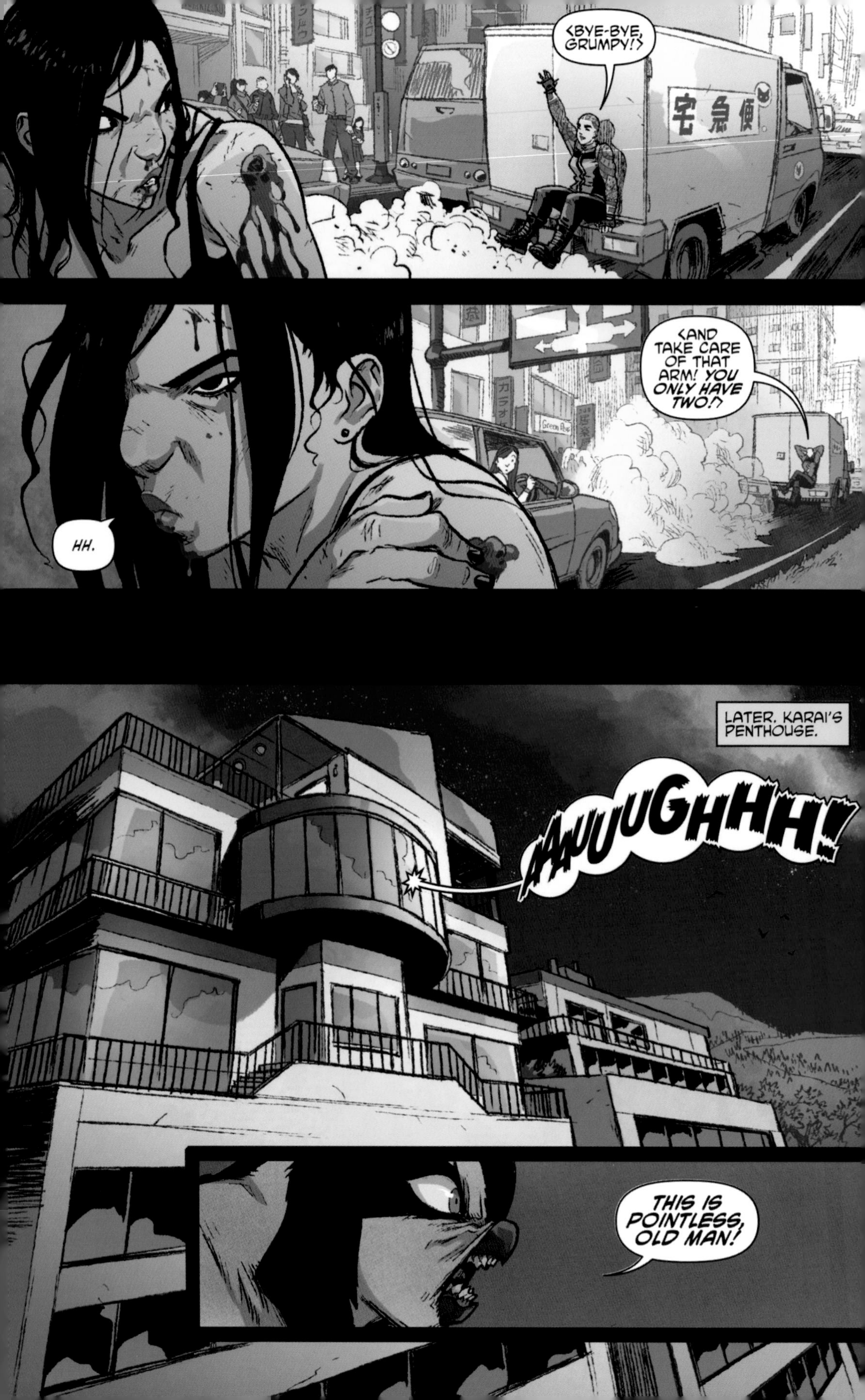

<BYE-BYE, GRUMPY!>
宅急便
<AND TAKE CARE OF THAT ARM! YOU ONLY HAVE TWO!>
HH.
LATER. KARAI'S PENTHOUSE.
AAAUUUGHHH!
THIS IS POINTLESS, OLD MAN!

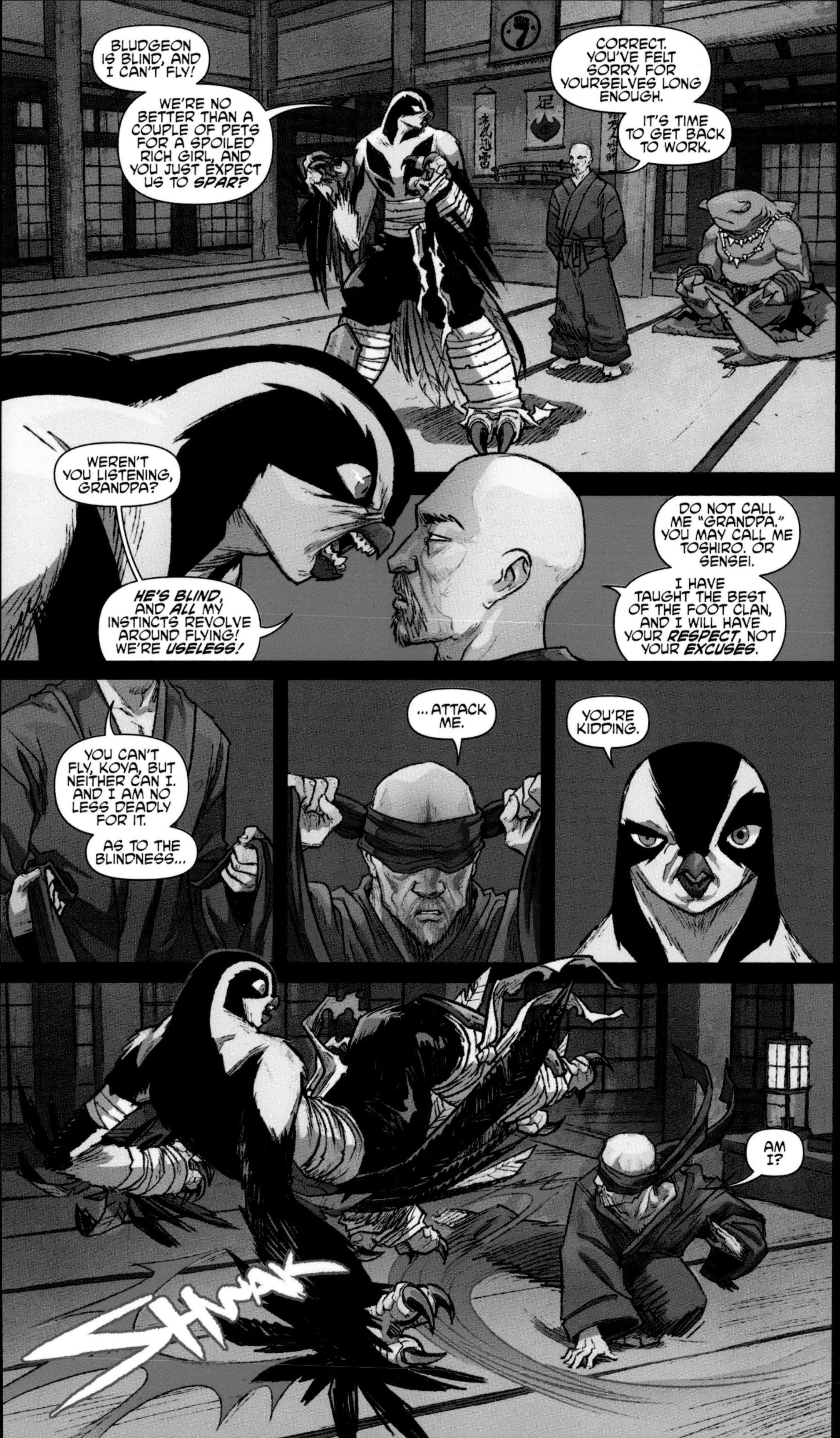

BLUDGEON IS BLIND, AND I CAN'T FLY!
WE'RE NO BETTER THAN A COUPLE OF PETS FOR A SPOILED RICH GIRL, AND YOU JUST EXPECT US TO *SPAR?*
CORRECT. YOU'VE FELT SORRY FOR YOURSELVES LONG ENOUGH.
IT'S TIME TO GET BACK TO WORK.
WEREN'T YOU LISTENING, GRANDPA?
HE'S BLIND, AND *ALL* MY INSTINCTS REVOLVE AROUND FLYING! WE'RE *USELESS!*
DO NOT CALL ME "GRANDPA." YOU MAY CALL ME TOSHIRO. OR SENSEI.
I HAVE TAUGHT THE BEST OF THE FOOT CLAN, AND I WILL HAVE YOUR *RESPECT*, NOT YOUR *EXCUSES*.
YOU CAN'T FLY, KOYA, BUT NEITHER CAN I. AND I AM NO LESS DEADLY FOR IT.
AS TO THE BLINDNESS...
...ATTACK ME.
YOU'RE KIDDING.
AM I?
SHWAK

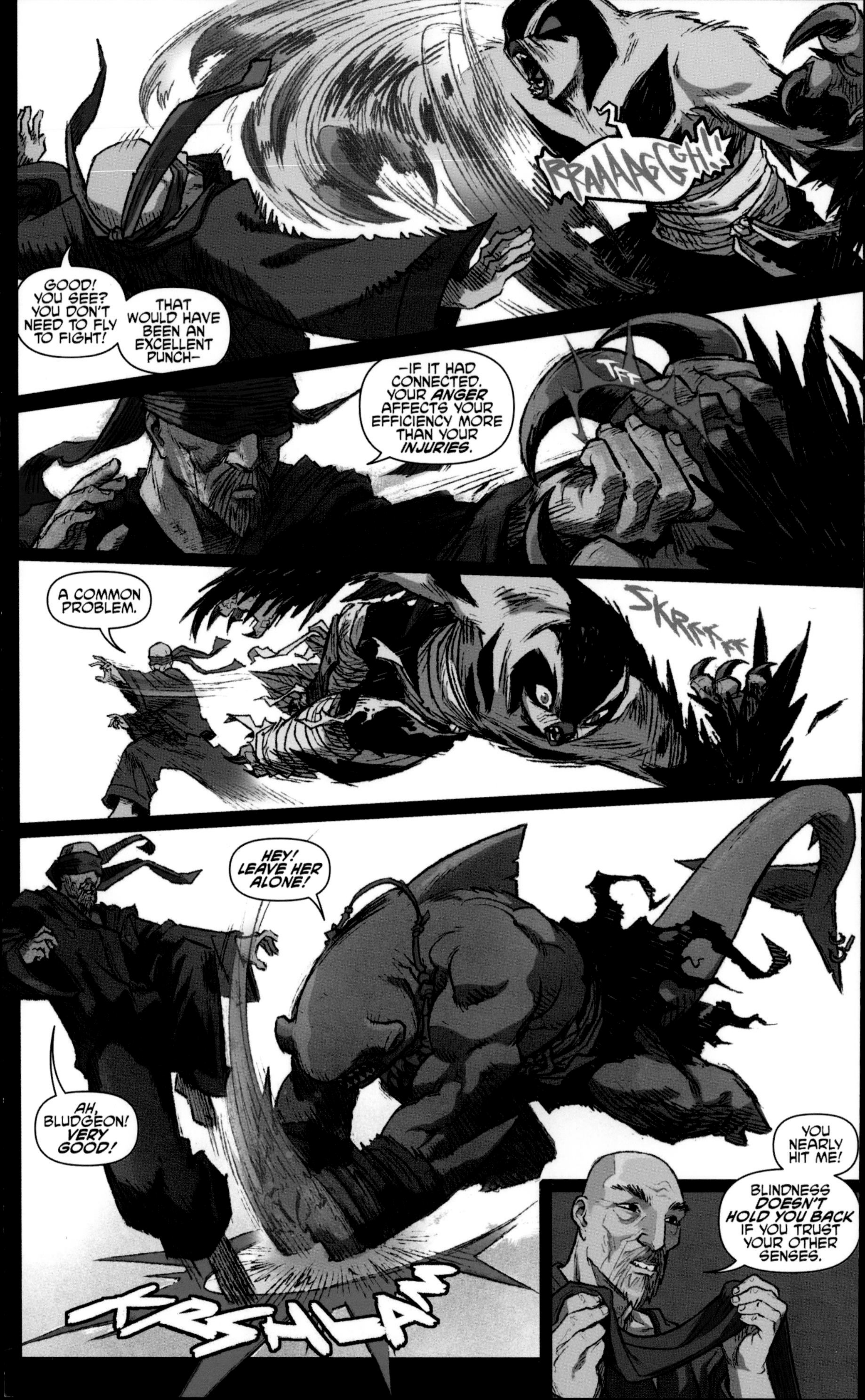
RRAAAAGGH!!
GOOD! YOU SEE? YOU DON'T NEED TO FLY TO FIGHT!
THAT WOULD HAVE BEEN AN EXCELLENT PUNCH–
–IF IT HAD CONNECTED. YOUR *ANGER* AFFECTS YOUR EFFICIENCY MORE THAN YOUR *INJURIES*.
A COMMON PROBLEM.
SKRFFFF
HEY! LEAVE HER ALONE!
AH, BLUDGEON! *VERY GOOD!*
KRSHLAM
YOU NEARLY HIT ME!
BLINDNESS *DOESN'T HOLD YOU BACK* IF YOU TRUST YOUR OTHER SENSES.

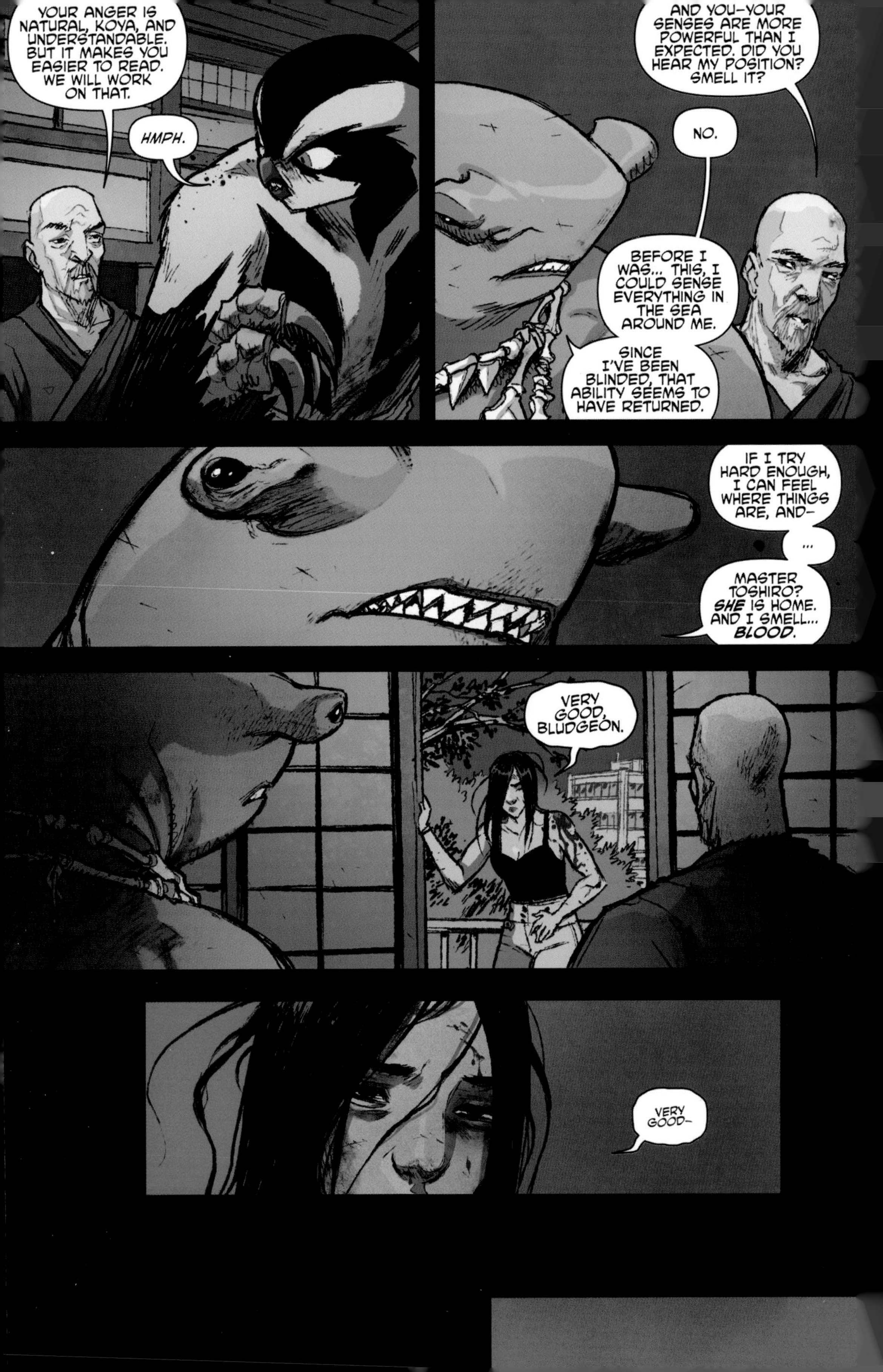
YOUR ANGER IS NATURAL, KOYA, AND UNDERSTANDABLE. BUT IT MAKES YOU EASIER TO READ. WE WILL WORK ON THAT.
HMPH.
AND YOU–YOUR SENSES ARE MORE POWERFUL THAN I EXPECTED. DID YOU HEAR MY POSITION? SMELL IT?
NO.
BEFORE I WAS... THIS, I COULD SENSE EVERYTHING IN THE SEA AROUND ME.
SINCE I'VE BEEN BLINDED, THAT ABILITY SEEMS TO HAVE RETURNED.
IF I TRY HARD ENOUGH, I CAN FEEL WHERE THINGS ARE, AND–
...
MASTER TOSHIRO? SHE IS HOME. AND I SMELL... BLOOD.
VERY GOOD, BLUDGEON.
VERY GOOD–

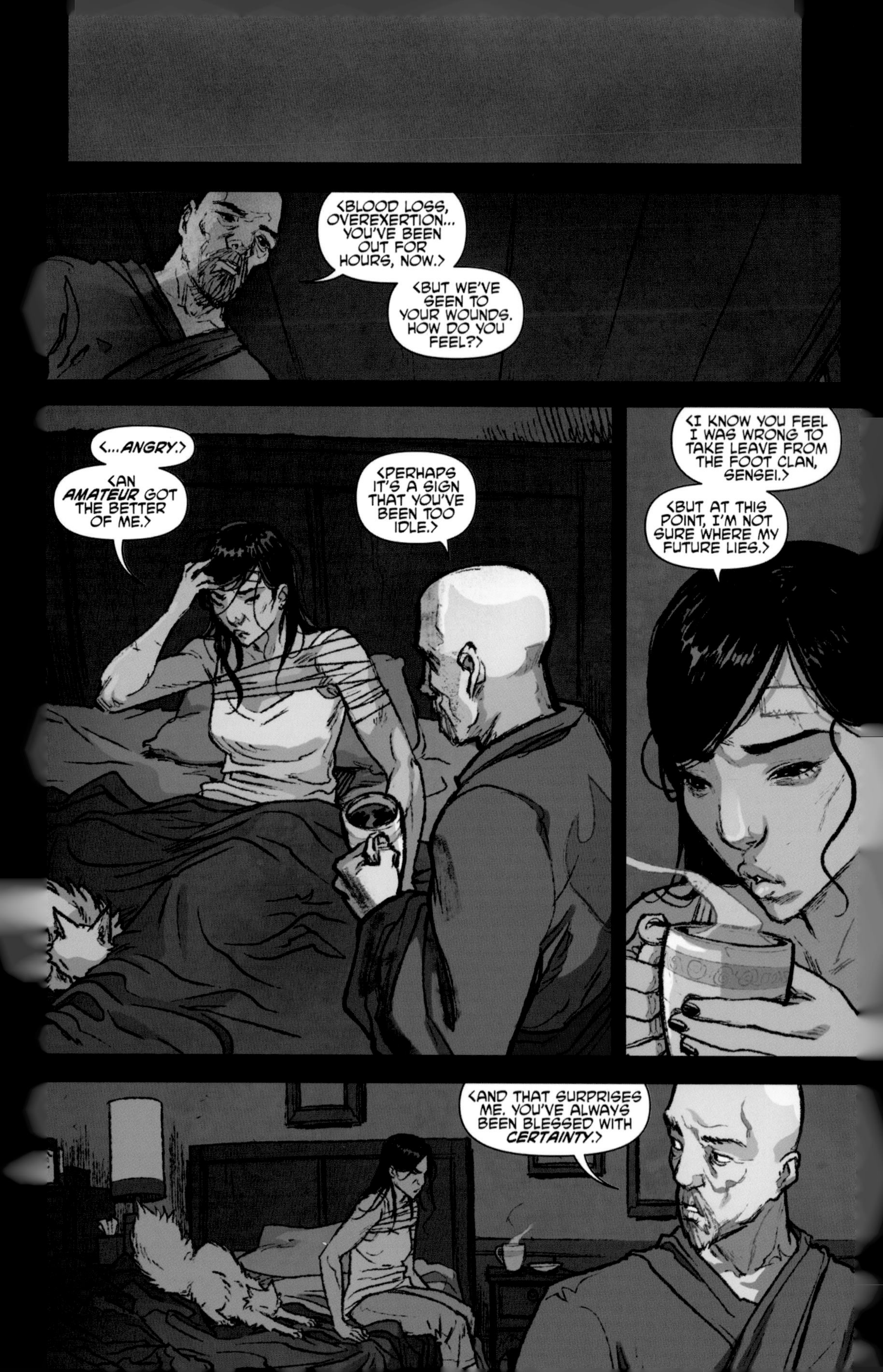
<BLOOD LOSS, OVEREXERTION... YOU'VE BEEN OUT FOR HOURS, NOW.>
<BUT WE'VE SEEN TO YOUR WOUNDS. HOW DO YOU FEEL?>
<...ANGRY.>
<AN AMATEUR GOT THE BETTER OF ME.>
<PERHAPS IT'S A SIGN THAT YOU'VE BEEN TOO IDLE.>
<I KNOW YOU FEEL I WAS WRONG TO TAKE LEAVE FROM THE FOOT CLAN, SENSEI.>
<BUT AT THIS POINT, I'M NOT SURE WHERE MY FUTURE LIES.>
<AND THAT SURPRISES ME. YOU'VE ALWAYS BEEN BLESSED WITH CERTAINTY.>

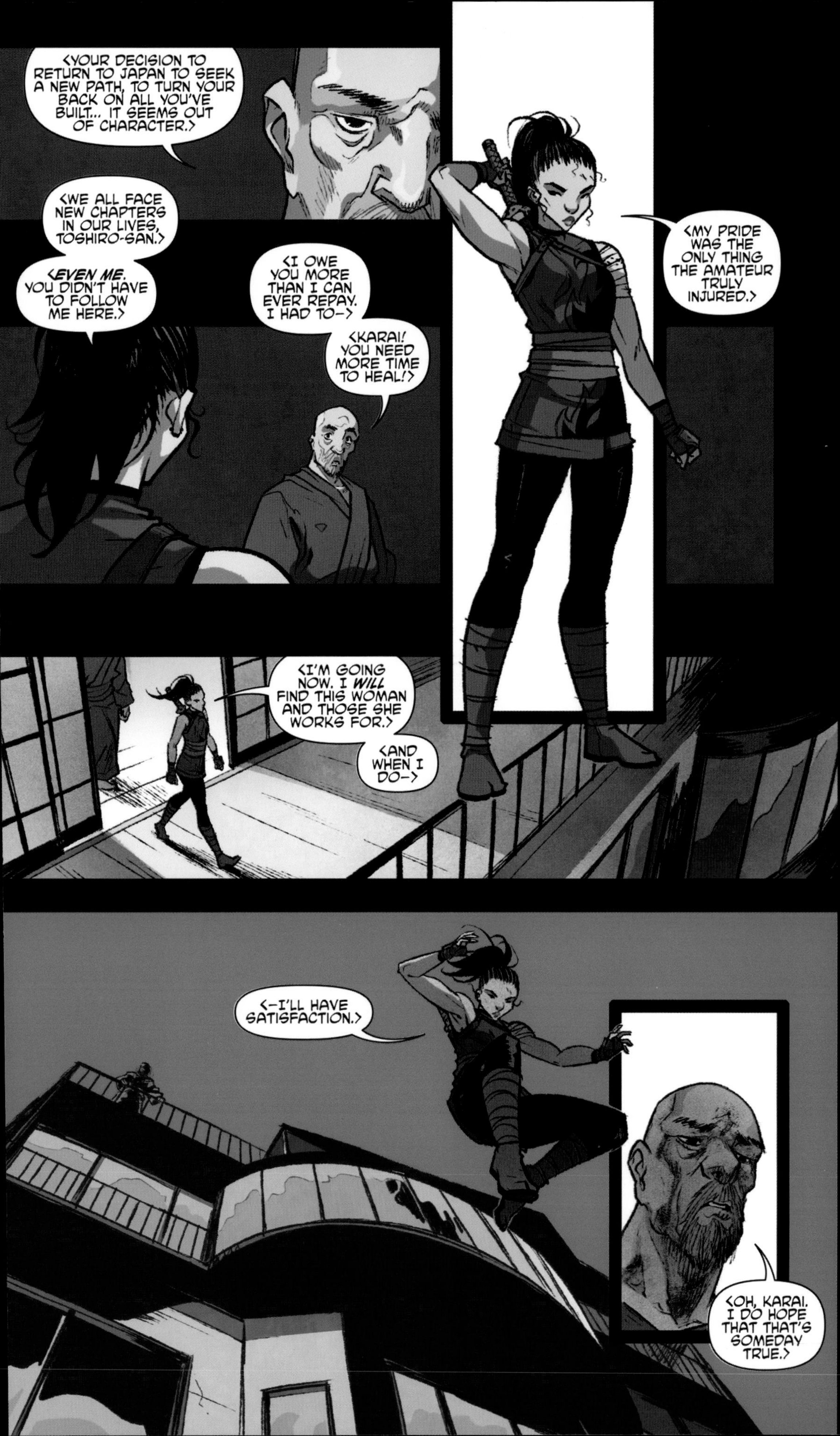
<YOUR DECISION TO RETURN TO JAPAN TO SEEK A NEW PATH, TO TURN YOUR BACK ON ALL YOU'VE BUILT... IT SEEMS OUT OF CHARACTER.>
<WE ALL FACE NEW CHAPTERS IN OUR LIVES, TOSHIRO-SAN.>
<MY PRIDE WAS THE ONLY THING THE AMATEUR TRULY INJURED.>
<*EVEN ME*. YOU DIDN'T HAVE TO FOLLOW ME HERE.>
<I OWE YOU MORE THAN I CAN EVER REPAY. I HAD TO–>
<KARAI! YOU NEED MORE TIME TO HEAL!>
<I'M GOING NOW. I ***WILL*** FIND THIS WOMAN AND THOSE SHE WORKS FOR.>
<AND WHEN I DO–>
<–I'LL HAVE SATISFACTION.>
<OH, KARAI. I DO HOPE THAT THAT'S SOMEDAY TRUE.>

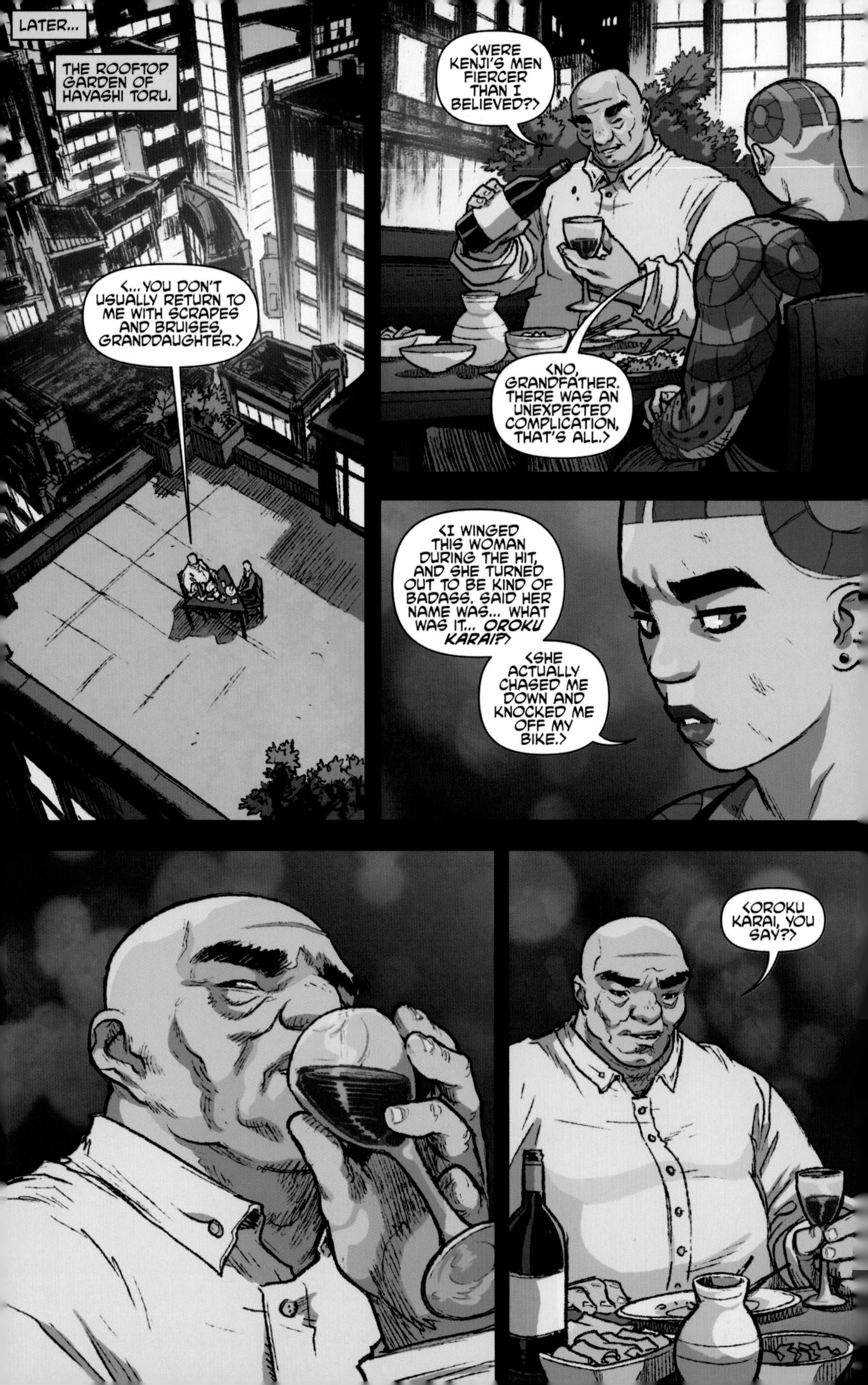
LATER...
THE ROOFTOP GARDEN OF HAYASHI TORU.
<...YOU DON'T USUALLY RETURN TO ME WITH SCRAPES AND BRUISES, GRANDDAUGHTER.>
<WERE KENJI'S MEN FIERCER THAN I BELIEVED?>
<NO, GRANDFATHER. THERE WAS AN UNEXPECTED COMPLICATION, THAT'S ALL.>
<I WINGED THIS WOMAN DURING THE HIT, AND SHE TURNED OUT TO BE KIND OF BADASS. SAID HER NAME WAS... WHAT WAS IT... OROKU KARAI?>
<SHE ACTUALLY CHASED ME DOWN AND KNOCKED ME OFF MY BIKE.>
<OROKU KARAI, YOU SAY?>

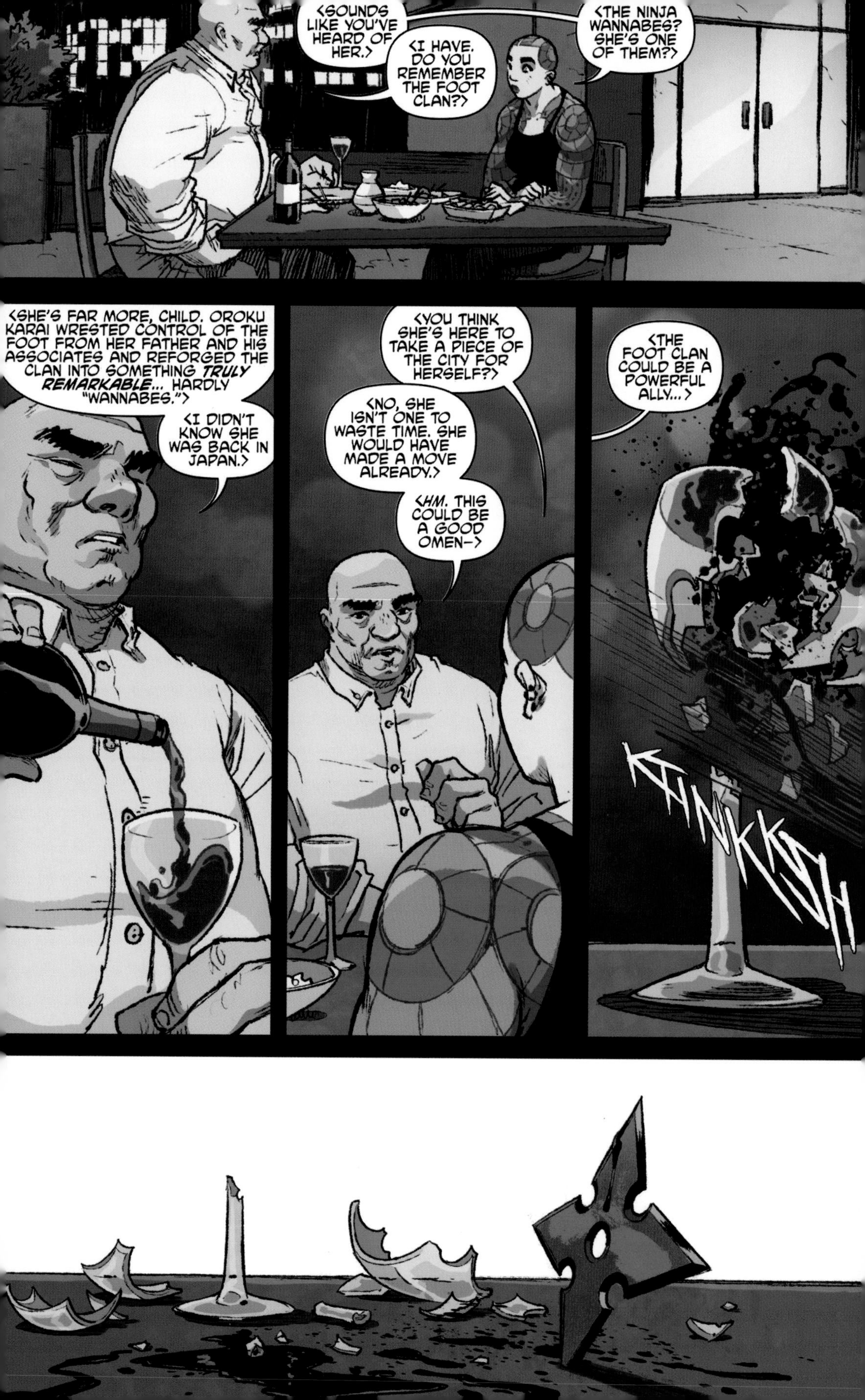

<SOUNDS LIKE YOU'VE HEARD OF HER.>
<THE NINJA WANNABES? SHE'S ONE OF THEM?>
<I HAVE. DO YOU REMEMBER THE FOOT CLAN?>
<SHE'S FAR MORE, CHILD. OROKU KARAI WRESTED CONTROL OF THE FOOT FROM HER FATHER AND HIS ASSOCIATES AND REFORGED THE CLAN INTO SOMETHING *TRULY REMARKABLE*... HARDLY "WANNABES.">
<I DIDN'T KNOW SHE WAS BACK IN JAPAN.>
<YOU THINK SHE'S HERE TO TAKE A PIECE OF THE CITY FOR HERSELF?>
<NO, SHE ISN'T ONE TO WASTE TIME. SHE WOULD HAVE MADE A MOVE ALREADY.>
<*HM.* THIS COULD BE A GOOD OMEN–>
<THE FOOT CLAN COULD BE A POWERFUL ALLY...>
KTINKKSH

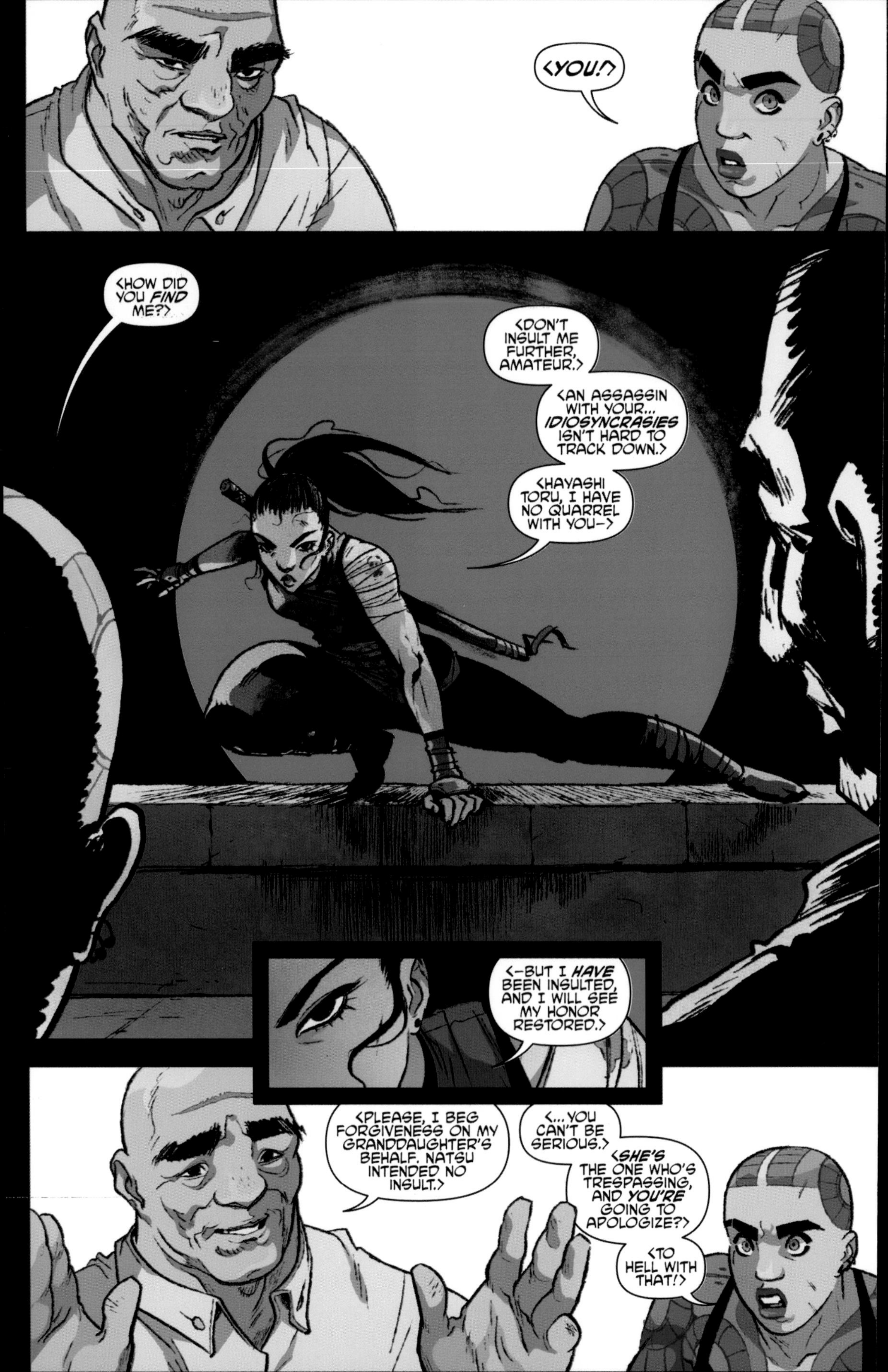
<YOU!?>
<HOW DID YOU FIND ME?>
<DON'T INSULT ME FURTHER, AMATEUR.>
<AN ASSASSIN WITH YOUR... IDIOSYNCRASIES ISN'T HARD TO TRACK DOWN.>
<HAYASHI TORU, I HAVE NO QUARREL WITH YOU–>
<–BUT I HAVE BEEN INSULTED, AND I WILL SEE MY HONOR RESTORED.>
<PLEASE, I BEG FORGIVENESS ON MY GRANDDAUGHTER'S BEHALF. NATSU INTENDED NO INSULT.>
<...YOU CAN'T BE SERIOUS.>
<SHE'S THE ONE WHO'S TRESPASSING, AND YOU'RE GOING TO APOLOGIZE?>
<TO HELL WITH THAT!>

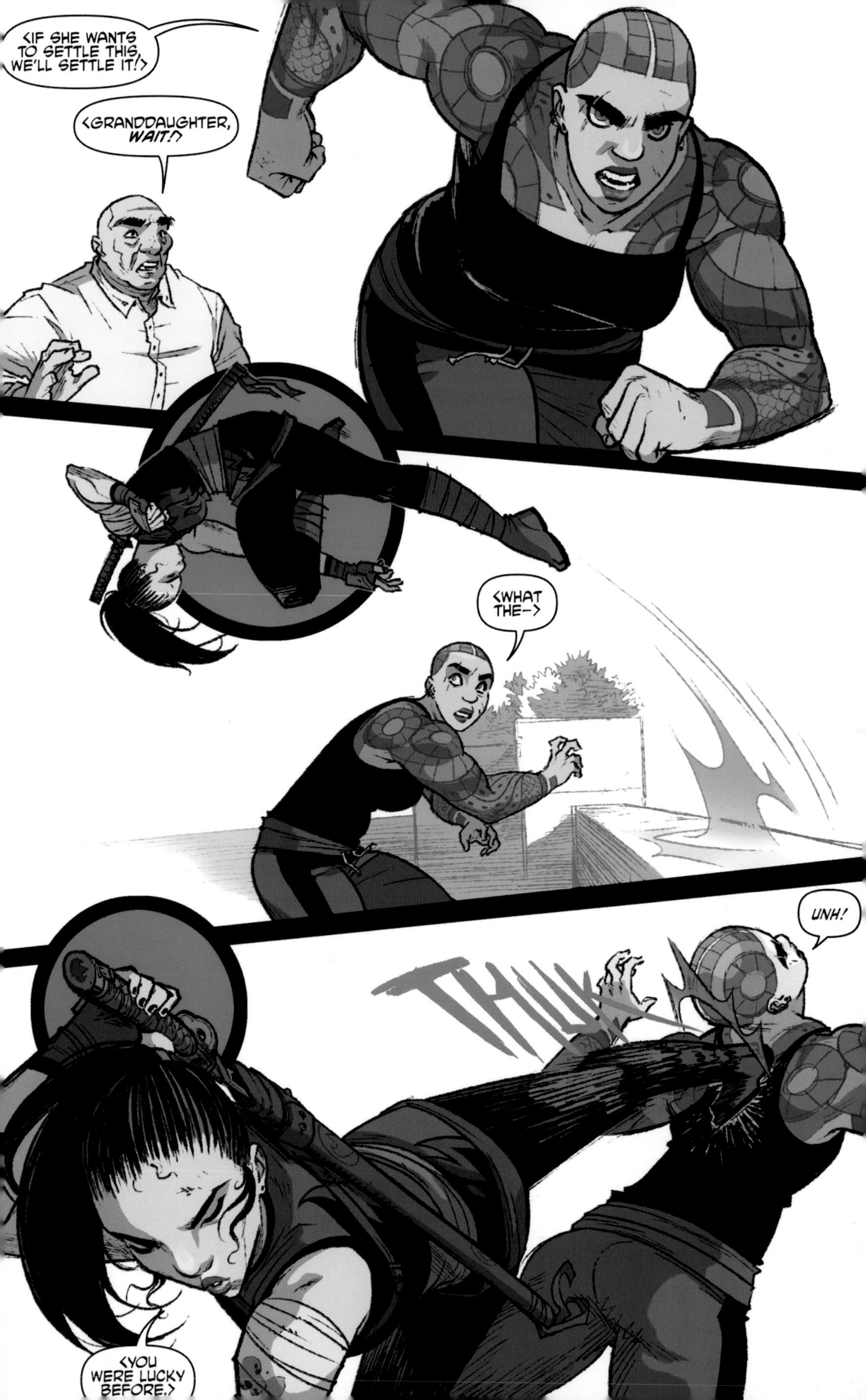
<IF SHE WANTS TO SETTLE THIS, WE'LL SETTLE IT!>
<GRANDDAUGHTER, *WAIT!*>
<WHAT THE-->
UNH!
THUK
<YOU WERE LUCKY BEFORE.>

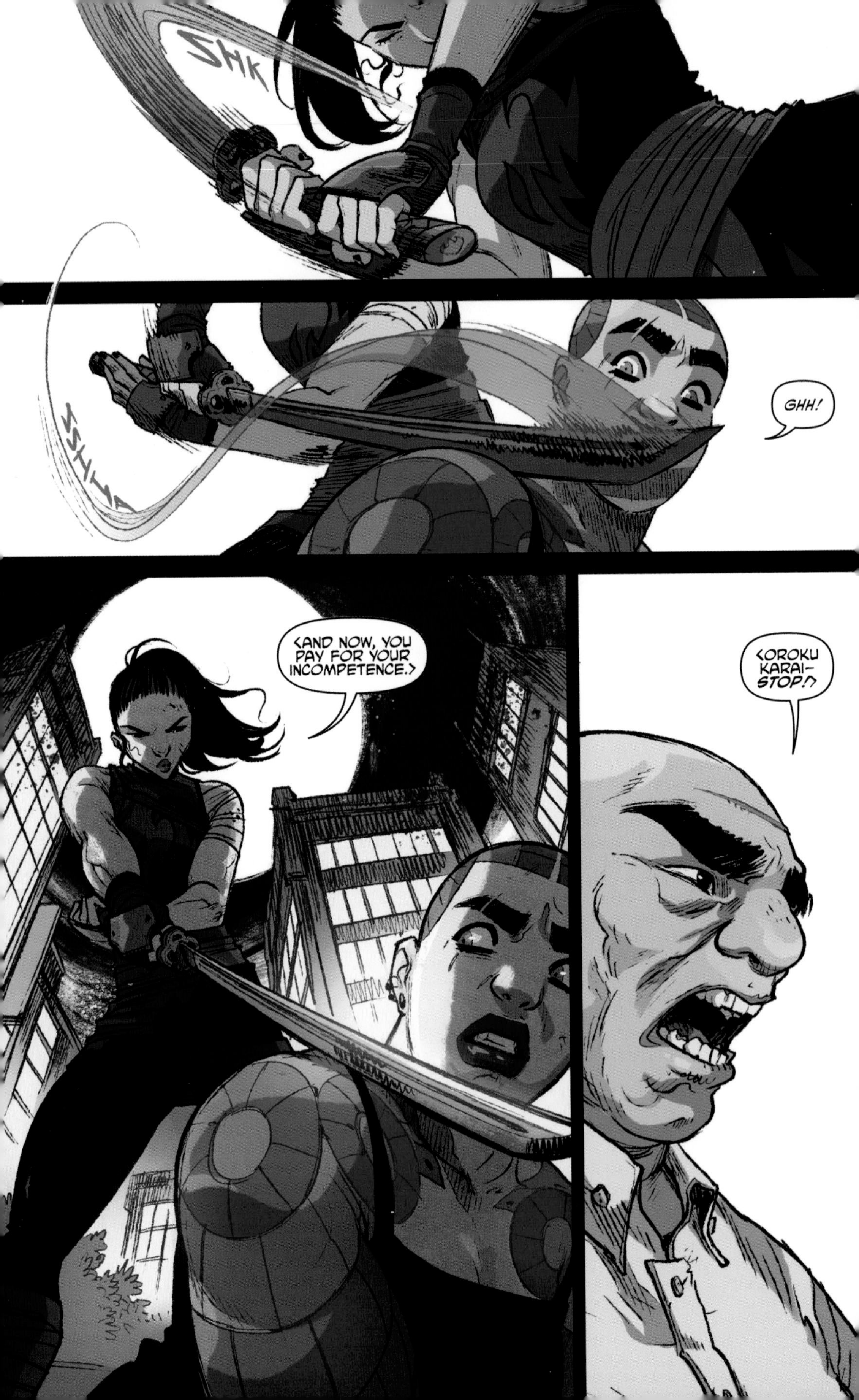
SHK
SSHHA
GHH!
<AND NOW, YOU PAY FOR YOUR INCOMPETENCE.>
<OROKU KARAI-STOP!?>

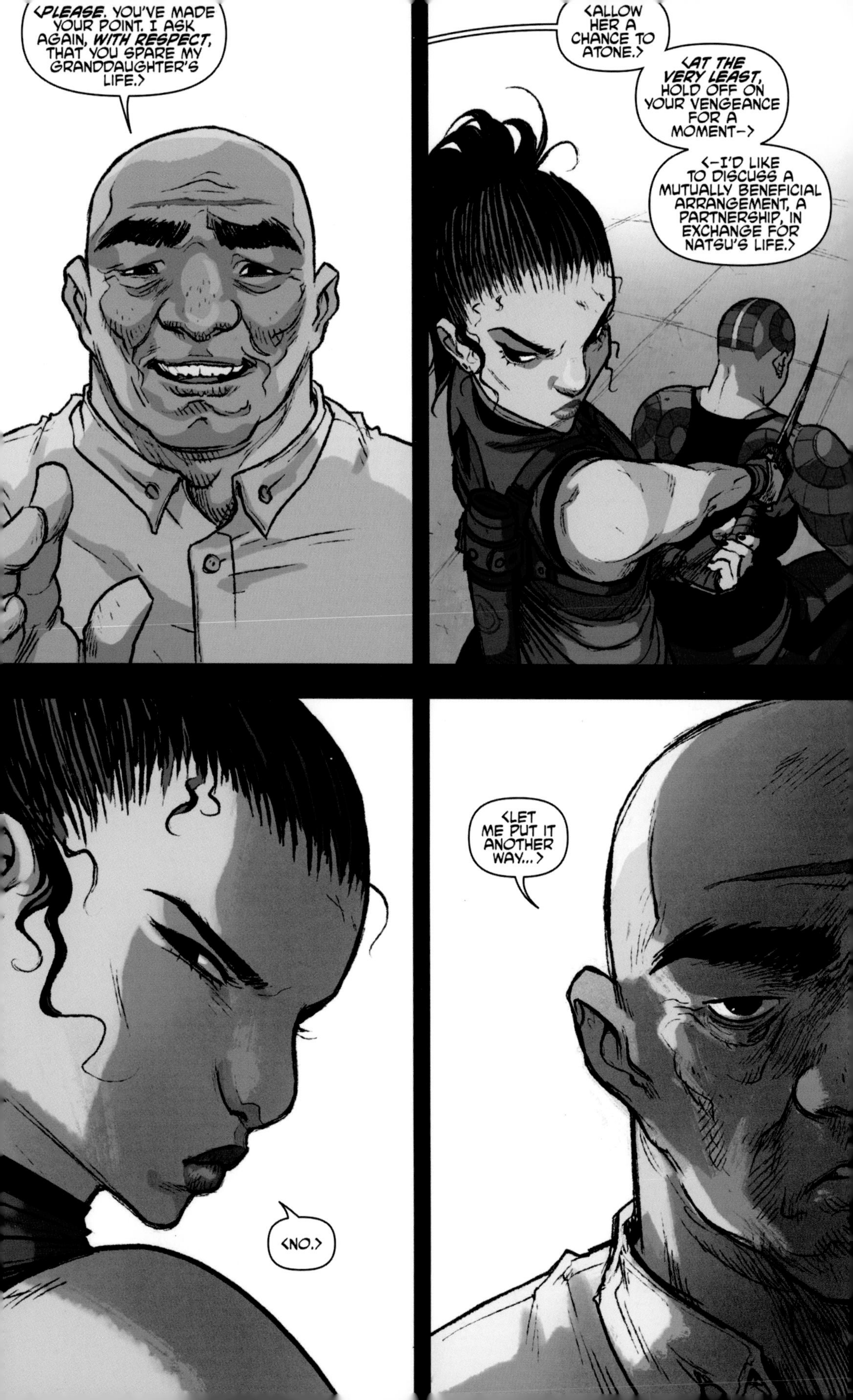
<PLEASE. YOU'VE MADE YOUR POINT. I ASK AGAIN, WITH RESPECT, THAT YOU SPARE MY GRANDDAUGHTER'S LIFE.>
<ALLOW HER A CHANCE TO ATONE.>
<AT THE VERY LEAST, HOLD OFF ON YOUR VENGEANCE FOR A MOMENT-->
<--I'D LIKE TO DISCUSS A MUTUALLY BENEFICIAL ARRANGEMENT, A PARTNERSHIP, IN EXCHANGE FOR NATSU'S LIFE.>
<NO.>
<LET ME PUT IT ANOTHER WAY...>

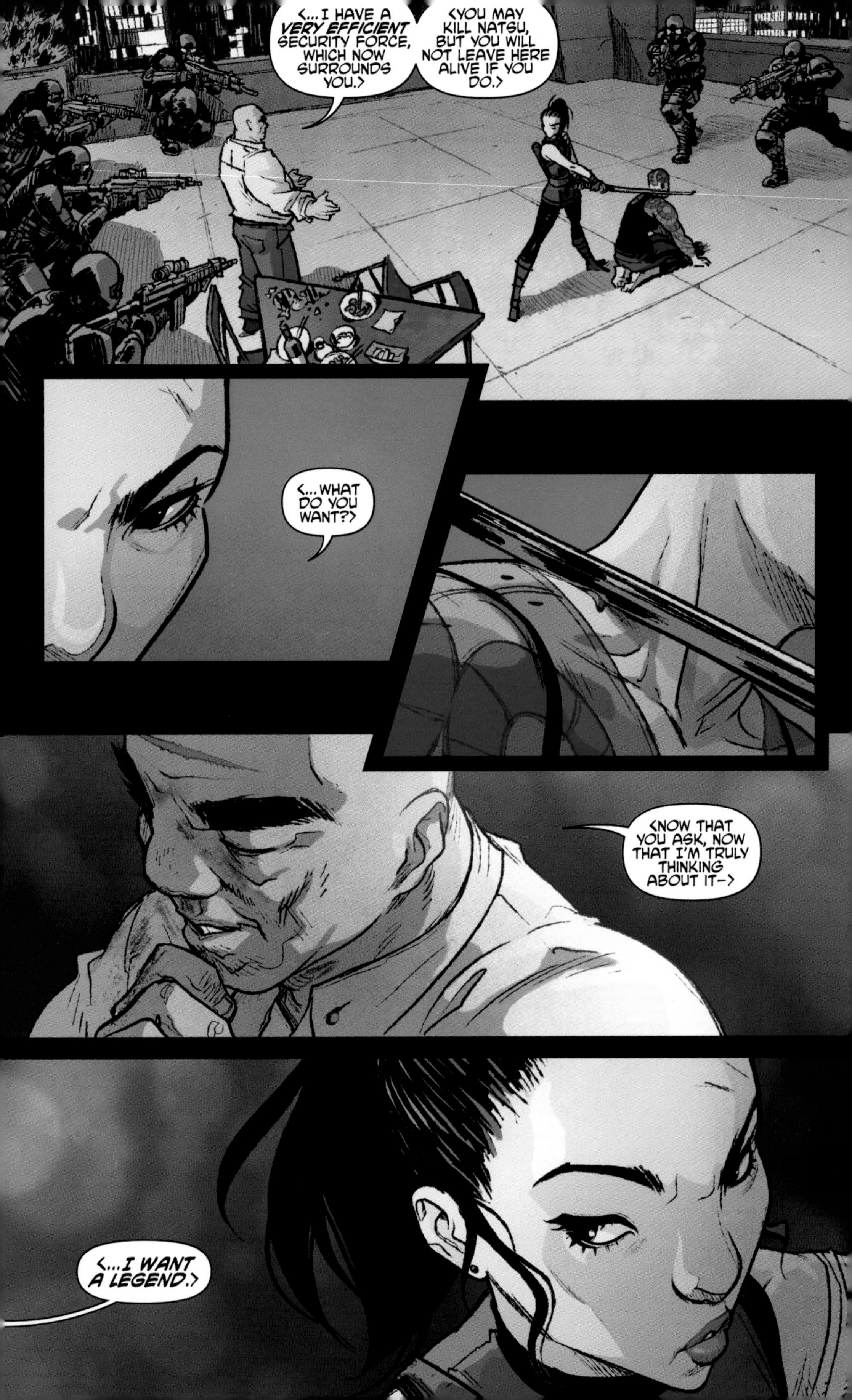
<...I HAVE A **VERY EFFICIENT** SECURITY FORCE, WHICH NOW SURROUNDS YOU.>
<YOU MAY KILL NATSU, BUT YOU WILL NOT LEAVE HERE ALIVE IF YOU DO.>
<...WHAT DO YOU WANT?>
<NOW THAT YOU ASK, NOW THAT I'M TRULY THINKING ABOUT IT-->
<...*I WANT A LEGEND.*>

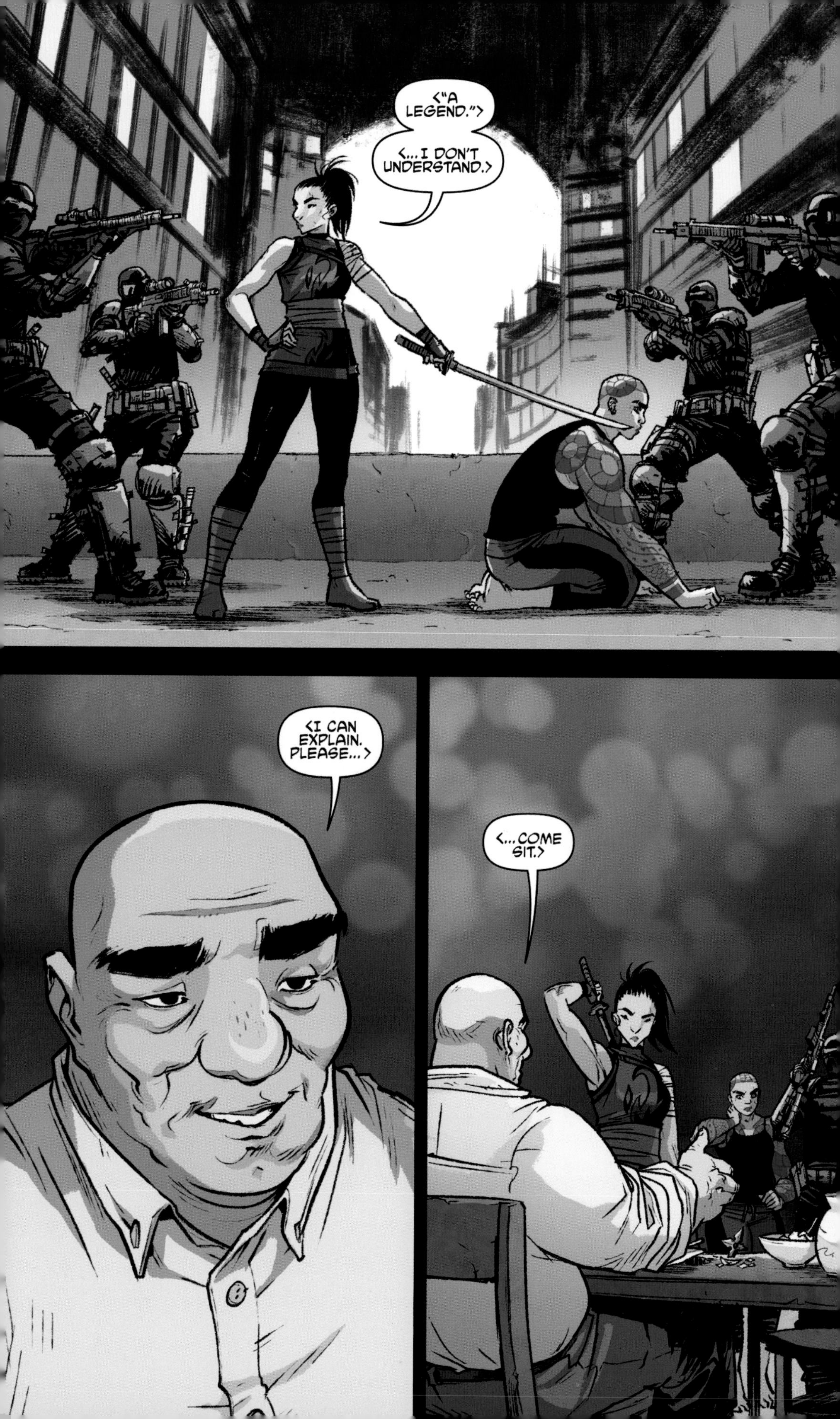
<"A LEGEND.">
<...I DON'T UNDERSTAND.>
<I CAN EXPLAIN. PLEASE...>
<...COME SIT.>

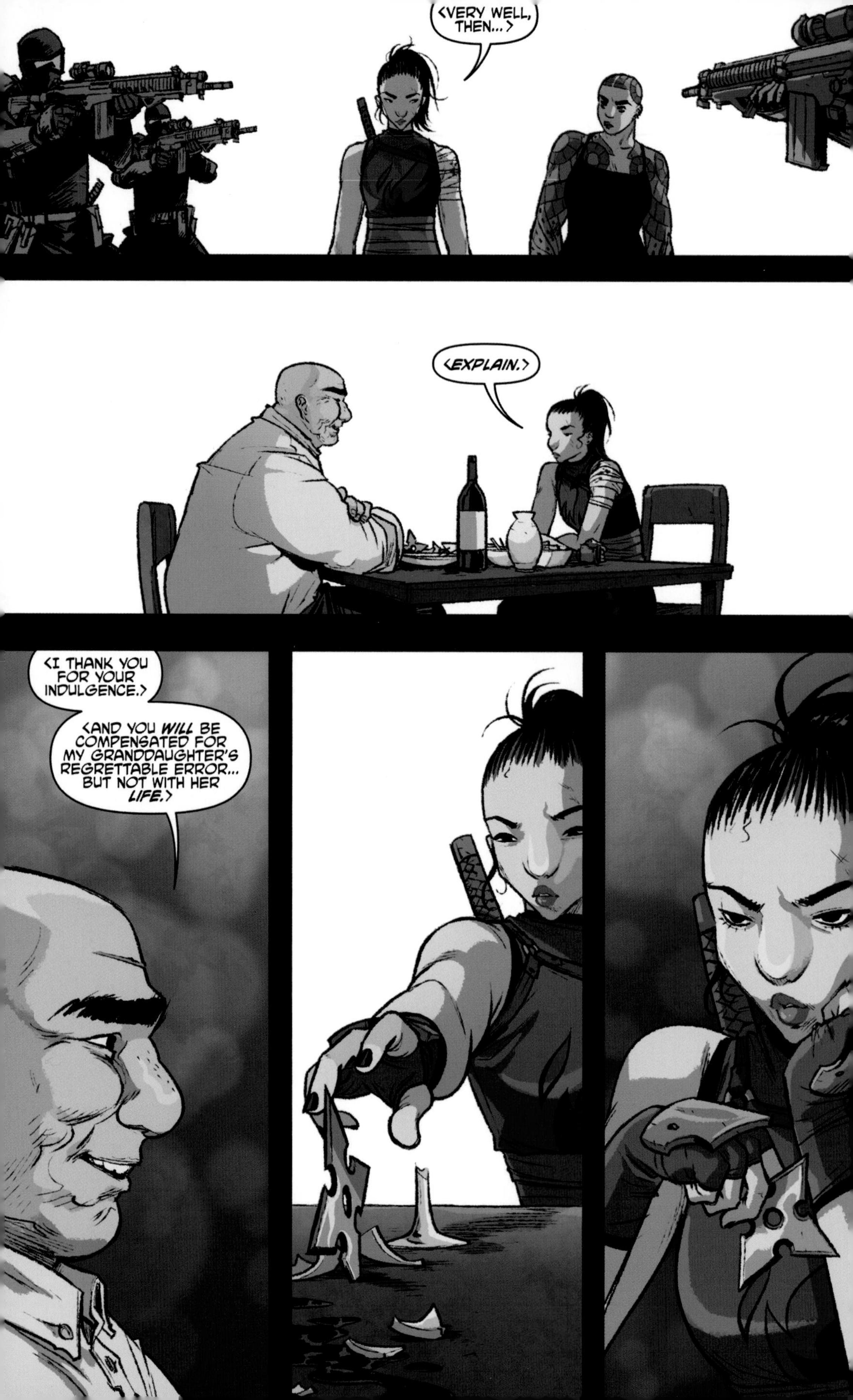
<VERY WELL, THEN...>
<EXPLAIN.>
<I THANK YOU FOR YOUR INDULGENCE.>
<AND YOU WILL BE COMPENSATED FOR MY GRANDDAUGHTER'S REGRETTABLE ERROR... BUT NOT WITH HER LIFE.>

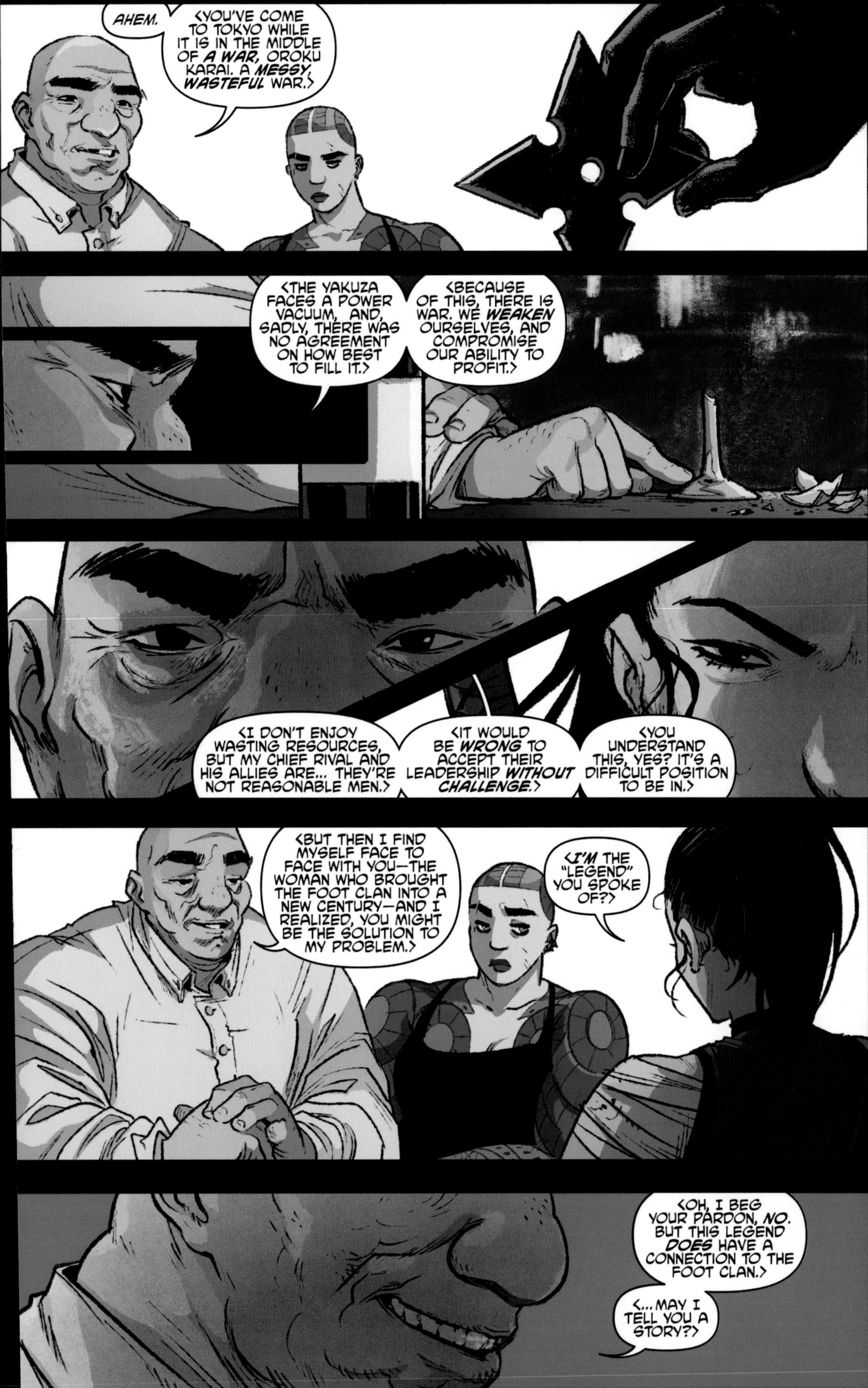
AHEM.
<YOU'VE COME TO TOKYO WHILE IT IS IN THE MIDDLE OF A WAR, OROKU KARAI. A MESSY, WASTEFUL WAR.>
<THE YAKUZA FACES A POWER VACUUM, AND, SADLY, THERE WAS NO AGREEMENT ON HOW BEST TO FILL IT.>
<BECAUSE OF THIS, THERE IS WAR. WE WEAKEN OURSELVES, AND COMPROMISE OUR ABILITY TO PROFIT.>
<I DON'T ENJOY WASTING RESOURCES, BUT MY CHIEF RIVAL AND HIS ALLIES ARE... THEY'RE NOT REASONABLE MEN.>
<IT WOULD BE WRONG TO ACCEPT THEIR LEADERSHIP WITHOUT CHALLENGE.>
<YOU UNDERSTAND THIS, YES? IT'S A DIFFICULT POSITION TO BE IN.>
<BUT THEN I FIND MYSELF FACE TO FACE WITH YOU—THE WOMAN WHO BROUGHT THE FOOT CLAN INTO A NEW CENTURY—AND I REALIZED, YOU MIGHT BE THE SOLUTION TO MY PROBLEM.>
<I'M THE "LEGEND" YOU SPOKE OF?>
<OH, I BEG YOUR PARDON, NO. BUT THIS LEGEND DOES HAVE A CONNECTION TO THE FOOT CLAN.>
<...MAY I TELL YOU A STORY?>

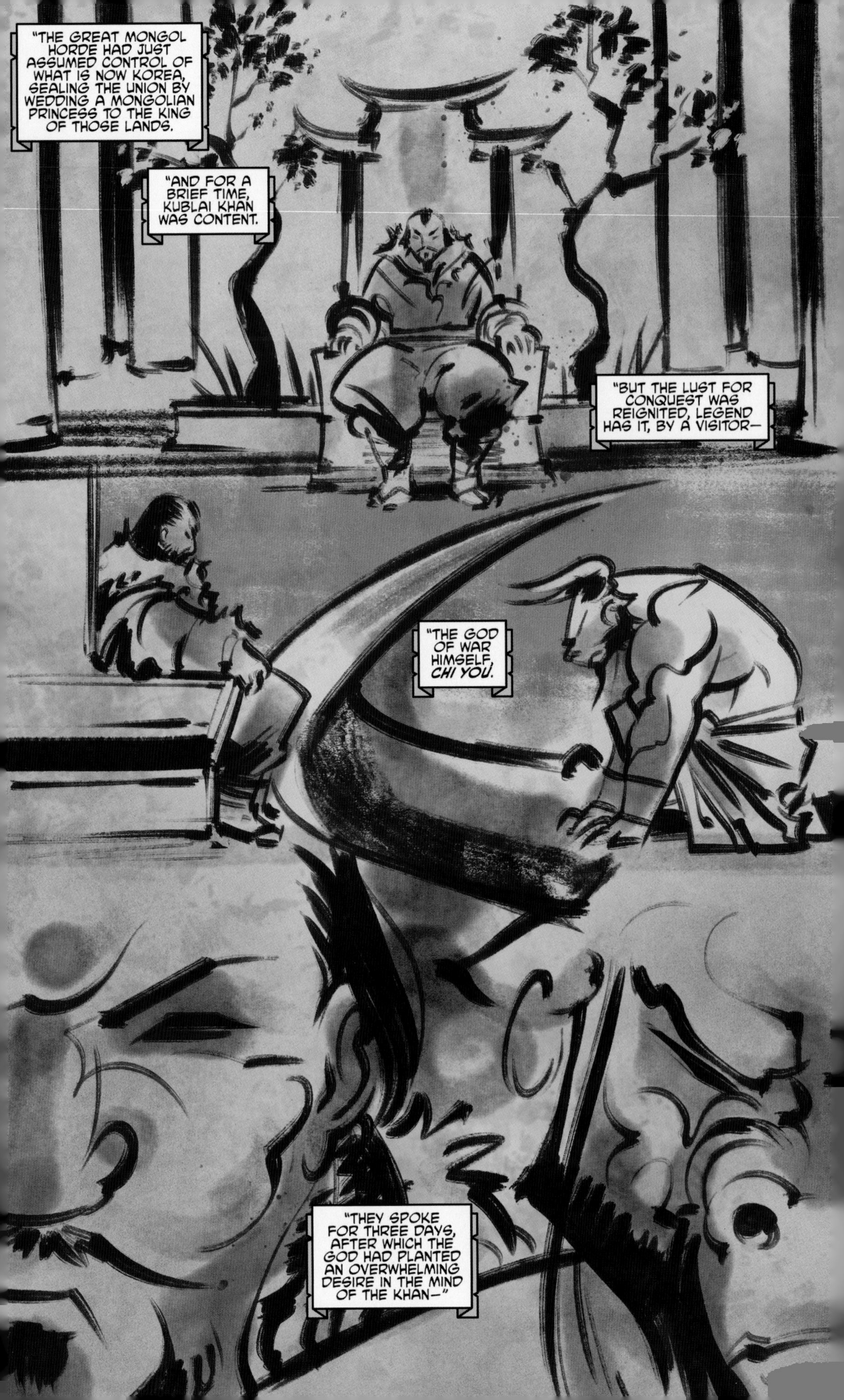
"THE GREAT MONGOL HORDE HAD JUST ASSUMED CONTROL OF WHAT IS NOW KOREA, SEALING THE UNION BY WEDDING A MONGOLIAN PRINCESS TO THE KING OF THOSE LANDS.
"AND FOR A BRIEF TIME, KUBLAI KHAN WAS CONTENT.
"BUT THE LUST FOR CONQUEST WAS REIGNITED, LEGEND HAS IT, BY A VISITOR—
"THE GOD OF WAR HIMSELF, *CHI YOU*.
"THEY SPOKE FOR THREE DAYS, AFTER WHICH THE GOD HAD PLANTED AN OVERWHELMING DESIRE IN THE MIND OF THE KHAN—"

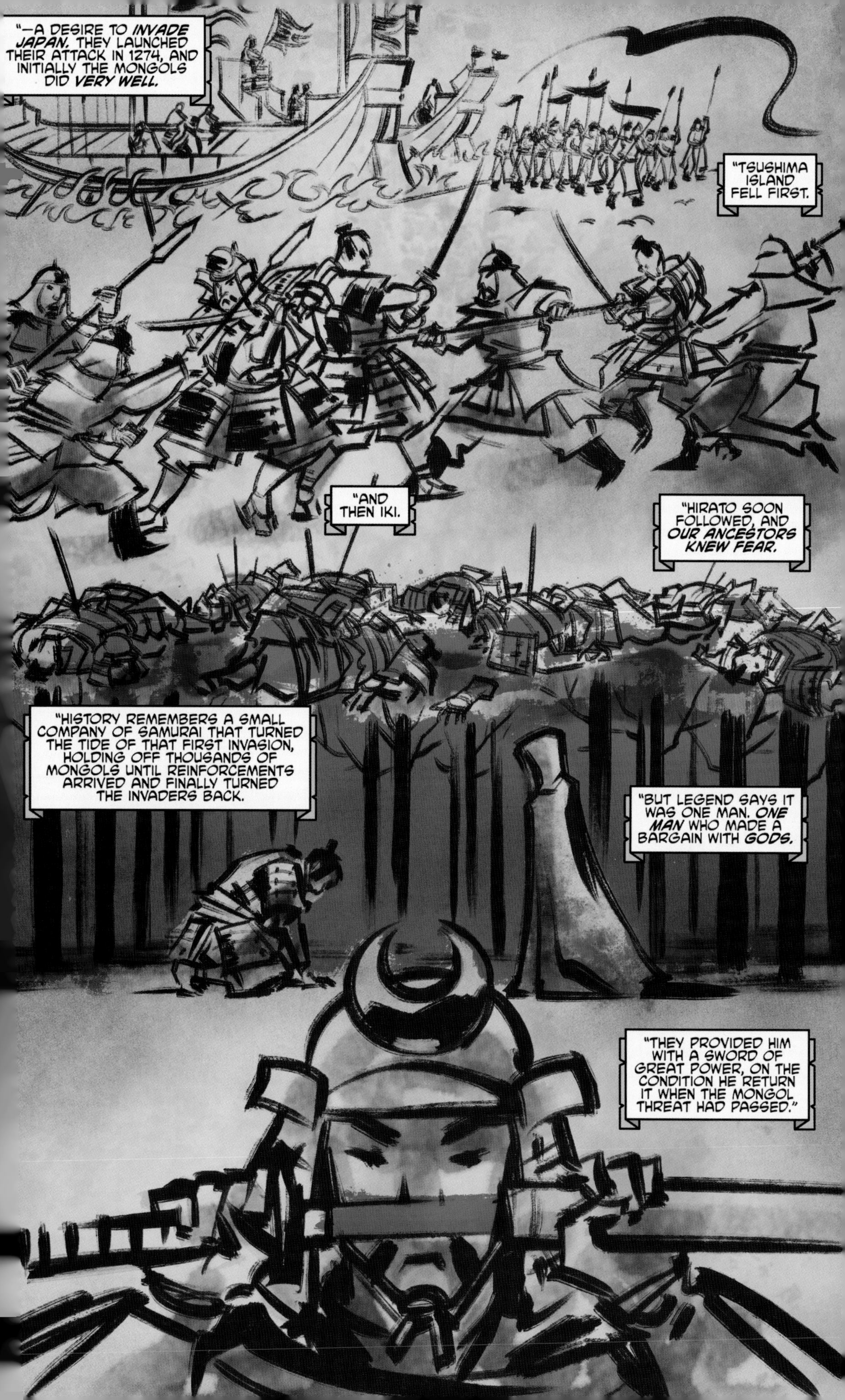
"—A DESIRE TO INVADE JAPAN. THEY LAUNCHED THEIR ATTACK IN 1274, AND INITIALLY THE MONGOLS DID VERY WELL.
"TSUSHIMA ISLAND FELL FIRST.
"AND THEN IKI.
"HIRATO SOON FOLLOWED, AND OUR ANCESTORS KNEW FEAR.
"HISTORY REMEMBERS A SMALL COMPANY OF SAMURAI THAT TURNED THE TIDE OF THAT FIRST INVASION, HOLDING OFF THOUSANDS OF MONGOLS UNTIL REINFORCEMENTS ARRIVED AND FINALLY TURNED THE INVADERS BACK.
"BUT LEGEND SAYS IT WAS ONE MAN. ONE MAN WHO MADE A BARGAIN WITH GODS.
"THEY PROVIDED HIM WITH A SWORD OF GREAT POWER, ON THE CONDITION HE RETURN IT WHEN THE MONGOL THREAT HAD PASSED."

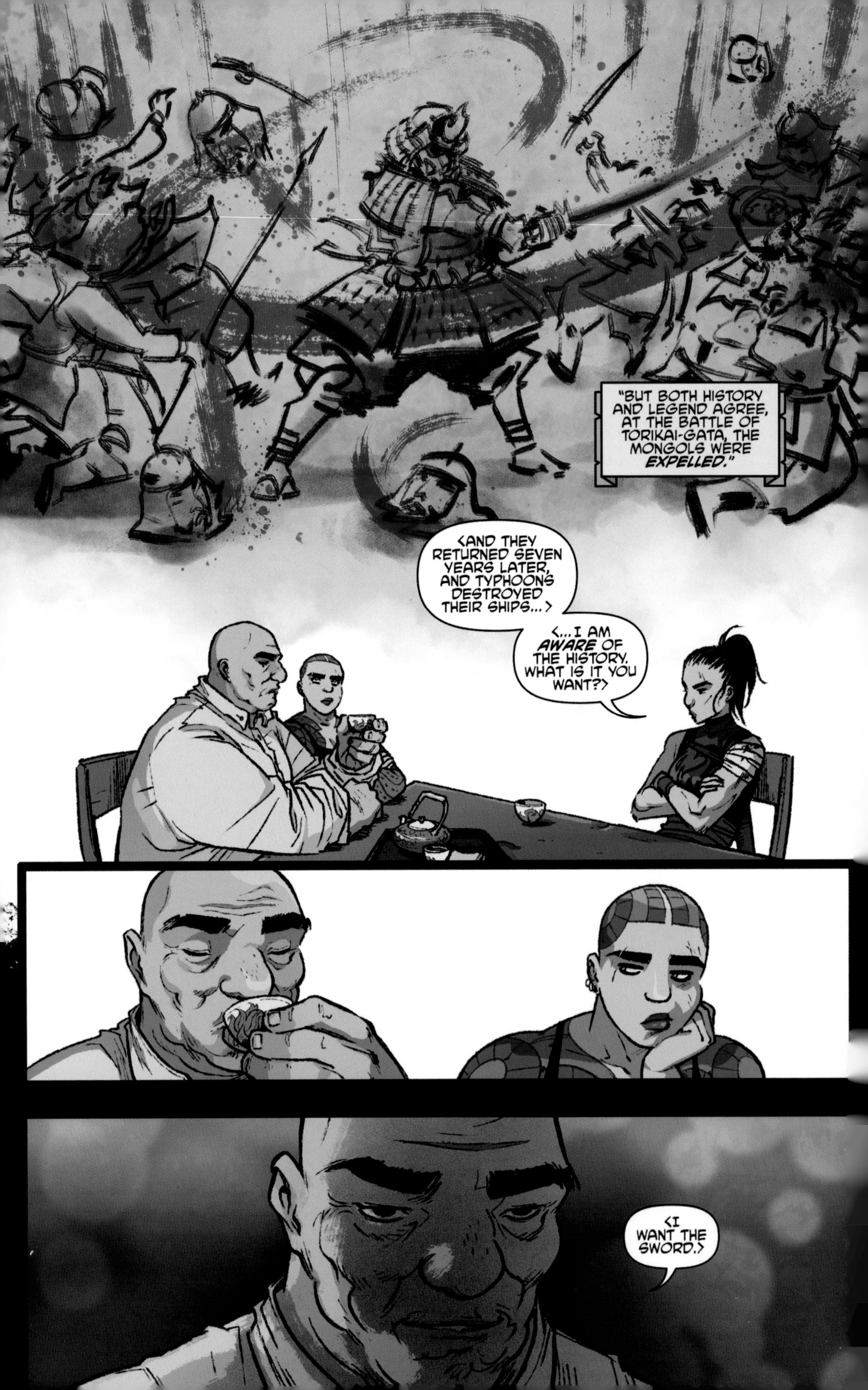
"BUT BOTH HISTORY AND LEGEND AGREE, AT THE BATTLE OF TORIKAI-GATA, THE MONGOLS WERE EXPELLED."
<AND THEY RETURNED SEVEN YEARS LATER, AND TYPHOONS DESTROYED THEIR SHIPS...>
<...I AM AWARE OF THE HISTORY. WHAT IS IT YOU WANT?>
<I WANT THE SWORD.>

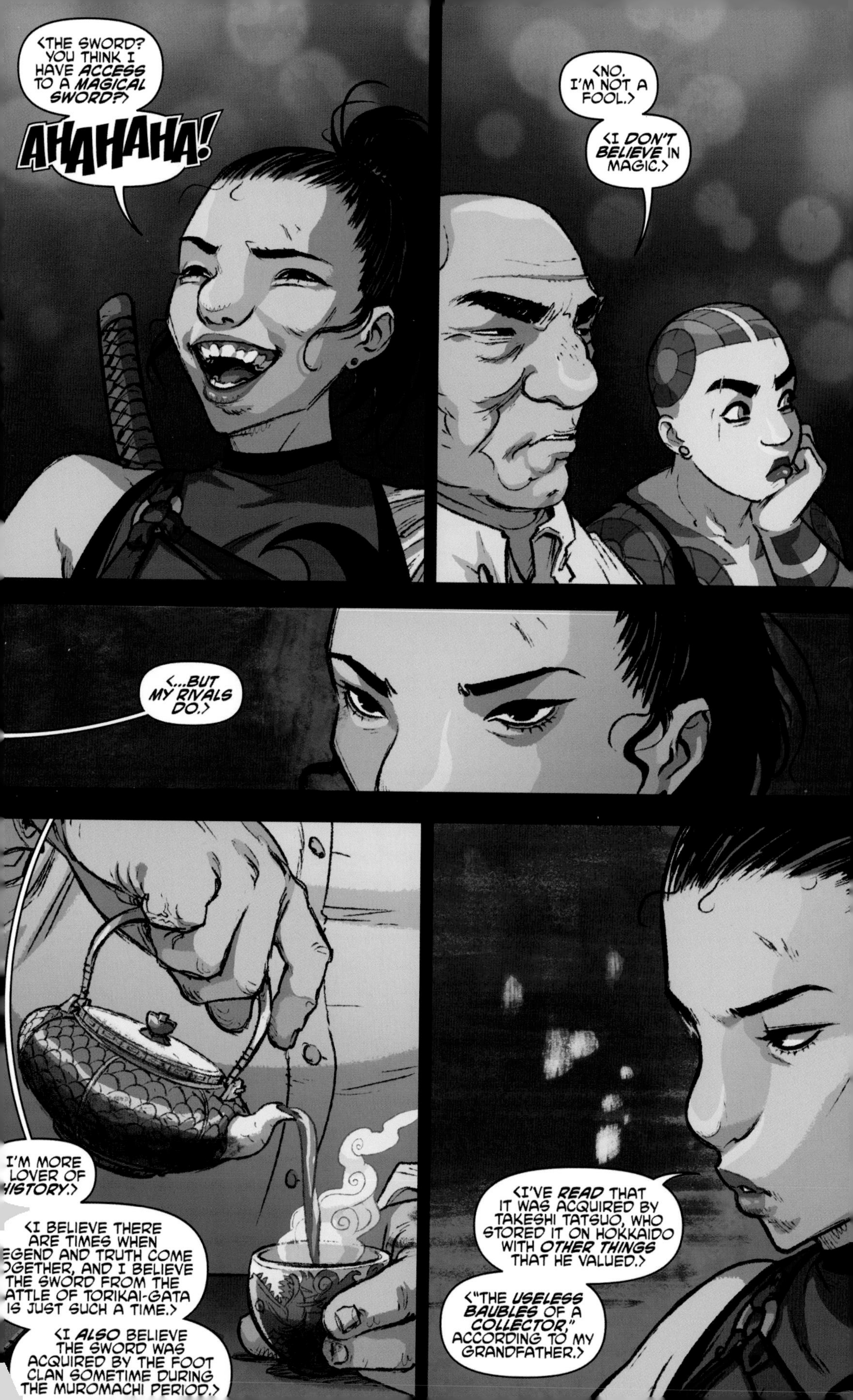
<THE SWORD? YOU THINK I HAVE ACCESS TO A MAGICAL SWORD?>
AHAHAHA!
<NO. I'M NOT A FOOL.>
<I DON'T BELIEVE IN MAGIC.>
<...BUT MY RIVALS DO.>
I'M MORE LOVER OF HISTORY.>
<I BELIEVE THERE ARE TIMES WHEN EGEND AND TRUTH COME OGETHER, AND I BELIEVE THE SWORD FROM THE ATTLE OF TORIKAI-GATA IS JUST SUCH A TIME.>
<I ALSO BELIEVE THE SWORD WAS ACQUIRED BY THE FOOT CLAN SOMETIME DURING THE MUROMACHI PERIOD.>
<I'VE READ THAT IT WAS ACQUIRED BY TAKESHI TATSUO, WHO STORED IT ON HOKKAIDO WITH OTHER THINGS THAT HE VALUED.>
<"THE USELESS BAUBLES OF A COLLECTOR," ACCORDING TO MY GRANDFATHER.>

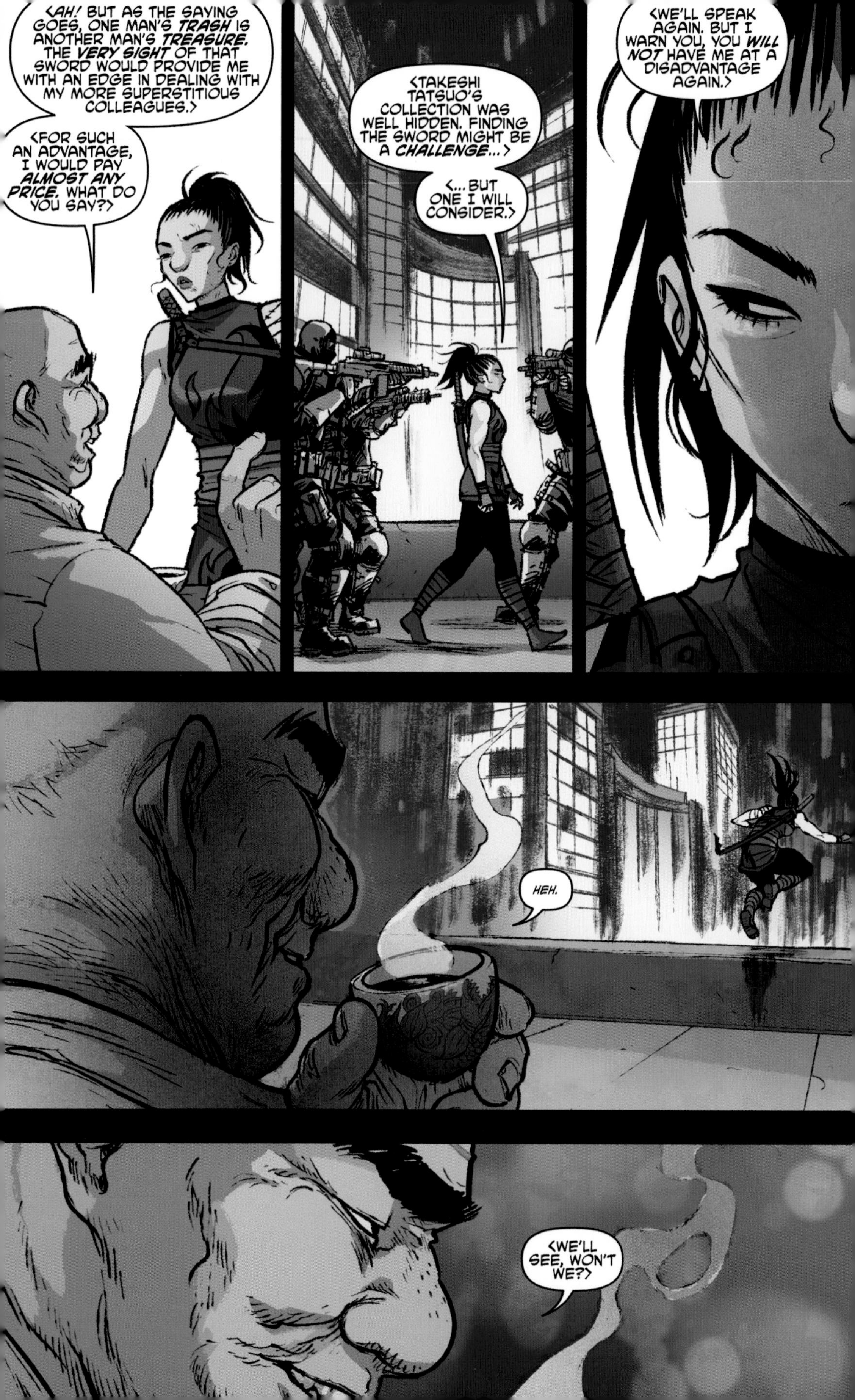
<AH! BUT AS THE SAYING GOES, ONE MAN'S TRASH IS ANOTHER MAN'S TREASURE. THE VERY SIGHT OF THAT SWORD WOULD PROVIDE ME WITH AN EDGE IN DEALING WITH MY MORE SUPERSTITIOUS COLLEAGUES.>
<FOR SUCH AN ADVANTAGE, I WOULD PAY ALMOST ANY PRICE. WHAT DO YOU SAY?>
<TAKESHI TATSUO'S COLLECTION WAS WELL HIDDEN. FINDING THE SWORD MIGHT BE A CHALLENGE...>
<...BUT ONE I WILL CONSIDER.>
<WE'LL SPEAK AGAIN. BUT I WARN YOU, YOU WILL NOT HAVE ME AT A DISADVANTAGE AGAIN.>
HEH.
<WE'LL SEE, WON'T WE?>

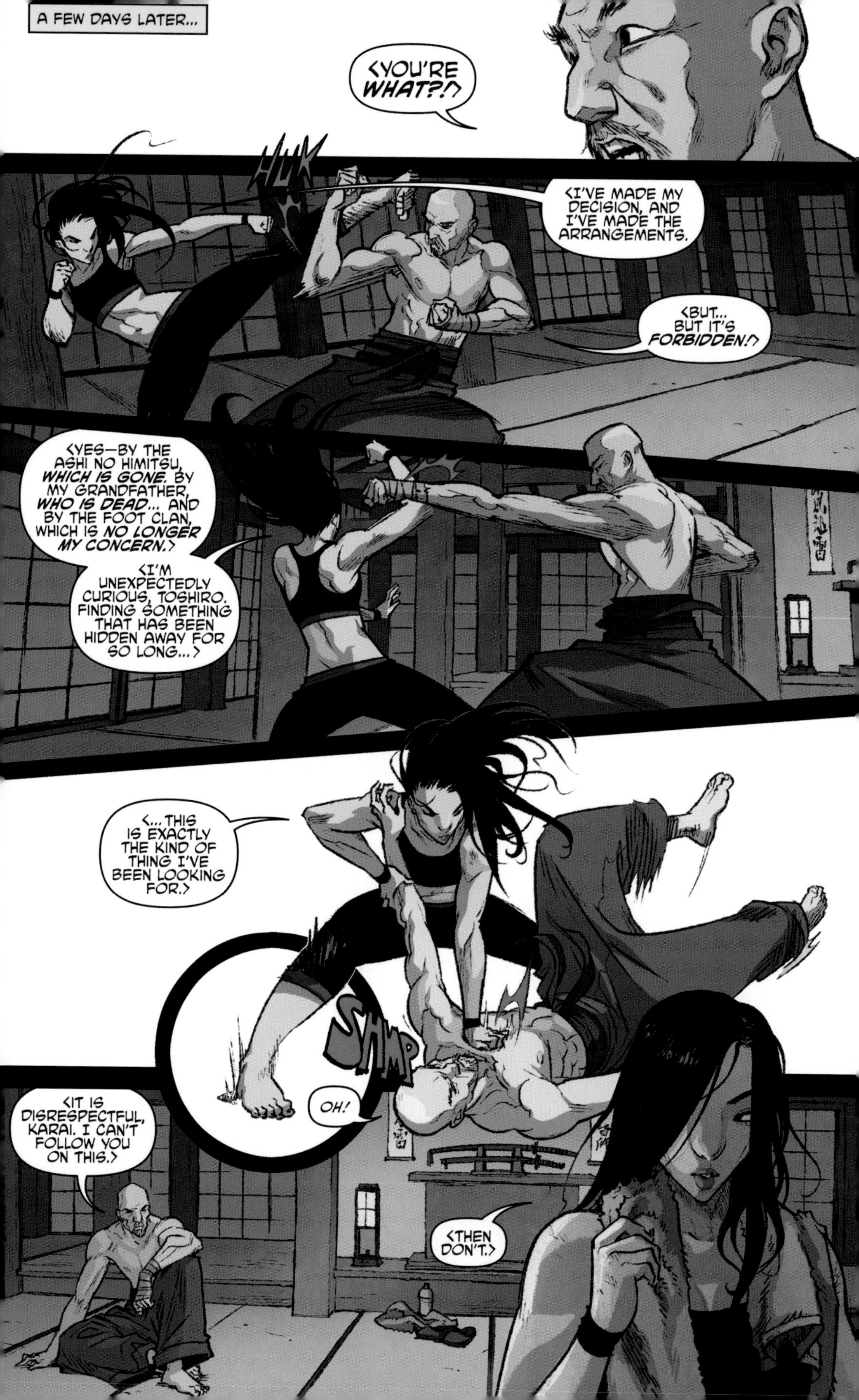
A FEW DAYS LATER...
<YOU'RE WHAT?!>
HUK
<I'VE MADE MY DECISION, AND I'VE MADE THE ARRANGEMENTS.
<BUT... BUT IT'S FORBIDDEN!>
<YES—BY THE ASHI NO HIMITSU, WHICH IS GONE. BY MY GRANDFATHER, WHO IS DEAD... AND BY THE FOOT CLAN, WHICH IS NO LONGER MY CONCERN.>
<I'M UNEXPECTEDLY CURIOUS, TOSHIRO. FINDING SOMETHING THAT HAS BEEN HIDDEN AWAY FOR SO LONG...>
<...THIS IS EXACTLY THE KIND OF THING I'VE BEEN LOOKING FOR.>
SHMP
OH!
<IT IS DISRESPECTFUL, KARAI. I CAN'T FOLLOW YOU ON THIS.>
<THEN DON'T.>

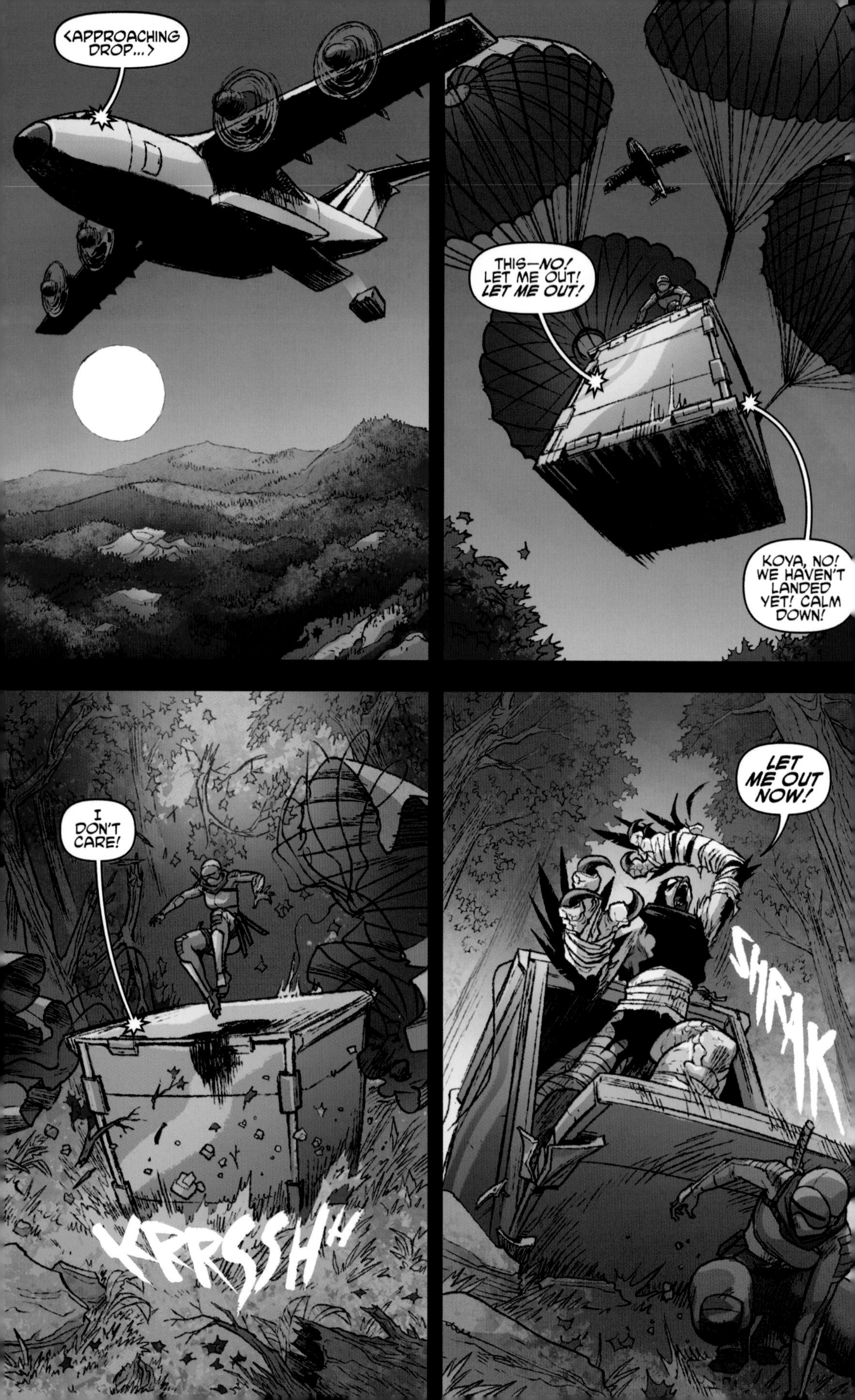
<APPROACHING DROP...>
THIS—NO! LET ME OUT! LET ME OUT!
KOYA, NO! WE HAVEN'T LANDED YET! CALM DOWN!
I DON'T CARE!
KRRSSHH
LET ME OUT NOW!
SHRAK

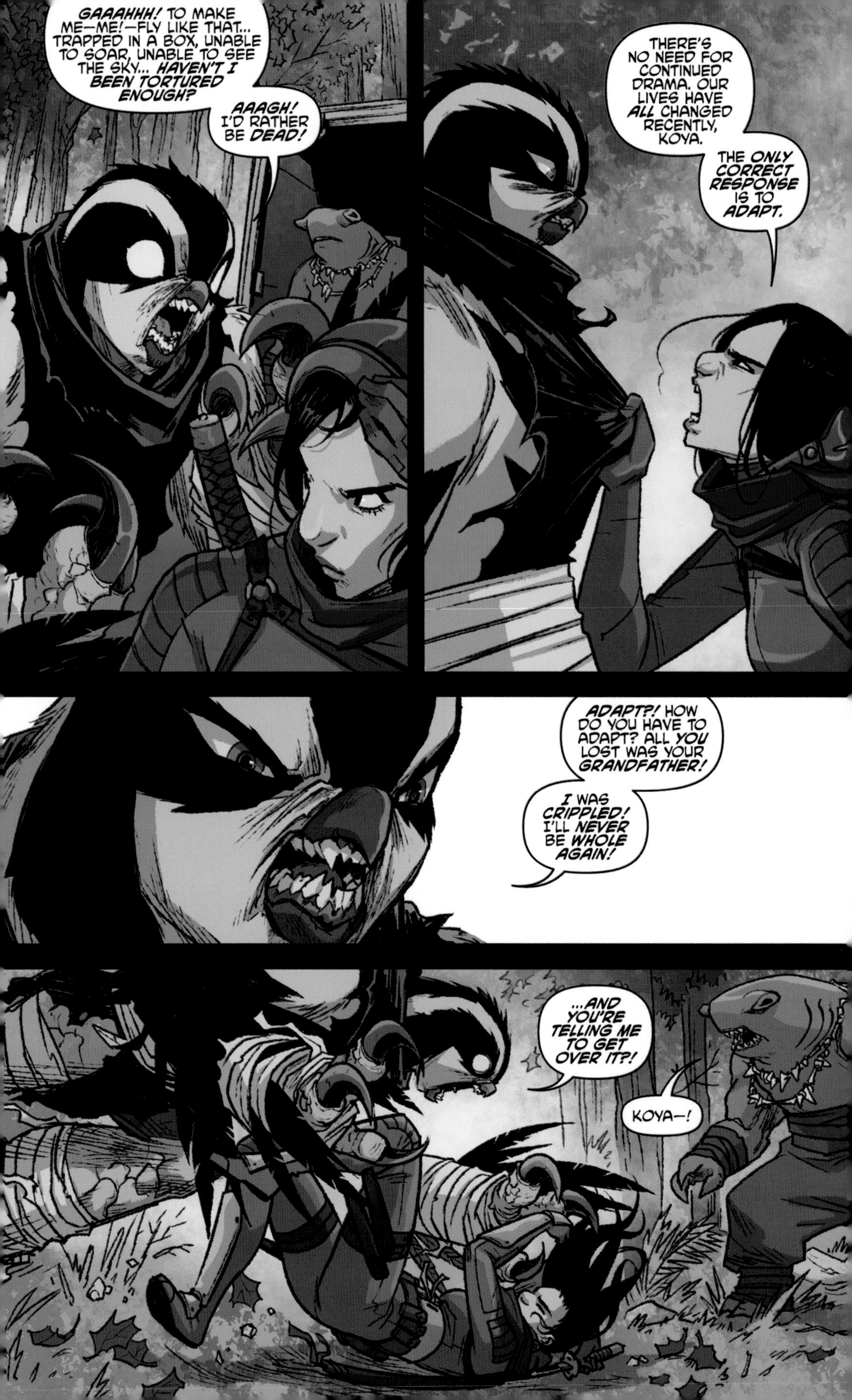
GAAAHHH! TO MAKE ME—ME!—FLY LIKE THAT... TRAPPED IN A BOX, UNABLE TO SOAR, UNABLE TO SEE THE SKY... HAVEN'T I BEEN TORTURED ENOUGH?
AAAGH! I'D RATHER BE DEAD!
THERE'S NO NEED FOR CONTINUED DRAMA. OUR LIVES HAVE ALL CHANGED RECENTLY, KOYA.
THE ONLY CORRECT RESPONSE IS TO ADAPT.
ADAPT?! HOW DO YOU HAVE TO ADAPT? ALL YOU LOST WAS YOUR GRANDFATHER!
I WAS CRIPPLED! I'LL NEVER BE WHOLE AGAIN!
...AND YOU'RE TELLING ME TO GET OVER IT?!
KOYA—!

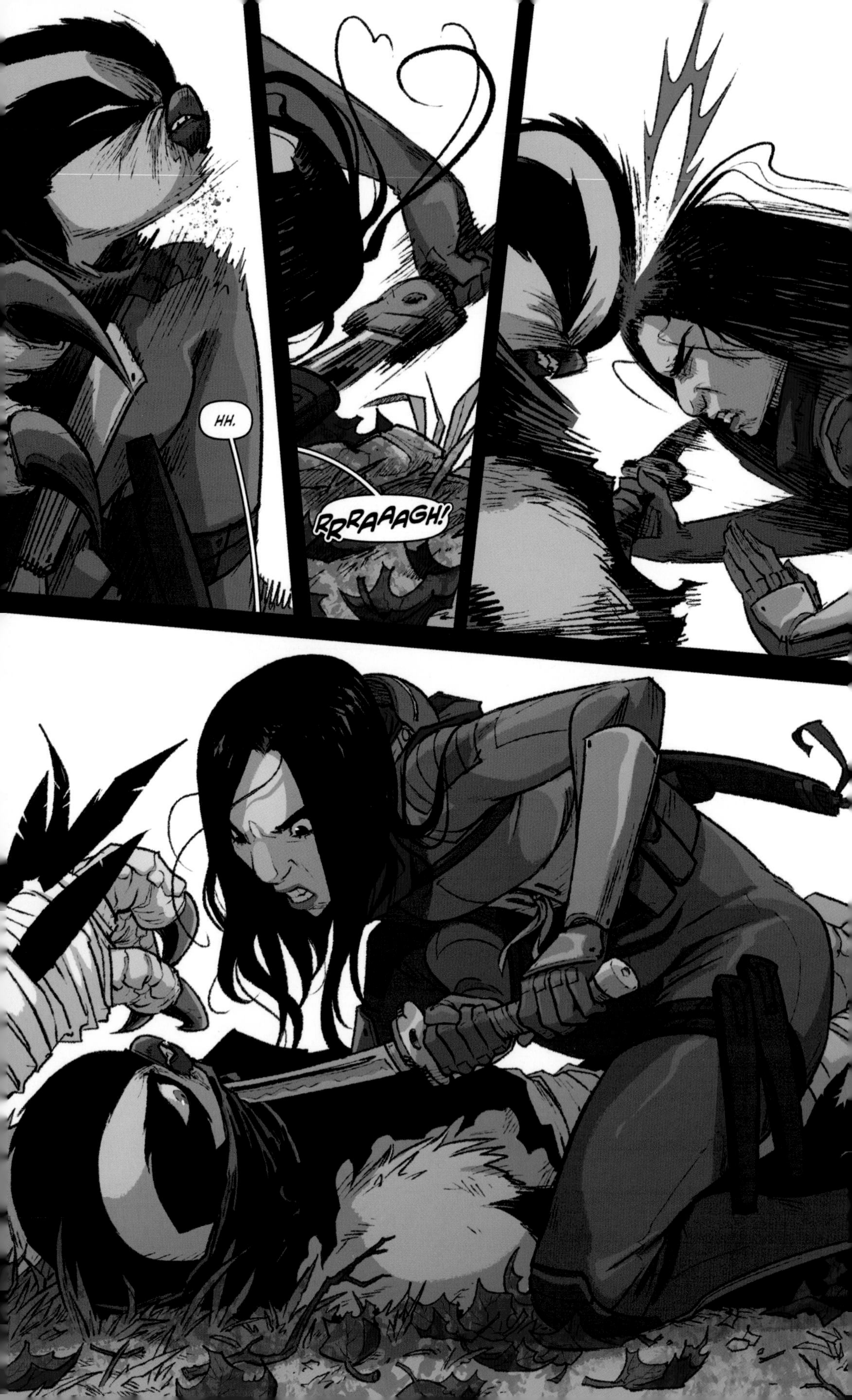
HH.
RRRAAAGH!

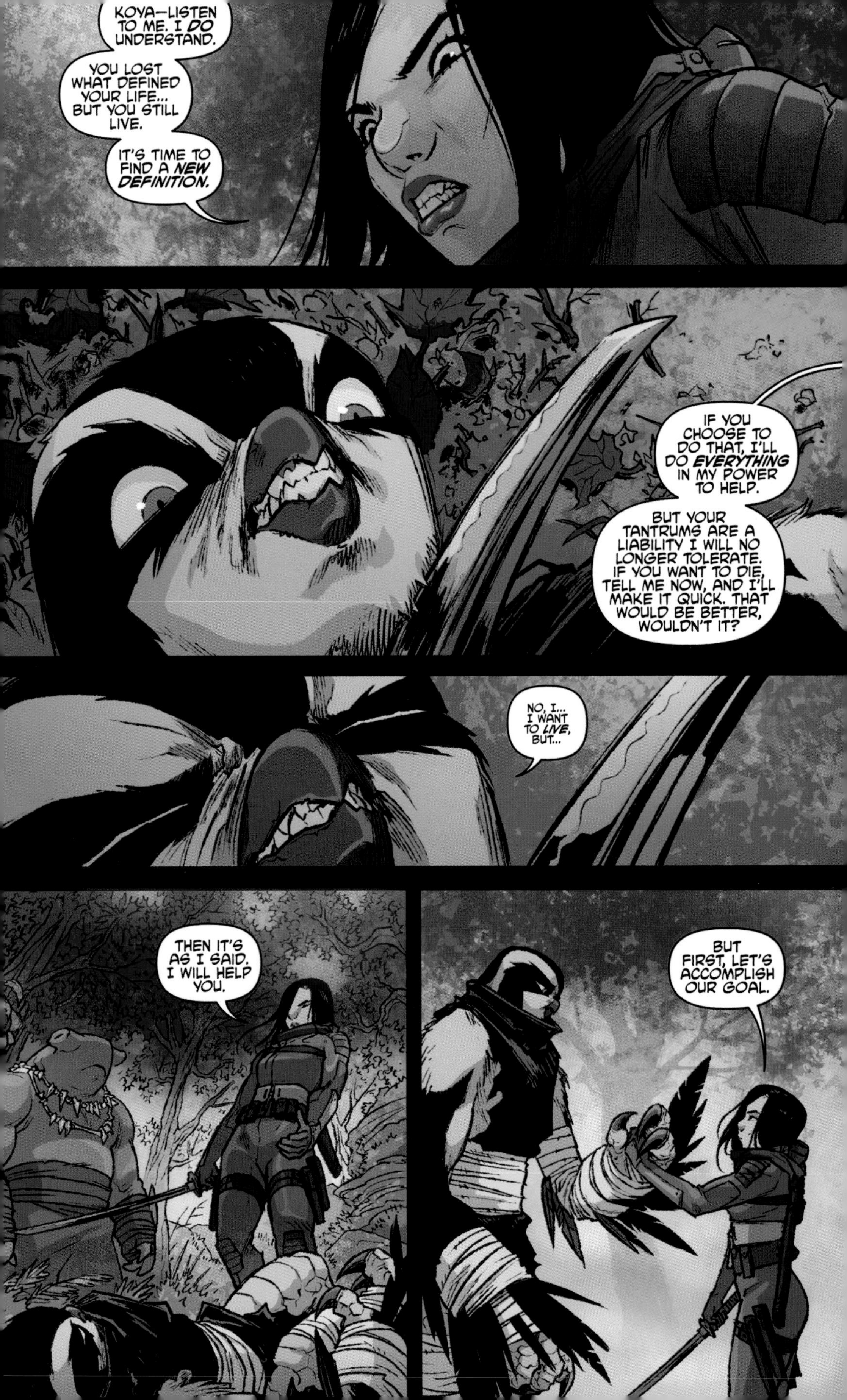
KOYA—LISTEN TO ME. I DO UNDERSTAND.
YOU LOST WHAT DEFINED YOUR LIFE... BUT YOU STILL LIVE.
IT'S TIME TO FIND A NEW DEFINITION.
IF YOU CHOOSE TO DO THAT, I'LL DO EVERYTHING IN MY POWER TO HELP.
BUT YOUR TANTRUMS ARE A LIABILITY I WILL NO LONGER TOLERATE. IF YOU WANT TO DIE, TELL ME NOW, AND I'LL MAKE IT QUICK. THAT WOULD BE BETTER, WOULDN'T IT?
NO, I... I WANT TO LIVE, BUT...
THEN IT'S AS I SAID. I WILL HELP YOU.
BUT FIRST, LET'S ACCOMPLISH OUR GOAL.

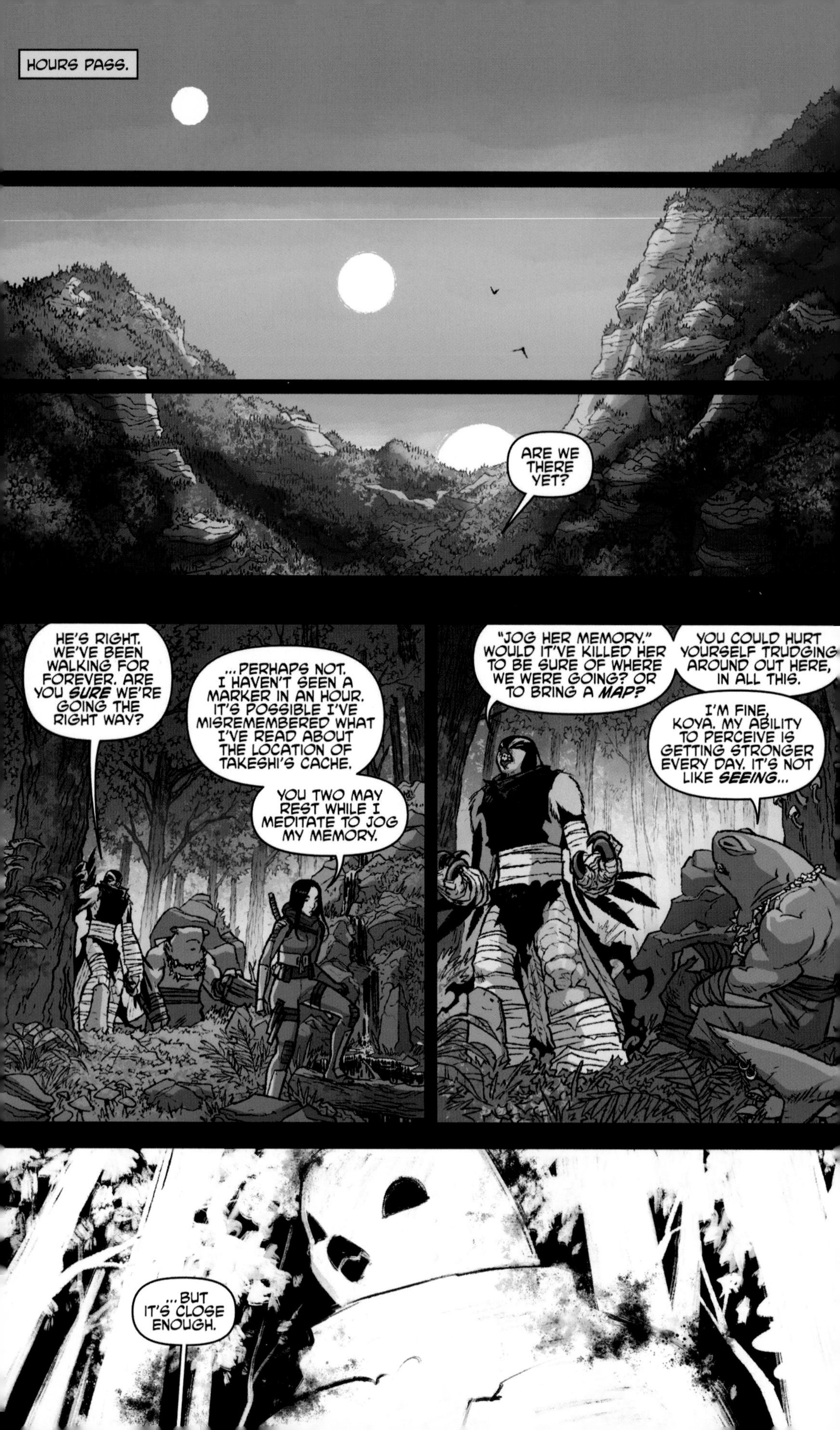
HOURS PASS.
ARE WE THERE YET?
HE'S RIGHT. WE'VE BEEN WALKING FOREVER. ARE YOU *SURE* WE'RE GOING THE RIGHT WAY?
...PERHAPS NOT. I HAVEN'T SEEN A MARKER IN AN HOUR. IT'S POSSIBLE I'VE MISREMEMBERED WHAT I'VE READ ABOUT THE LOCATION OF TAKESHI'S CACHE.
YOU TWO MAY REST WHILE I MEDITATE TO JOG MY MEMORY.
"JOG HER MEMORY." WOULD IT'VE KILLED HER TO BE SURE OF WHERE WE WERE GOING? OR TO BRING A *MAP?*
YOU COULD HURT YOURSELF TRUDGING AROUND OUT HERE, IN ALL THIS.
I'M FINE, KOYA. MY ABILITY TO PERCEIVE IS GETTING STRONGER EVERY DAY. IT'S NOT LIKE *SEEING*...
...BUT IT'S CLOSE ENOUGH.

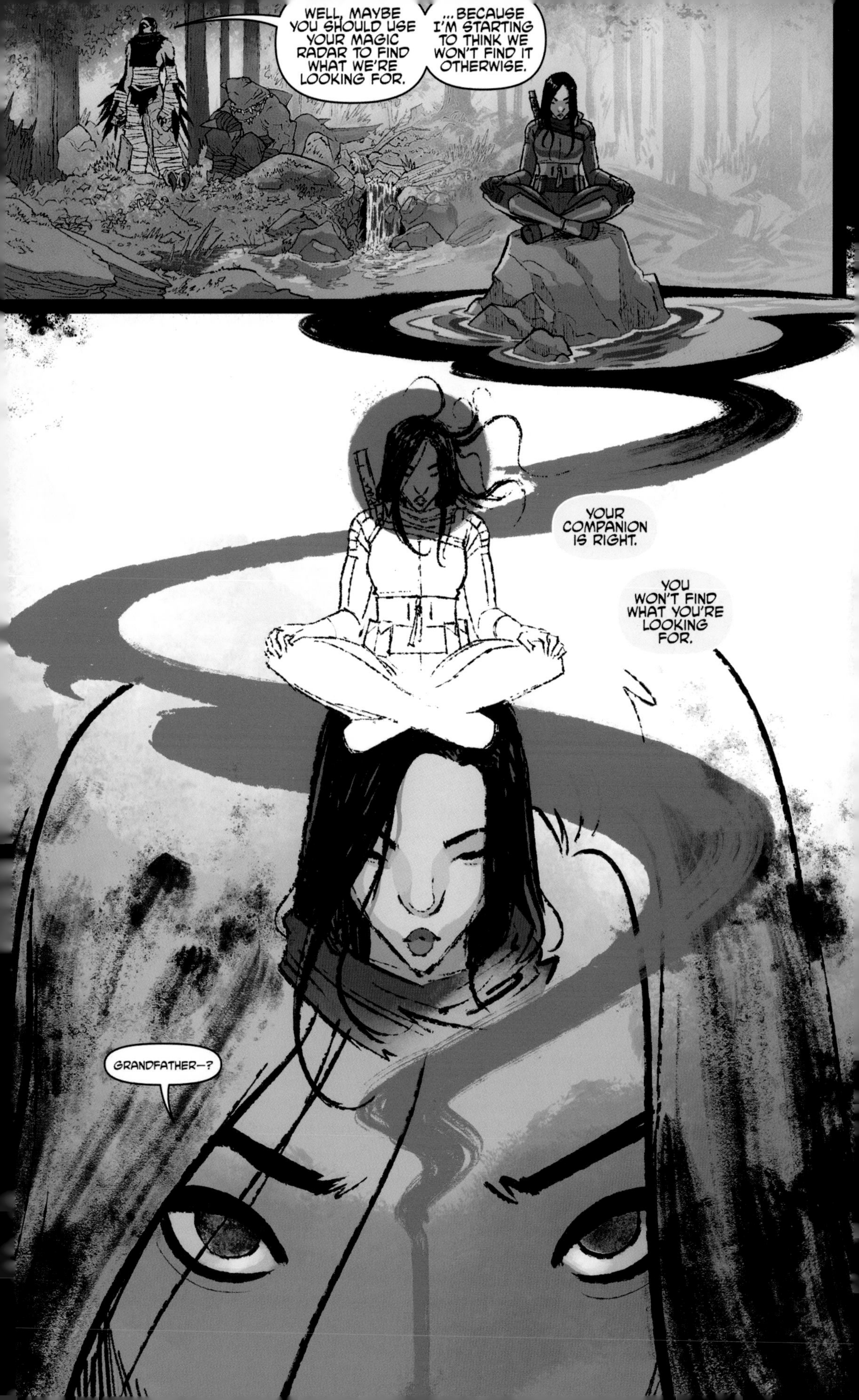
WELL, MAYBE YOU SHOULD USE YOUR MAGIC RADAR TO FIND WHAT WE'RE LOOKING FOR.
...BECAUSE I'M STARTING TO THINK WE WON'T FIND IT OTHERWISE.
YOUR COMPANION IS RIGHT.
YOU WON'T FIND WHAT YOU'RE LOOKING FOR.
GRANDFATHER—?

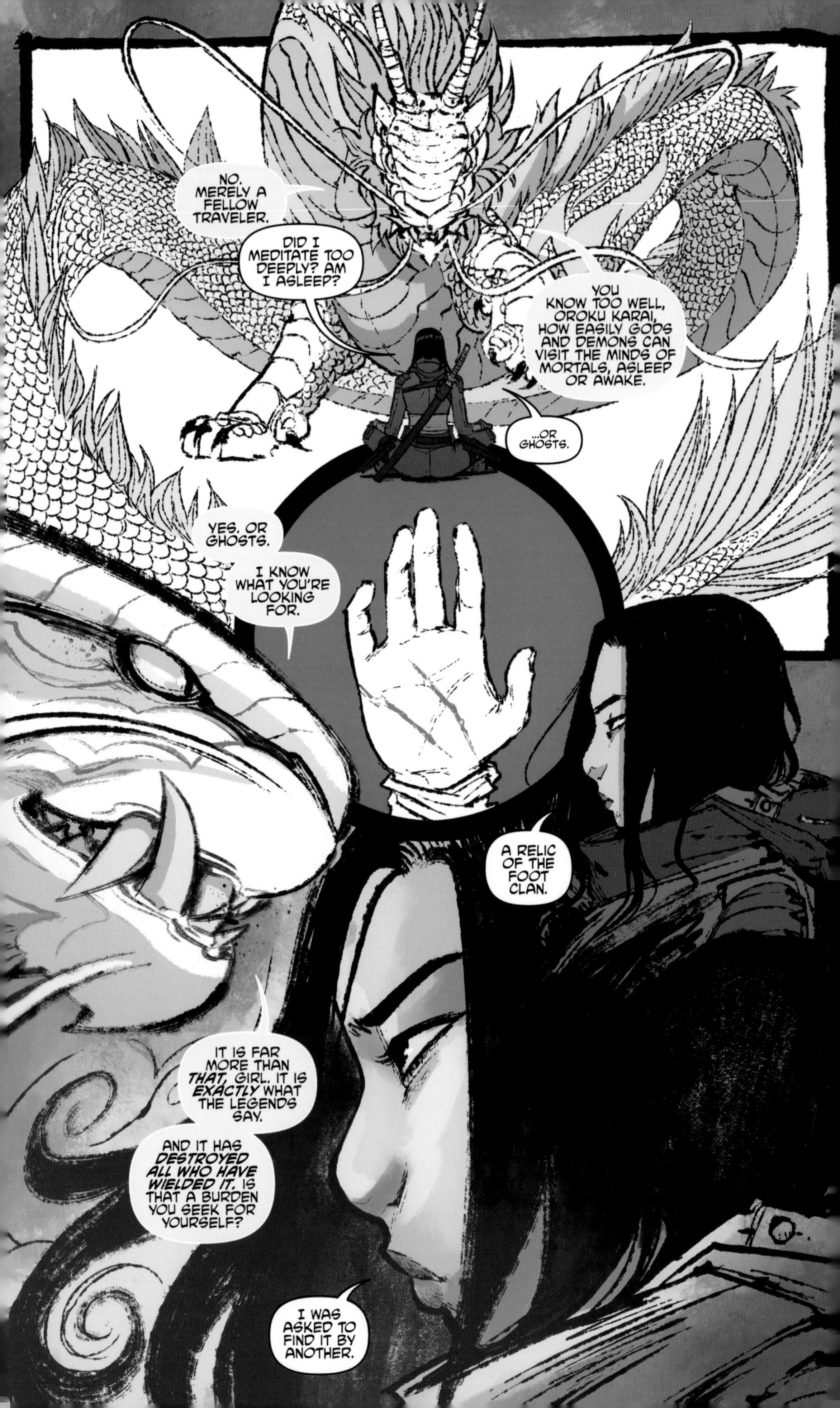

DID I MEDITATE TOO DEEPLY? AM I ASLEEP?
NO. MERELY A FELLOW TRAVELER.
YOU KNOW TOO WELL, OROKU KARAI, HOW EASILY GODS AND DEMONS CAN VISIT THE MINDS OF MORTALS, ASLEEP OR AWAKE.
...OR GHOSTS.
YES. OR GHOSTS.
I KNOW WHAT YOU'RE LOOKING FOR.
A RELIC OF THE FOOT CLAN.
IT IS FAR MORE THAN *THAT,* GIRL. IT IS *EXACTLY* WHAT THE LEGENDS SAY.
AND IT HAS ***DESTROYED ALL WHO HAVE WIELDED IT.*** IS THAT A BURDEN YOU SEEK FOR YOURSELF?
I WAS ASKED TO FIND IT BY ANOTHER.

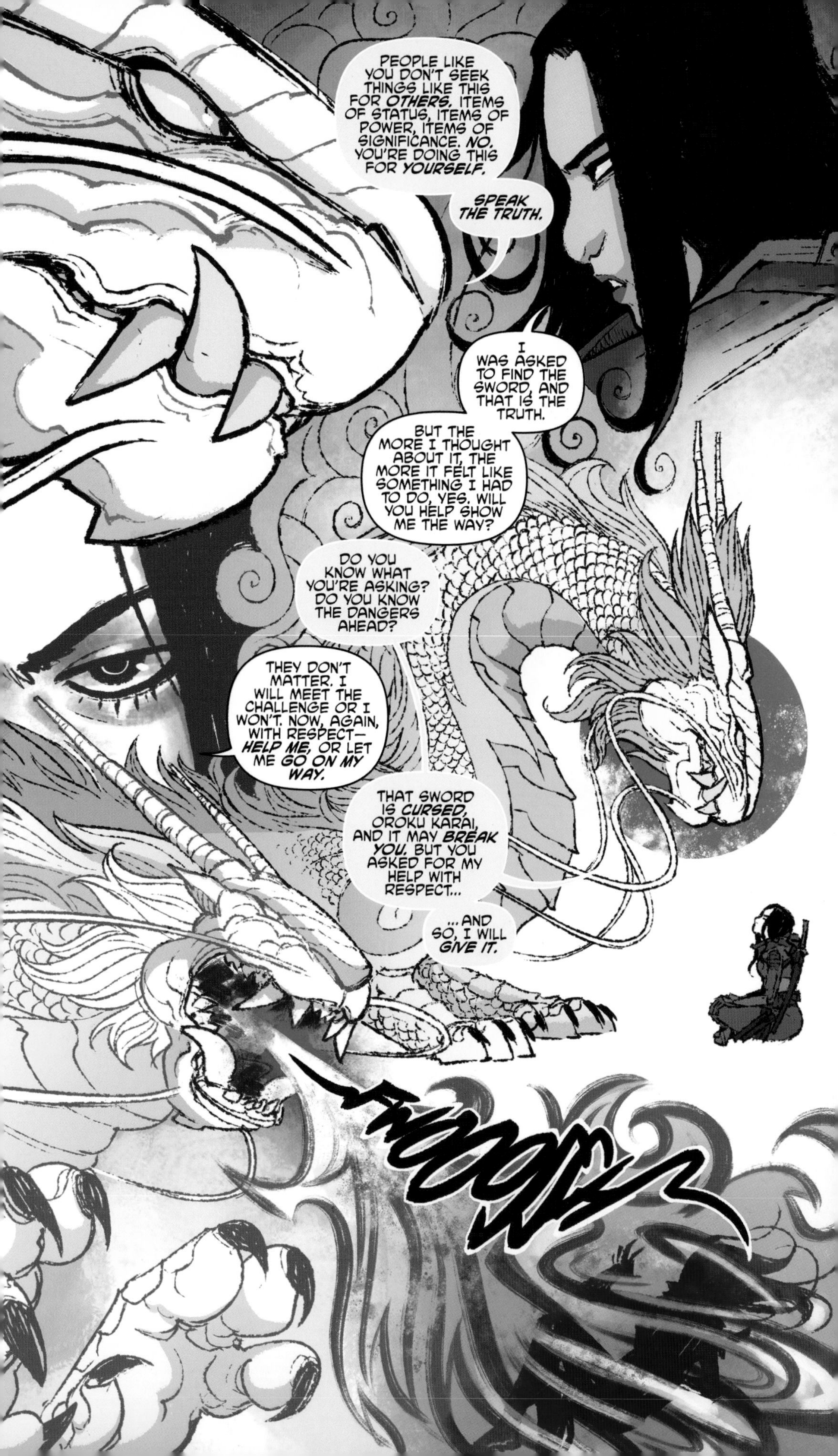
PEOPLE LIKE YOU DON'T SEEK THINGS LIKE THIS FOR *OTHERS.* ITEMS OF STATUS, ITEMS OF POWER, ITEMS OF SIGNIFICANCE. *NO.* YOU'RE DOING THIS FOR *YOURSELF.*
SPEAK THE TRUTH.
I WAS ASKED TO FIND THE SWORD, AND THAT IS THE TRUTH.
BUT THE MORE I THOUGHT ABOUT IT, THE MORE IT FELT LIKE SOMETHING I HAD TO DO, YES. WILL YOU HELP SHOW ME THE WAY?
DO YOU KNOW WHAT YOU'RE ASKING? DO YOU KNOW THE DANGERS AHEAD?
THEY DON'T MATTER. I WILL MEET THE CHALLENGE OR I WON'T. NOW, AGAIN, WITH RESPECT— *HELP ME,* OR LET ME *GO ON MY WAY.*
THAT SWORD IS *CURSED,* OROKU KARAI, AND IT MAY *BREAK YOU.* BUT YOU ASKED FOR MY HELP WITH RESPECT...
...AND SO, I WILL *GIVE IT.*

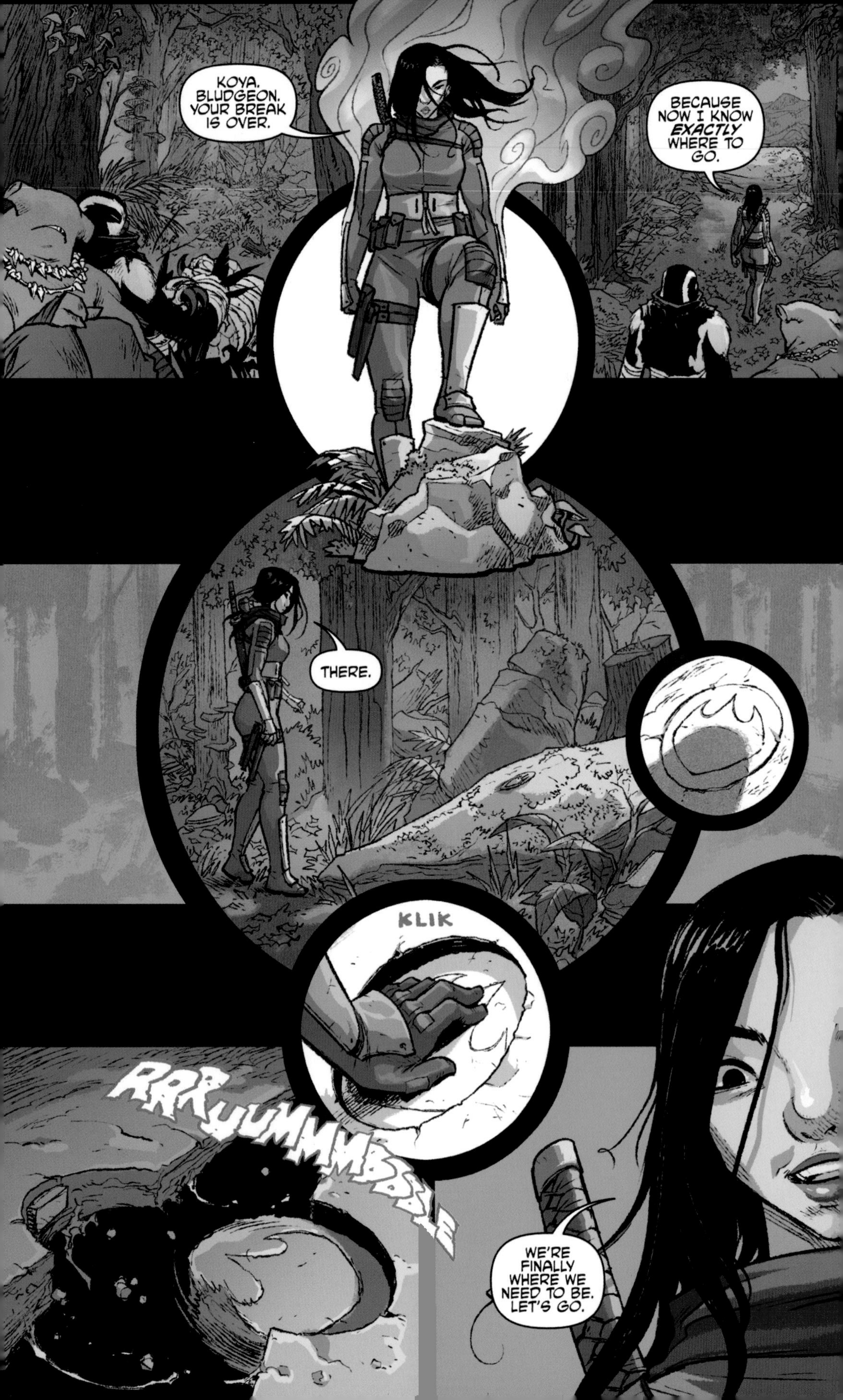
KOYA. BLUDGEON. YOUR BREAK IS OVER.
BECAUSE NOW I KNOW EXACTLY WHERE TO GO.
THERE.
KLIK
RRRUUMMMBBLE
WE'RE FINALLY WHERE WE NEED TO BE. LET'S GO.

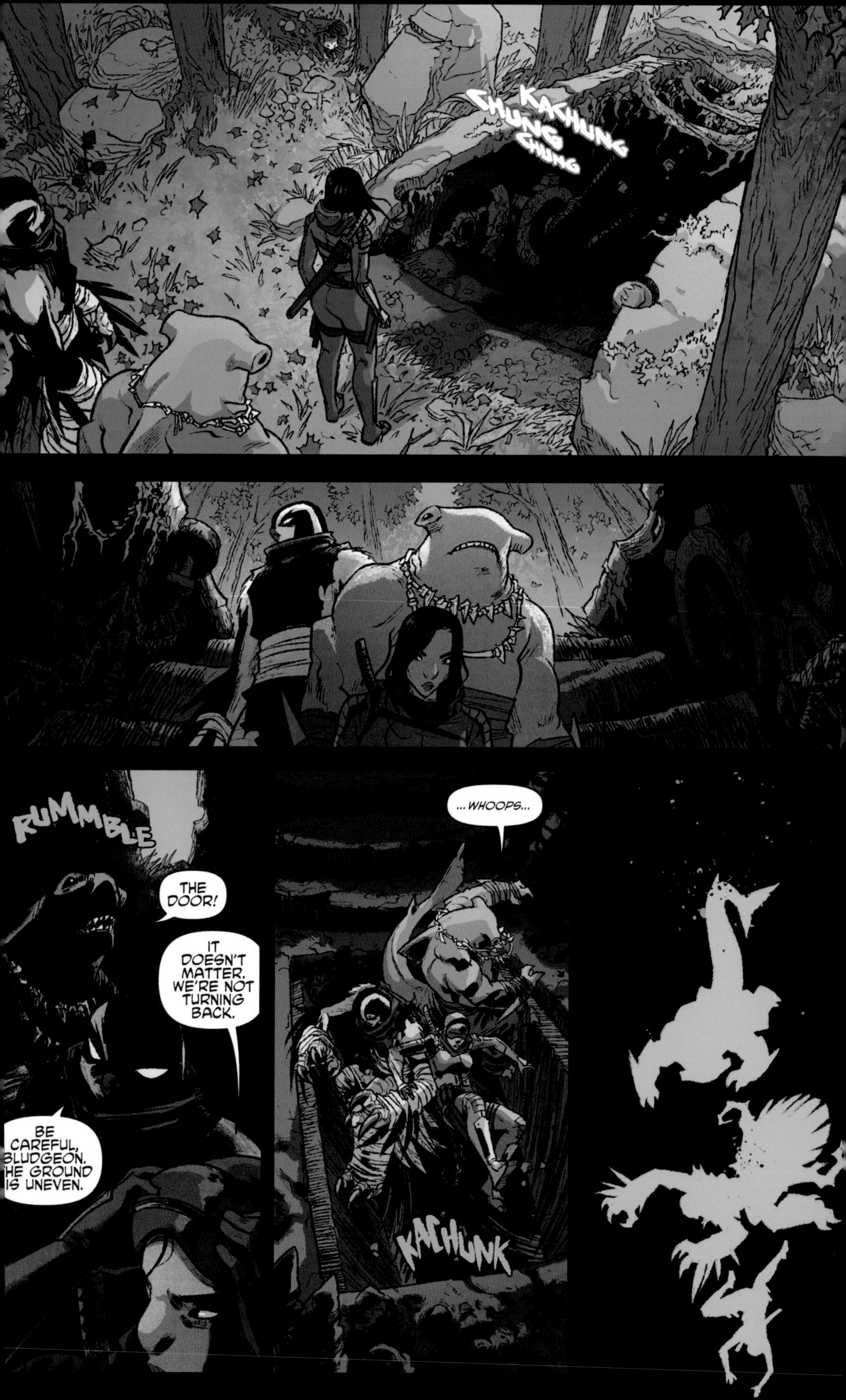
KACHUNG
CHUNG
CHUNG
RUMMBLE
THE DOOR!
IT DOESN'T MATTER. WE'RE NOT TURNING BACK.
BE CAREFUL, BLUDGEON. THE GROUND IS UNEVEN.
...WHOOPS...
KACHUNK

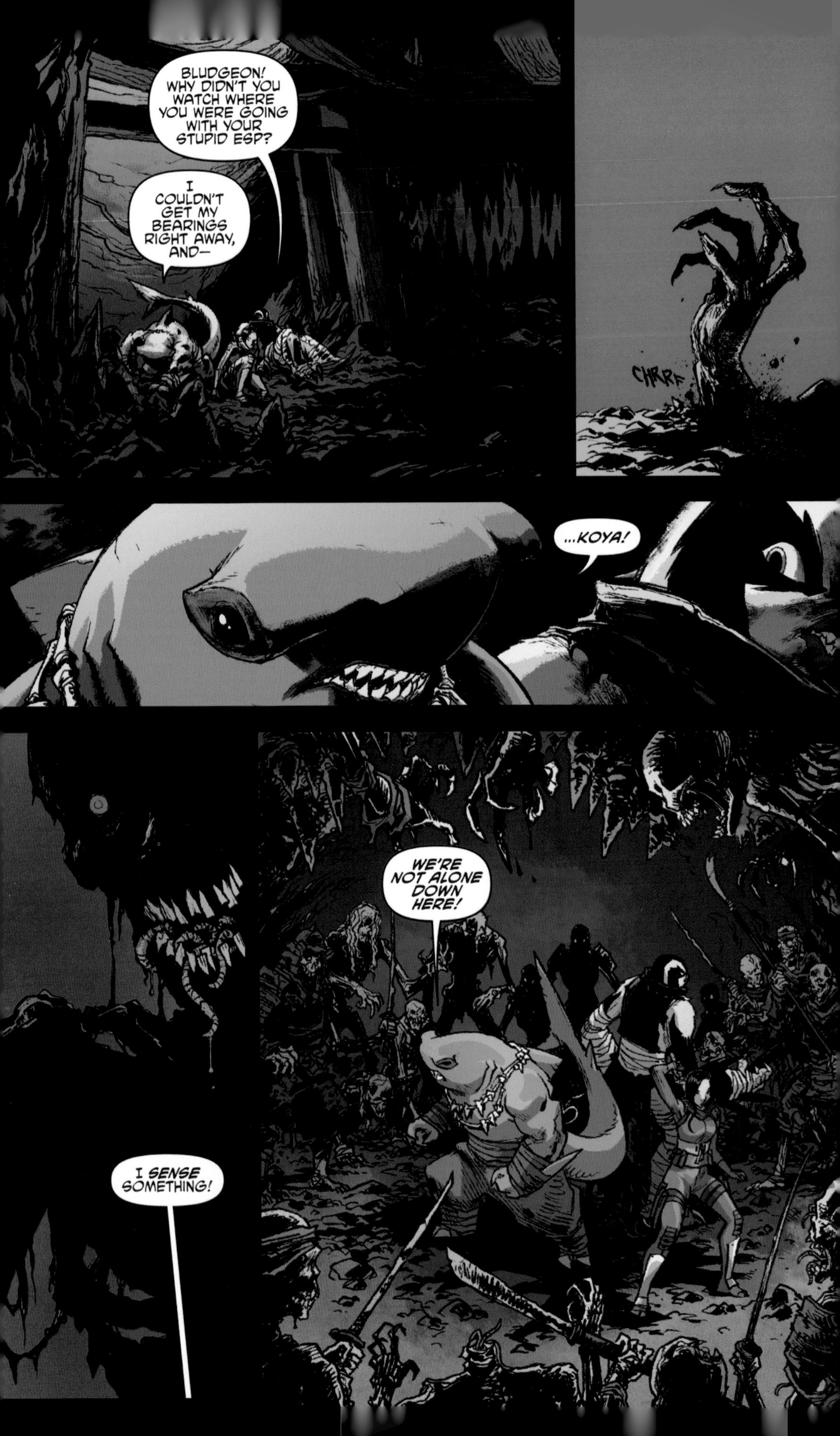

BLUDGEON! WHY DIDN'T YOU WATCH WHERE YOU WERE GOING WITH YOUR STUPID ESP?
I COULDN'T GET MY BEARINGS RIGHT AWAY, AND—
CHRRF
...KOYA!
I SENSE SOMETHING!
WE'RE NOT ALONE DOWN HERE!

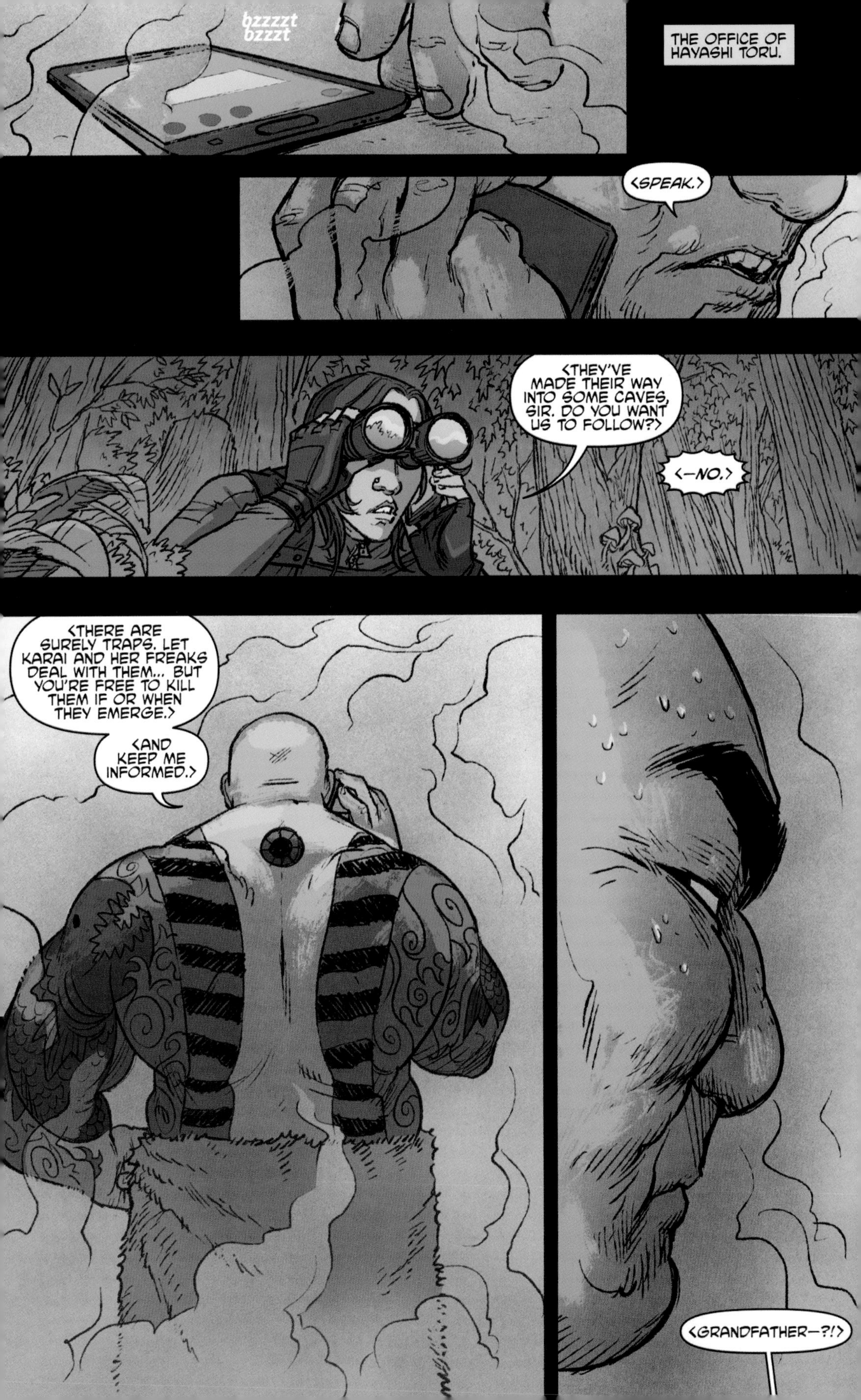
bzzzzt
bzzzt
THE OFFICE OF HAYASHI TORU.
<SPEAK.>
<THEY'VE MADE THEIR WAY INTO SOME CAVES, SIR. DO YOU WANT US TO FOLLOW?>
<--NO.>
<THERE ARE SURELY TRAPS. LET KARAI AND HER FREAKS DEAL WITH THEM... BUT YOU'RE FREE TO KILL THEM IF OR WHEN THEY EMERGE.>
<AND KEEP ME INFORMED.>
<GRANDFATHER--?!>

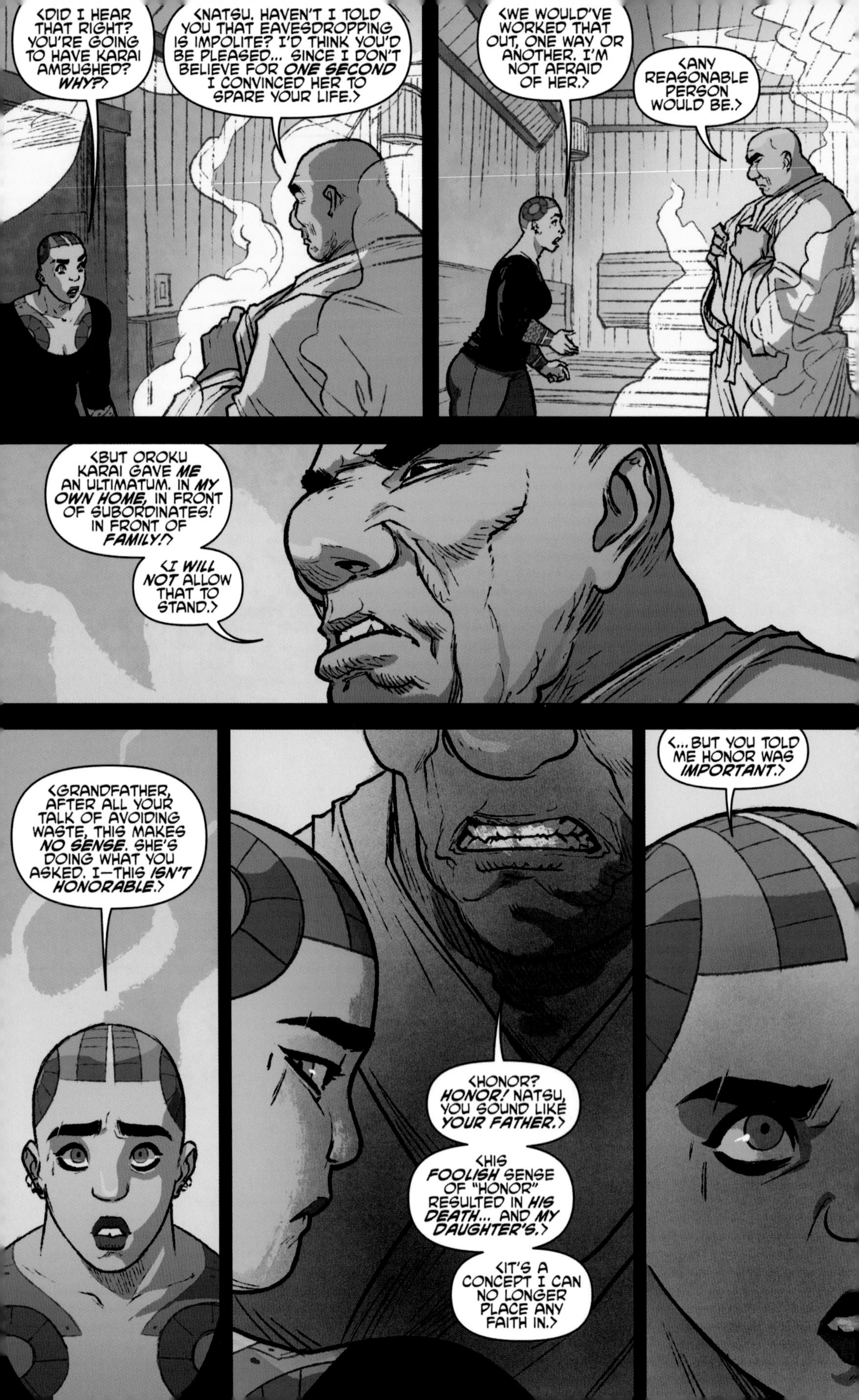

<DID I HEAR THAT RIGHT? YOU'RE GOING TO HAVE KARAI AMBUSHED? *WHY?*>
<NATSU. HAVEN'T I TOLD YOU THAT EAVESDROPPING IS IMPOLITE? I'D THINK YOU'D BE PLEASED... SINCE I DON'T BELIEVE FOR *ONE SECOND* I CONVINCED HER TO SPARE YOUR LIFE.>
<WE WOULD'VE WORKED THAT OUT, ONE WAY OR ANOTHER. I'M NOT AFRAID OF HER.>
<ANY REASONABLE PERSON WOULD BE.>
<BUT OROKU KARAI GAVE *ME* AN ULTIMATUM. IN *MY OWN HOME,* IN FRONT OF SUBORDINATES! IN FRONT OF *FAMILY!*>
<*I WILL NOT* ALLOW THAT TO STAND.>
<GRANDFATHER, AFTER ALL YOUR TALK OF AVOIDING WASTE, THIS MAKES *NO SENSE.* SHE'S DOING WHAT YOU ASKED. I—THIS *ISN'T HONORABLE.*>
<HONOR? *HONOR!* NATSU, YOU SOUND LIKE *YOUR FATHER.*>
<HIS *FOOLISH* SENSE OF "HONOR" RESULTED IN *HIS DEATH*... AND *MY DAUGHTER'S.*>
<IT'S A CONCEPT I CAN NO LONGER PLACE ANY FAITH IN.>
<...BUT YOU TOLD ME HONOR WAS *IMPORTANT.*>

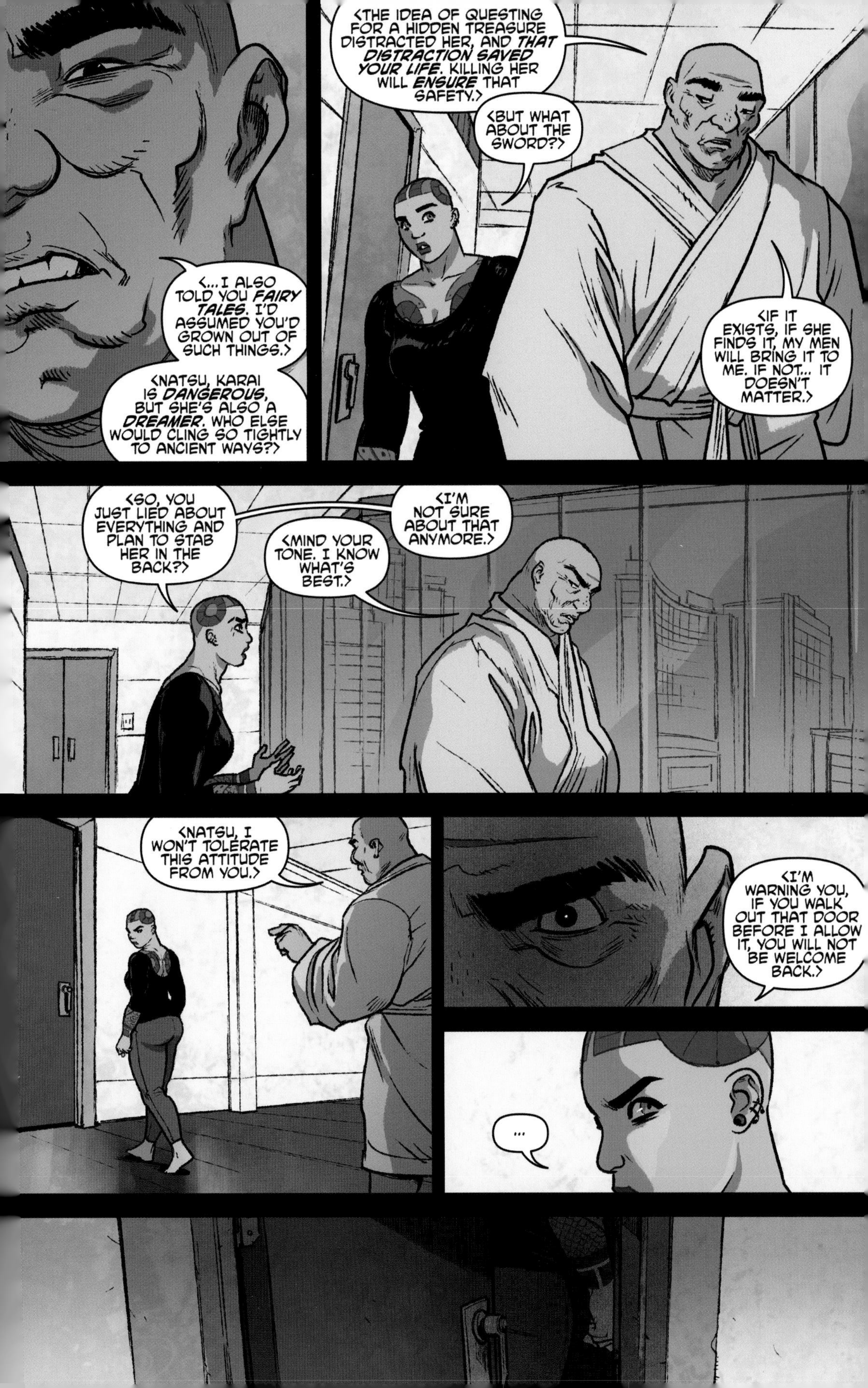
<...I ALSO TOLD YOU FAIRY TALES. I'D ASSUMED YOU'D GROWN OUT OF SUCH THINGS.>
<NATSU, KARAI IS DANGEROUS, BUT SHE'S ALSO A DREAMER. WHO ELSE WOULD CLING SO TIGHTLY TO ANCIENT WAYS?>
<THE IDEA OF QUESTING FOR A HIDDEN TREASURE DISTRACTED HER, AND THAT DISTRACTION SAVED YOUR LIFE. KILLING HER WILL ENSURE THAT SAFETY.>
<BUT WHAT ABOUT THE SWORD?>
<IF IT EXISTS, IF SHE FINDS IT, MY MEN WILL BRING IT TO ME. IF NOT... IT DOESN'T MATTER.>
<SO, YOU JUST LIED ABOUT EVERYTHING AND PLAN TO STAB HER IN THE BACK?>
<I'M NOT SURE ABOUT THAT ANYMORE.>
<MIND YOUR TONE. I KNOW WHAT'S BEST.>
<NATSU, I WON'T TOLERATE THIS ATTITUDE FROM YOU.>
<I'M WARNING YOU, IF YOU WALK OUT THAT DOOR BEFORE I ALLOW IT, YOU WILL NOT BE WELCOME BACK.>
...

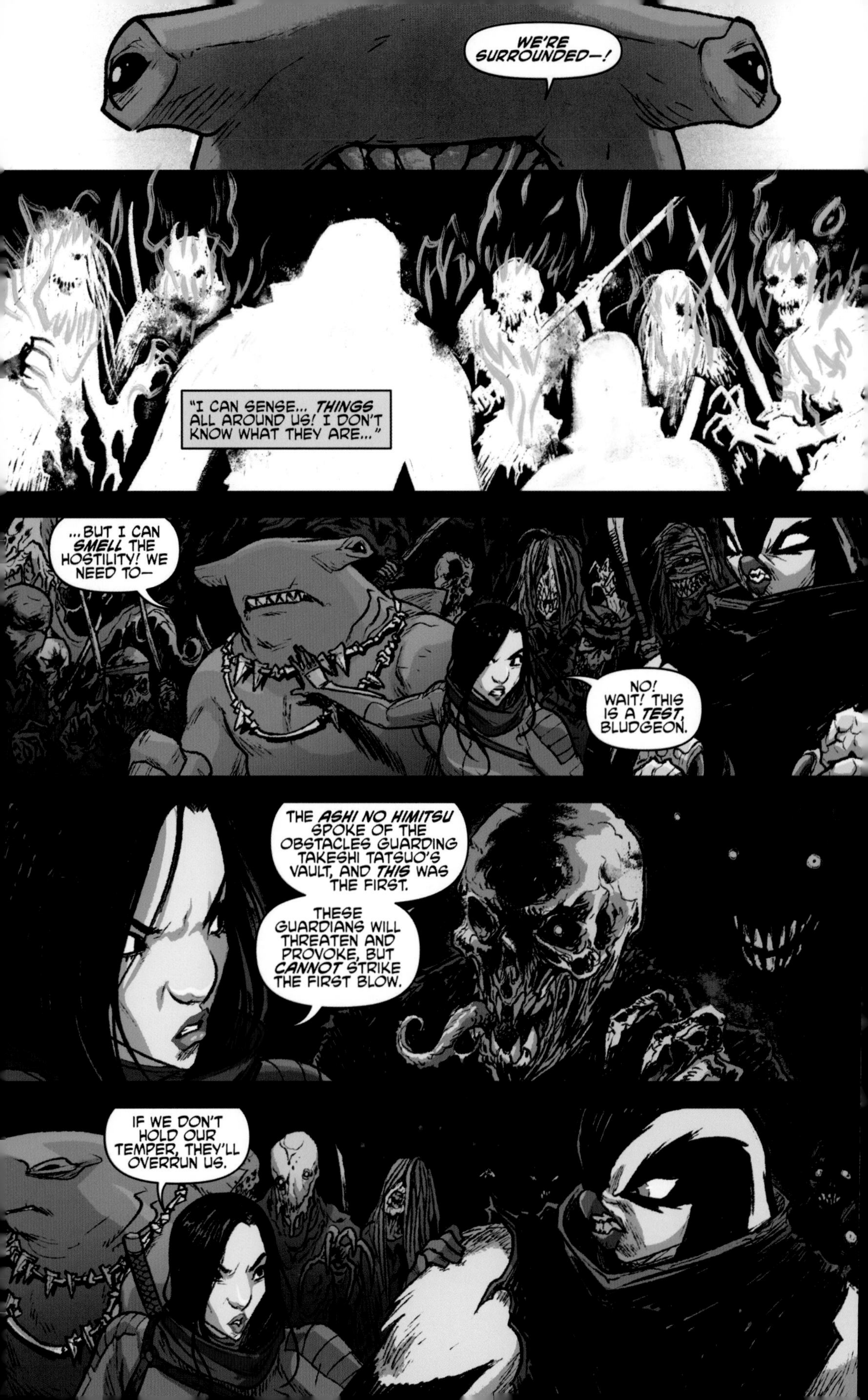
WE'RE SURROUNDED—!
"I CAN SENSE... THINGS ALL AROUND US! I DON'T KNOW WHAT THEY ARE..."
...BUT I CAN SMELL THE HOSTILITY! WE NEED TO—
NO! WAIT! THIS IS A TEST, BLUDGEON.
THE ASHI NO HIMITSU SPOKE OF THE OBSTACLES GUARDING TAKESHI TATSUO'S VAULT, AND THIS WAS THE FIRST.
THESE GUARDIANS WILL THREATEN AND PROVOKE, BUT CANNOT STRIKE THE FIRST BLOW.
IF WE DON'T HOLD OUR TEMPER, THEY'LL OVERRUN US.

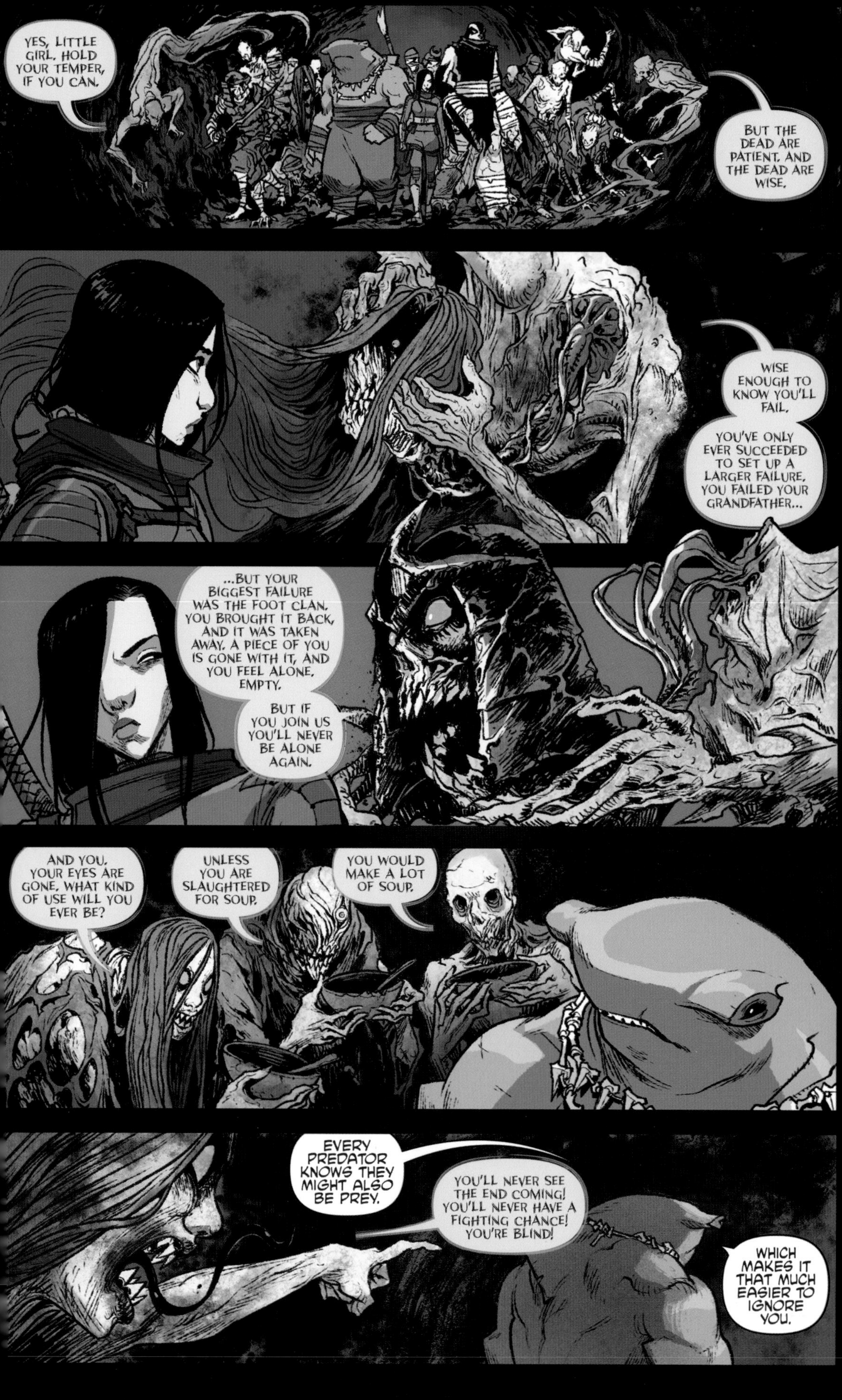
YES, LITTLE GIRL. HOLD YOUR TEMPER, IF YOU CAN.
BUT THE DEAD ARE PATIENT. AND THE DEAD ARE WISE.
WISE ENOUGH TO KNOW YOU'LL FAIL.
YOU'VE ONLY EVER SUCCEEDED TO SET UP A LARGER FAILURE. YOU FAILED YOUR GRANDFATHER...
...BUT YOUR BIGGEST FAILURE WAS THE FOOT CLAN. YOU BROUGHT IT BACK, AND IT WAS TAKEN AWAY. A PIECE OF YOU IS GONE WITH IT, AND YOU FEEL ALONE, EMPTY.
BUT IF YOU JOIN US YOU'LL NEVER BE ALONE AGAIN.
AND YOU. YOUR EYES ARE GONE. WHAT KIND OF USE WILL YOU EVER BE?
UNLESS YOU ARE SLAUGHTERED FOR SOUP.
YOU WOULD MAKE A LOT OF SOUP.
EVERY PREDATOR KNOWS THEY MIGHT ALSO BE PREY.
YOU'LL NEVER SEE THE END COMING! YOU'LL NEVER HAVE A FIGHTING CHANCE! YOU'RE BLIND!
WHICH MAKES IT THAT MUCH EASIER TO IGNORE YOU.

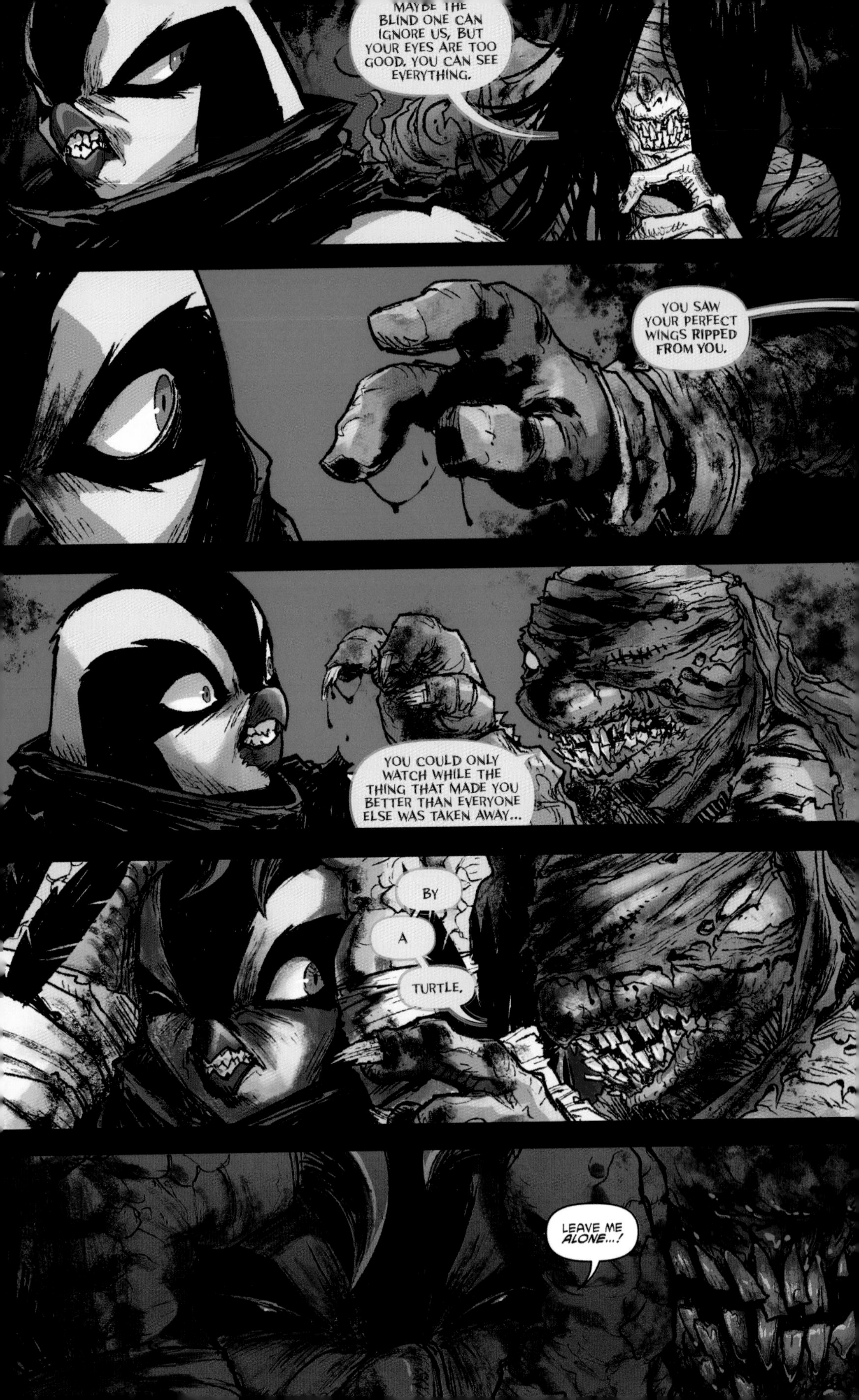
MAYBE THE BLIND ONE CAN IGNORE US, BUT YOUR EYES ARE TOO GOOD. YOU CAN SEE EVERYTHING.
YOU SAW YOUR PERFECT WINGS RIPPED FROM YOU.
YOU COULD ONLY WATCH WHILE THE THING THAT MADE YOU BETTER THAN EVERYONE ELSE WAS TAKEN AWAY...
BY
A
TURTLE.
LEAVE ME *ALONE*...!

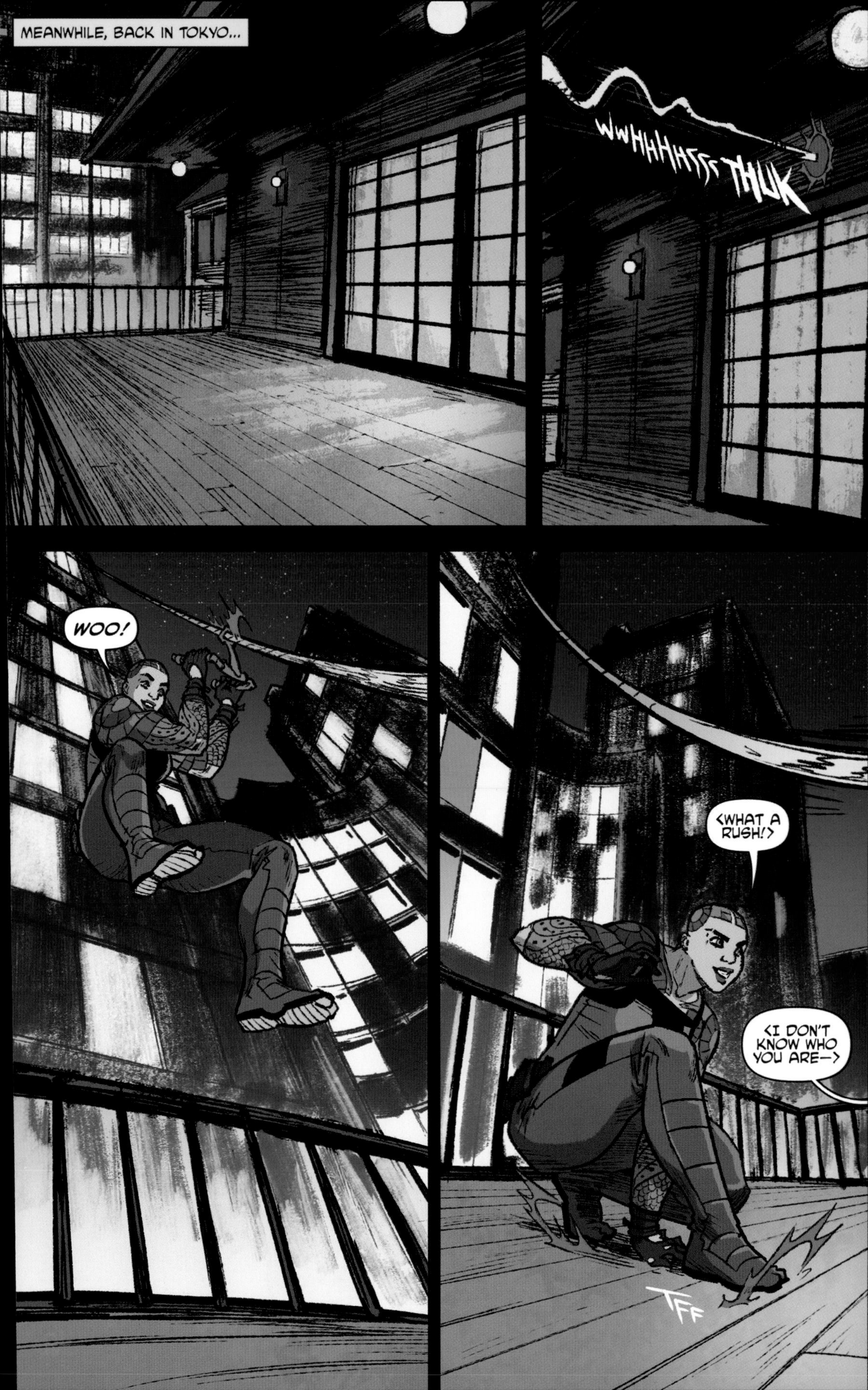
MEANWHILE, BACK IN TOKYO...
WWHHHHZZZZ THUK
WOO!
<WHAT A RUSH!>
<I DON'T KNOW WHO YOU ARE—>
TFF

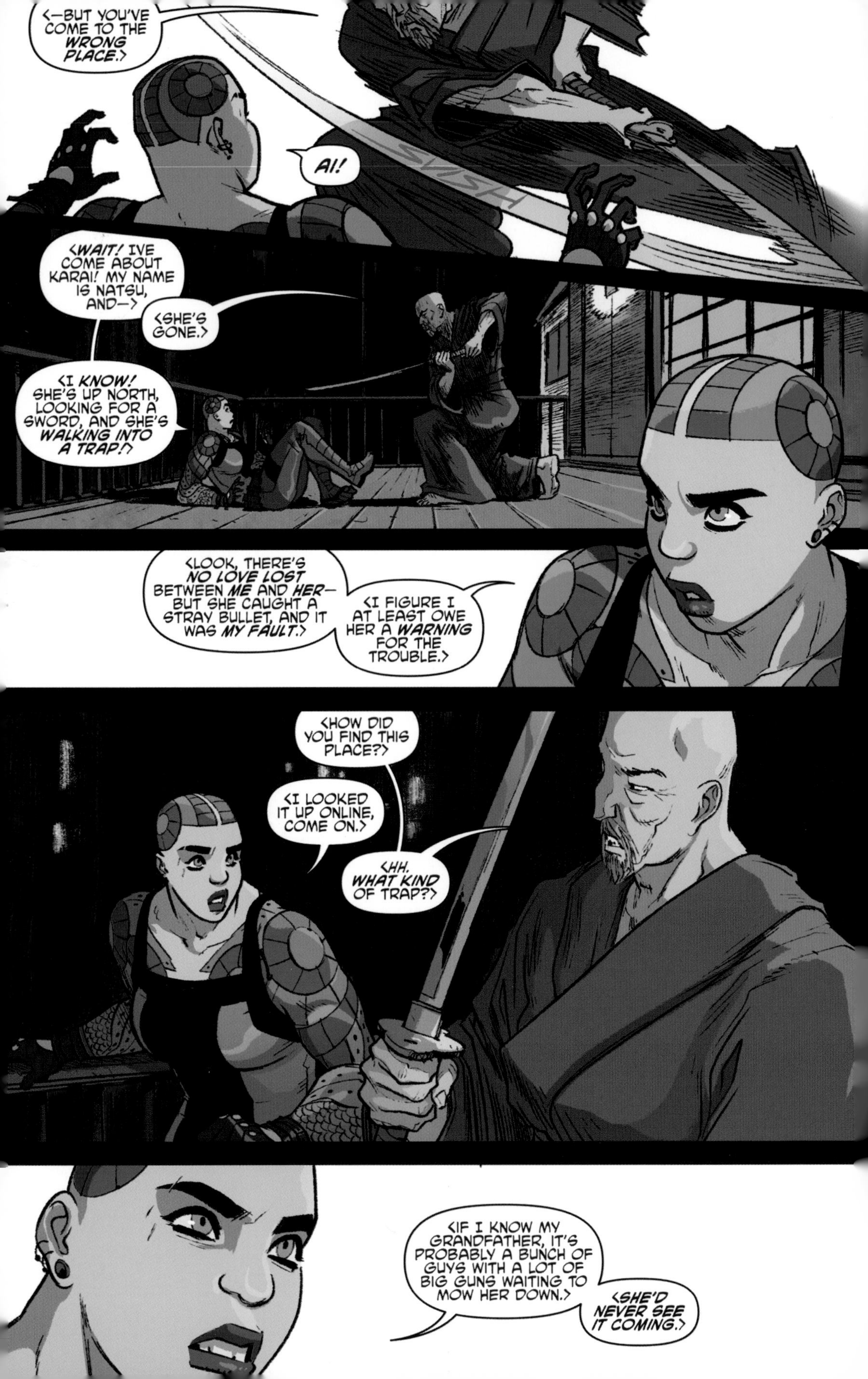
<—BUT YOU'VE COME TO THE WRONG PLACE.>
AI!
SWISH
<WAIT! IVE COME ABOUT KARAI! MY NAME IS NATSU, AND—>
<SHE'S GONE.>
<I KNOW! SHE'S UP NORTH, LOOKING FOR A SWORD, AND SHE'S WALKING INTO A TRAP!>
<LOOK, THERE'S NO LOVE LOST BETWEEN ME AND HER—BUT SHE CAUGHT A STRAY BULLET, AND IT WAS MY FAULT.>
<I FIGURE I AT LEAST OWE HER A WARNING FOR THE TROUBLE.>
<HOW DID YOU FIND THIS PLACE?>
<I LOOKED IT UP ONLINE, COME ON.>
<HH. WHAT KIND OF TRAP?>
<IF I KNOW MY GRANDFATHER, IT'S PROBABLY A BUNCH OF GUYS WITH A LOT OF BIG GUNS WAITING TO MOW HER DOWN.>
<SHE'D NEVER SEE IT COMING.>

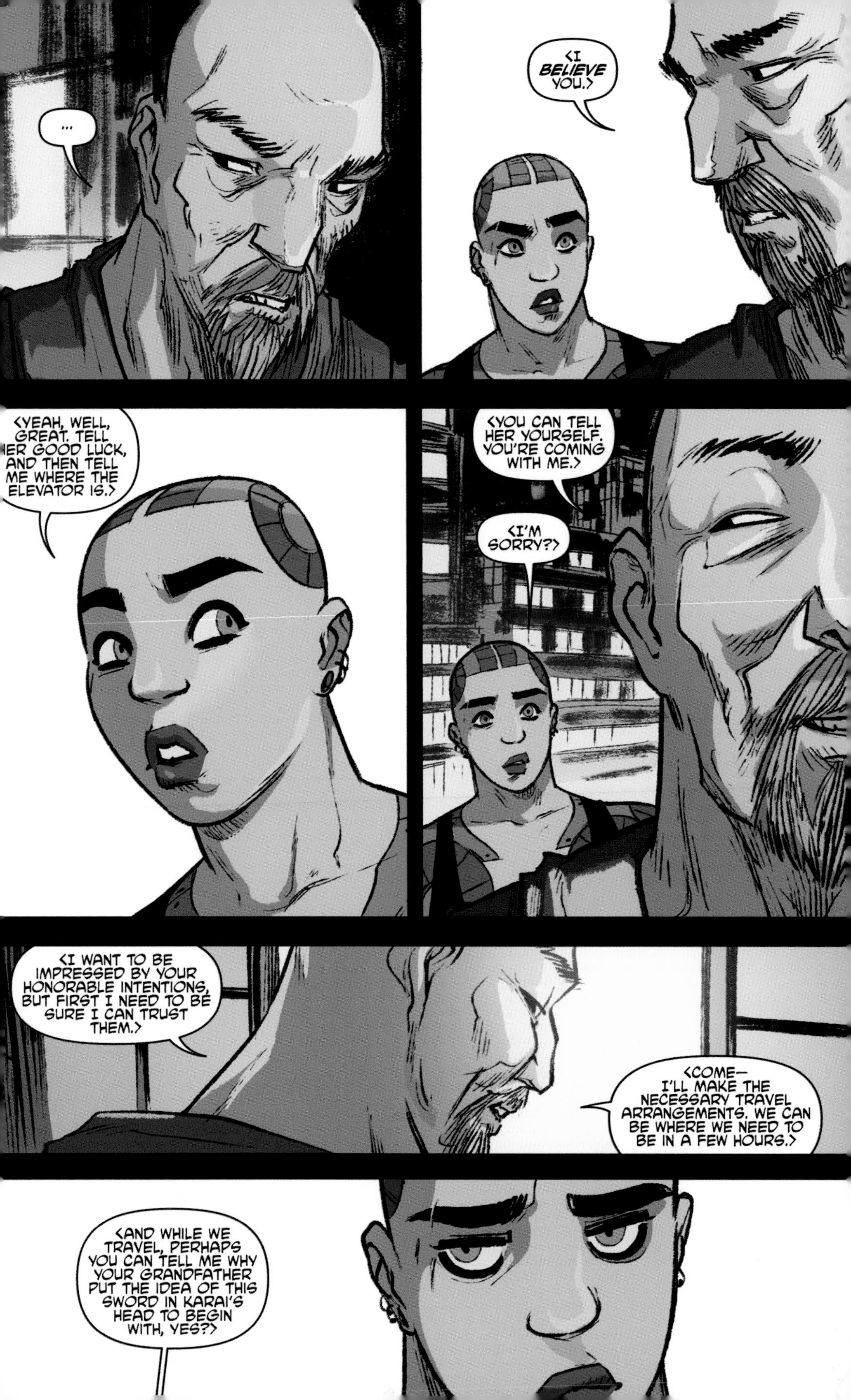
...
<I BELIEVE YOU.>
<YEAH, WELL, GREAT. TELL ER GOOD LUCK, AND THEN TELL ME WHERE THE ELEVATOR IS.>
<YOU CAN TELL HER YOURSELF. YOU'RE COMING WITH ME.>
<I'M SORRY?>
<I WANT TO BE IMPRESSED BY YOUR HONORABLE INTENTIONS, BUT FIRST I NEED TO BE SURE I CAN TRUST THEM.>
<COME— I'LL MAKE THE NECESSARY TRAVEL ARRANGEMENTS. WE CAN BE WHERE WE NEED TO BE IN A FEW HOURS.>
<AND WHILE WE TRAVEL, PERHAPS YOU CAN TELL ME WHY YOUR GRANDFATHER PUT THE IDEA OF THIS SWORD IN KARAI'S HEAD TO BEGIN WITH, YES?>

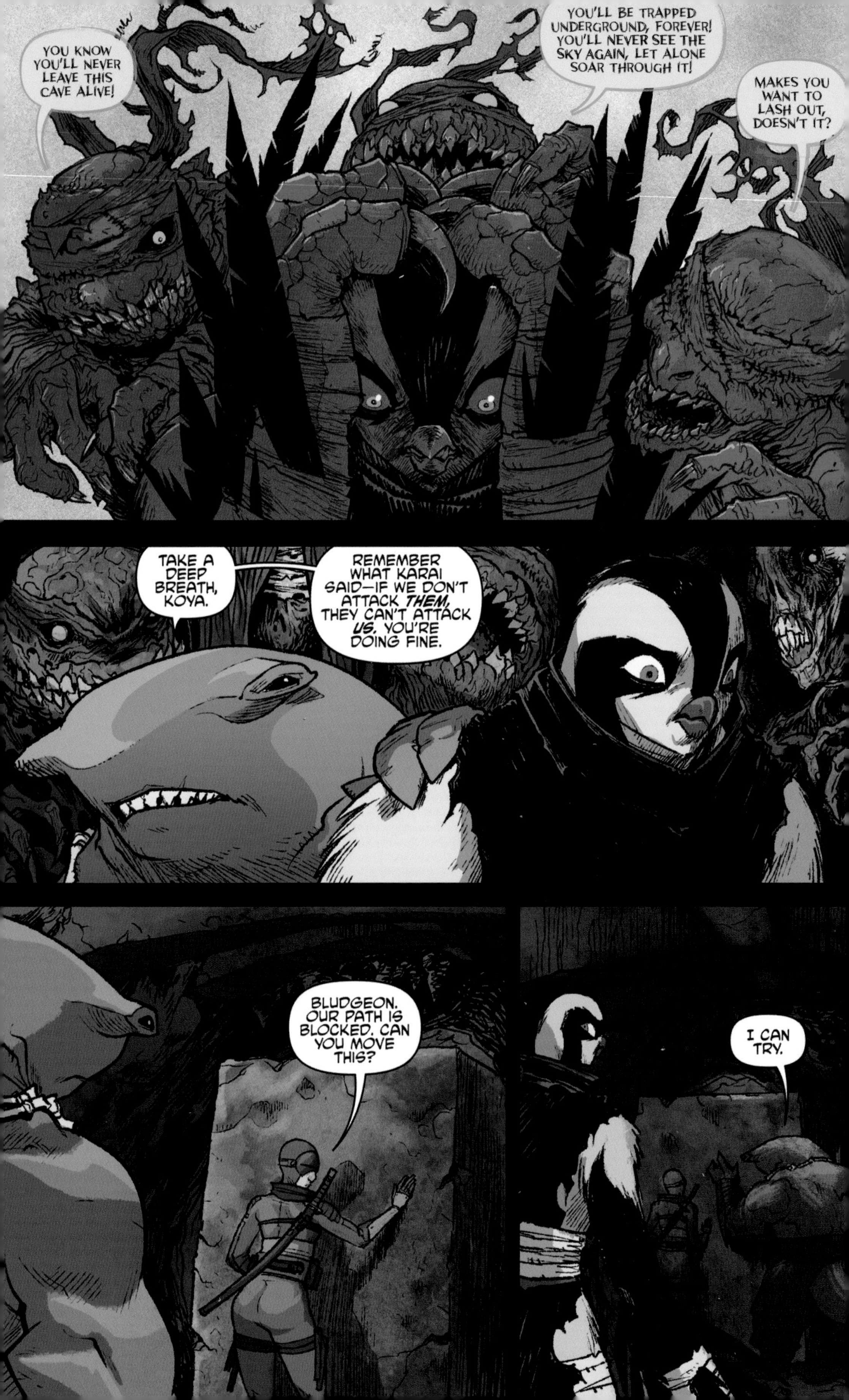

YOU KNOW YOU'LL NEVER LEAVE THIS CAVE ALIVE!
YOU'LL BE TRAPPED UNDERGROUND, FOREVER! YOU'LL NEVER SEE THE SKY AGAIN, LET ALONE SOAR THROUGH IT!
MAKES YOU WANT TO LASH OUT, DOESN'T IT?
TAKE A DEEP BREATH, KOYA.
REMEMBER WHAT KARAI SAID—IF WE DON'T ATTACK *THEM,* THEY CAN'T ATTACK *US.* YOU'RE DOING FINE.
BLUDGEON. OUR PATH IS BLOCKED. CAN YOU MOVE THIS?
I CAN TRY.

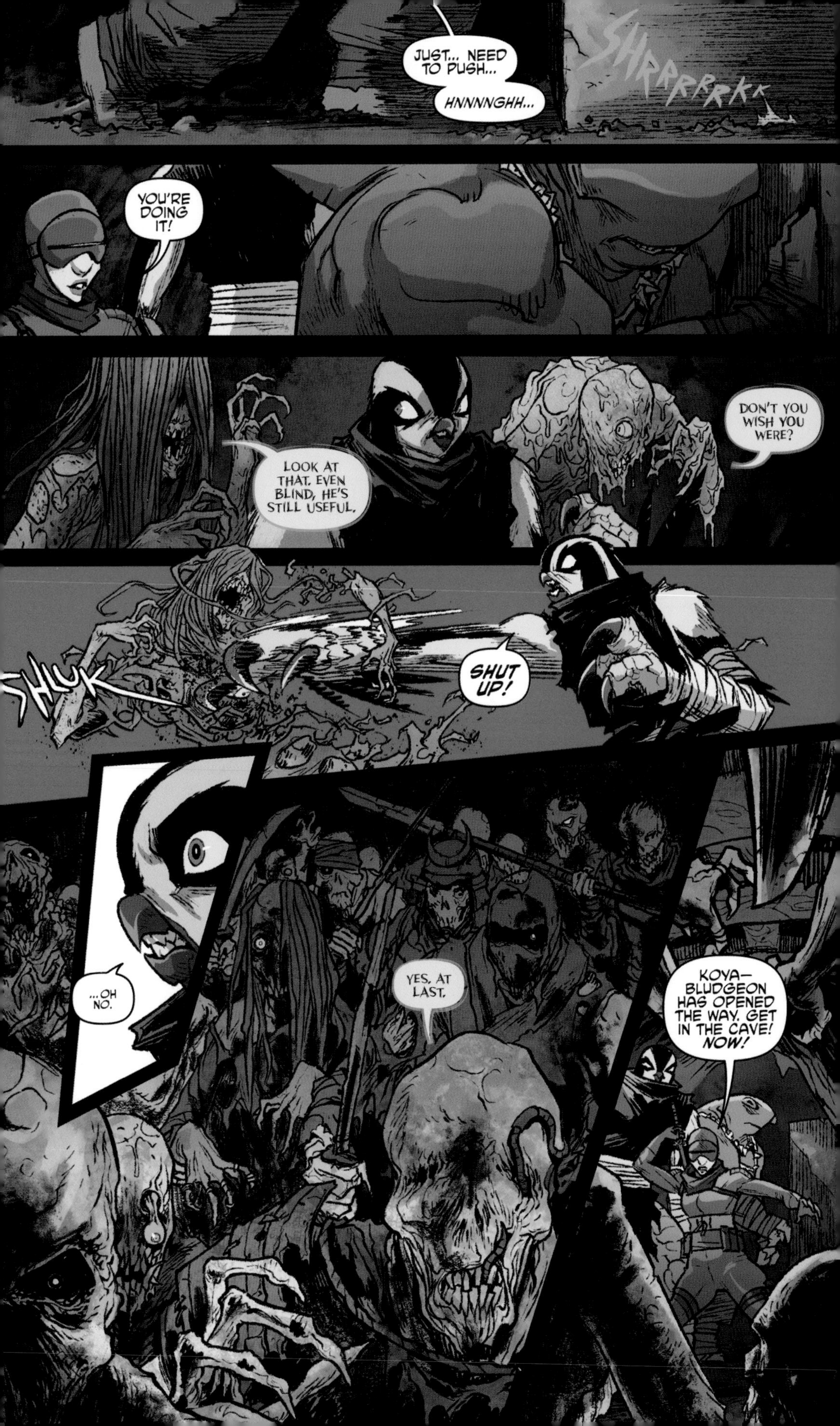
JUST... NEED TO PUSH...
HNNNNGHH...
SHRRRRRKK
YOU'RE DOING IT!
LOOK AT THAT. EVEN BLIND, HE'S STILL USEFUL.
DON'T YOU WISH YOU WERE?
SHLUK
SHUT UP!
...OH NO.
YES, AT LAST.
KOYA— BLUDGEON HAS OPENED THE WAY. GET IN THE CAVE! NOW!

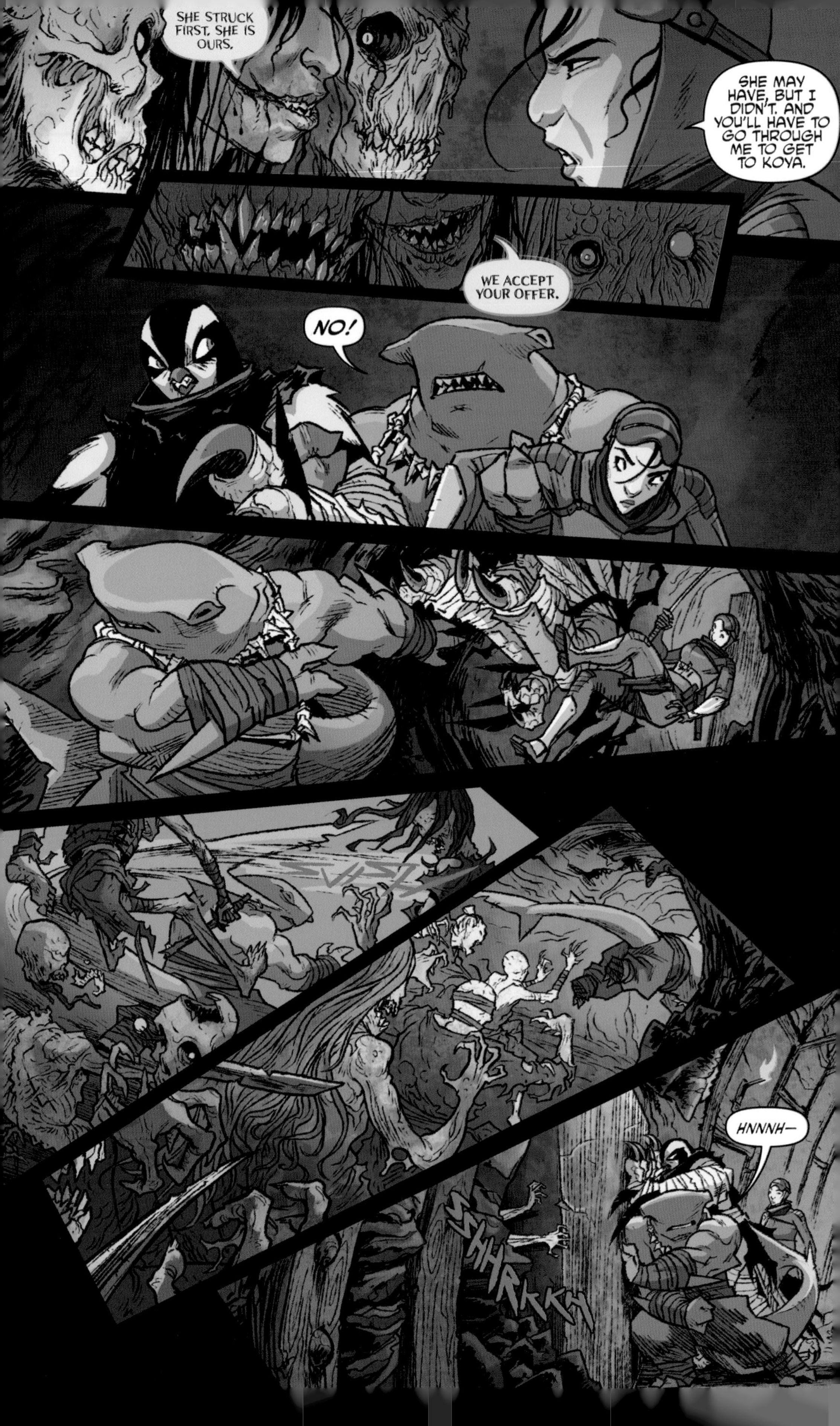
SHE STRUCK FIRST. SHE IS OURS.
SHE MAY HAVE, BUT I DIDN'T. AND YOU'LL HAVE TO GO THROUGH ME TO GET TO KOYA.
WE ACCEPT YOUR OFFER.
NO!
SSHHRKKKH
HNNNH—

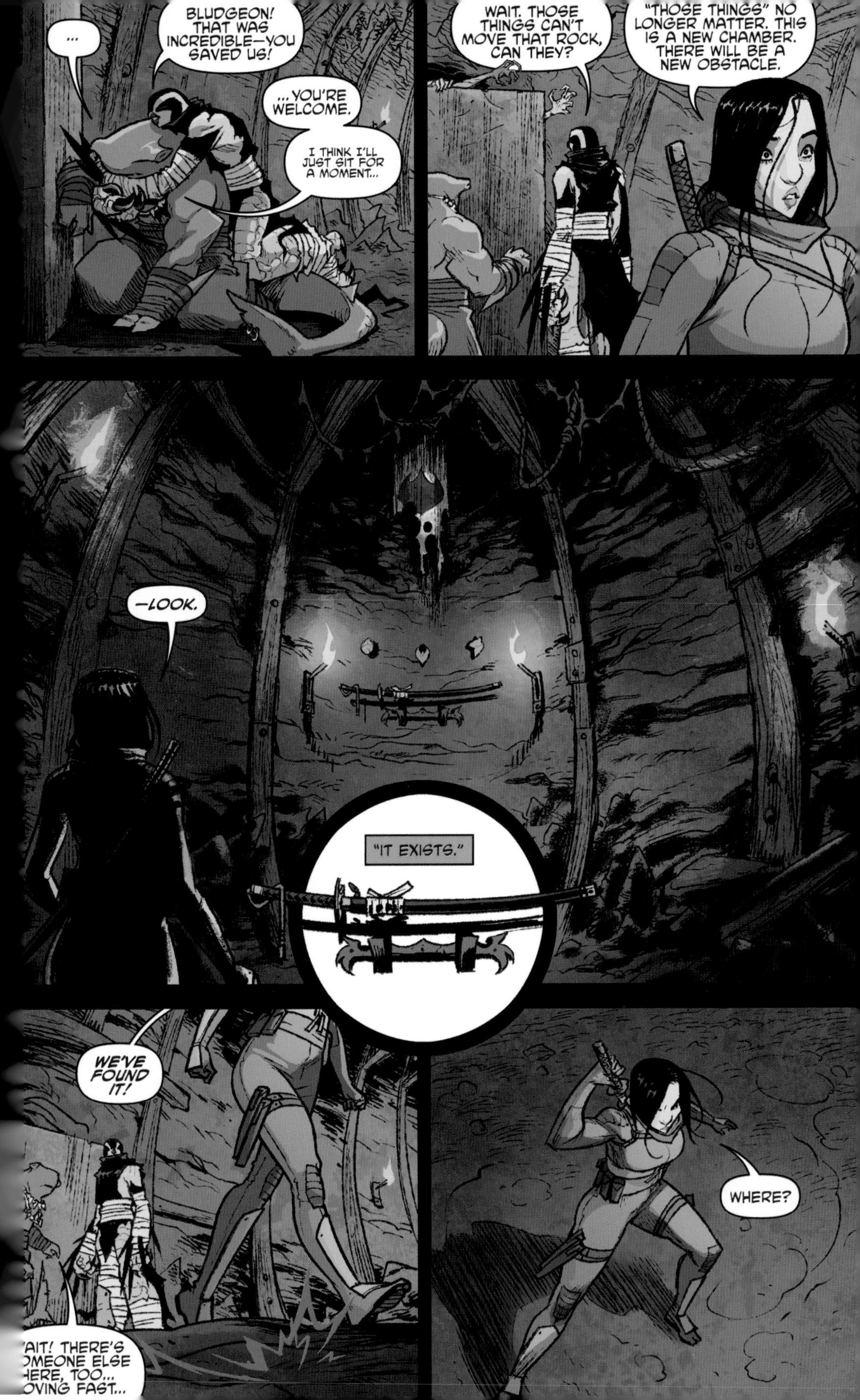
...
BLUDGEON! THAT WAS INCREDIBLE—YOU SAVED US!
...YOU'RE WELCOME.
I THINK I'LL JUST SIT FOR A MOMENT...
WAIT. THOSE THINGS CAN'T MOVE THAT ROCK, CAN THEY?
"THOSE THINGS" NO LONGER MATTER. THIS IS A NEW CHAMBER. THERE WILL BE A NEW OBSTACLE.
—LOOK.
"IT EXISTS."
WE'VE FOUND IT!
AIT! THERE'S OMEONE ELSE HERE, TOO... OVING FAST...
WHERE?

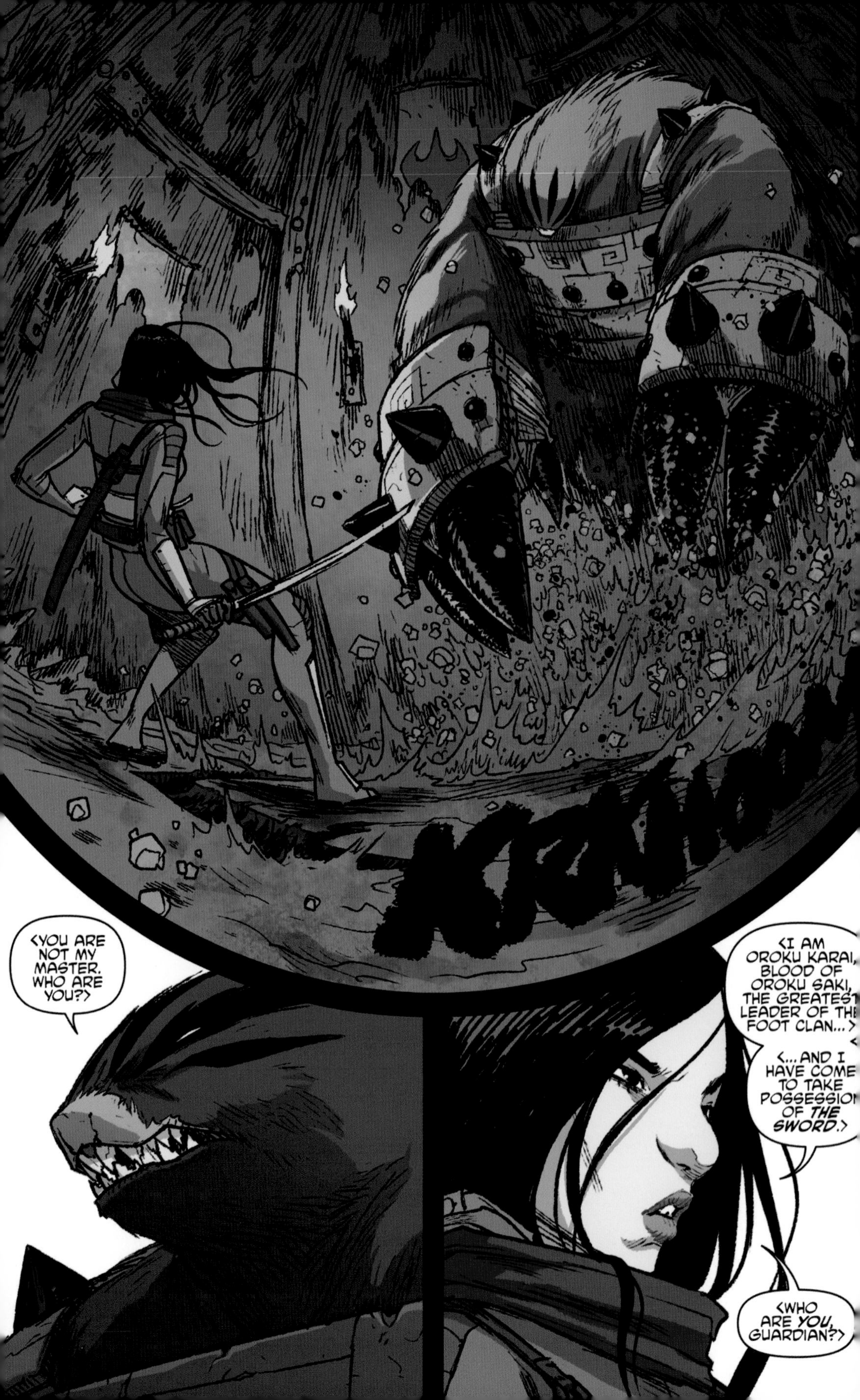
<YOU ARE NOT MY MASTER. WHO ARE YOU?>
<I AM OROKU KARAI, BLOOD OF OROKU SAKI, THE GREATEST LEADER OF THE FOOT CLAN...>
<...AND I HAVE COME TO TAKE POSSESSIO OF THE SWORD.>
<WHO ARE YOU, GUARDIAN?>

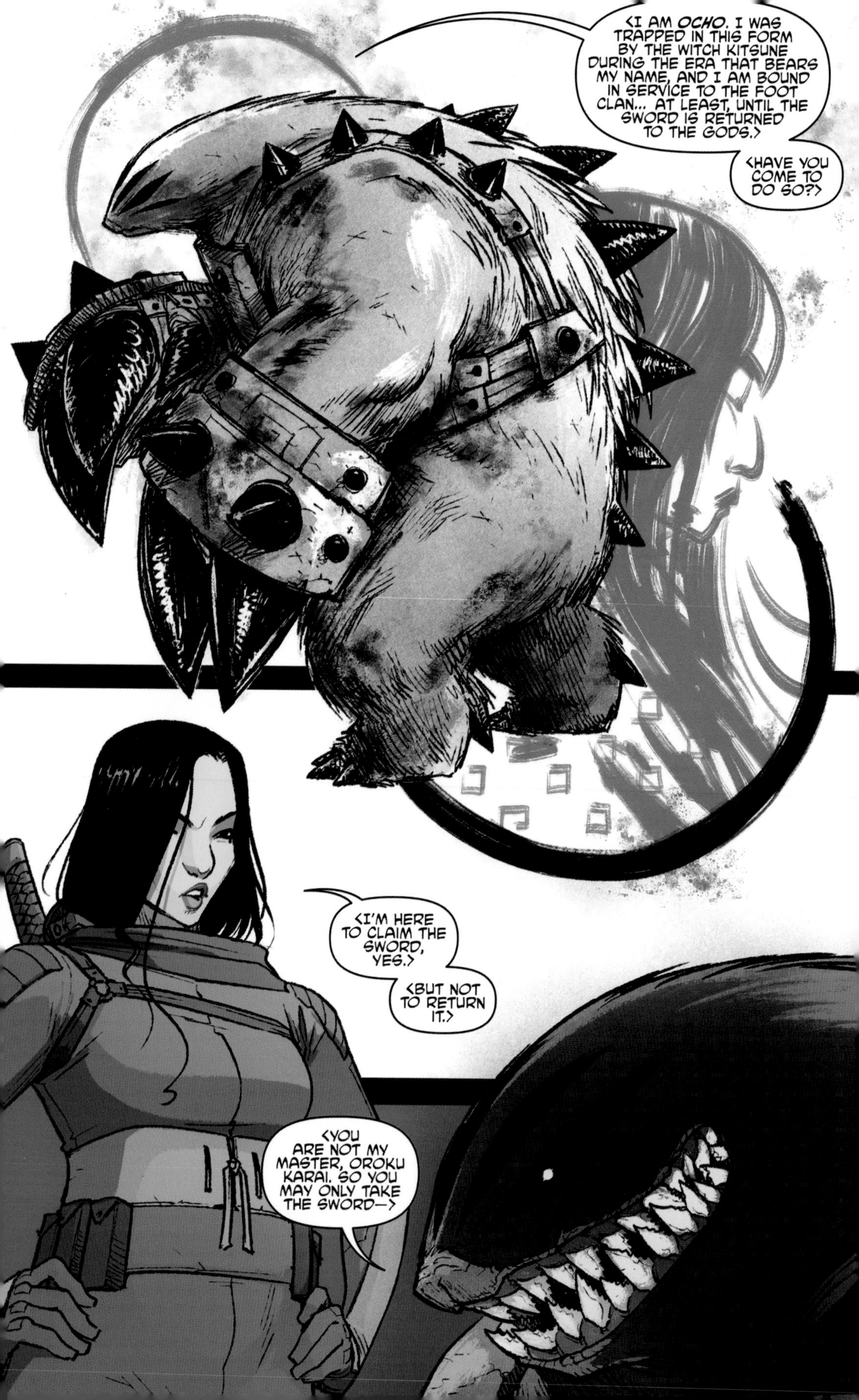
<I AM OCHO. I WAS TRAPPED IN THIS FORM BY THE WITCH KITSUNE DURING THE ERA THAT BEARS MY NAME, AND I AM BOUND IN SERVICE TO THE FOOT CLAN... AT LEAST, UNTIL THE SWORD IS RETURNED TO THE GODS.>
<HAVE YOU COME TO DO SO?>
<I'M HERE TO CLAIM THE SWORD, YES.>
<BUT NOT TO RETURN IT.>
<YOU ARE NOT MY MASTER, OROKU KARAI. SO YOU MAY ONLY TAKE THE SWORD—>

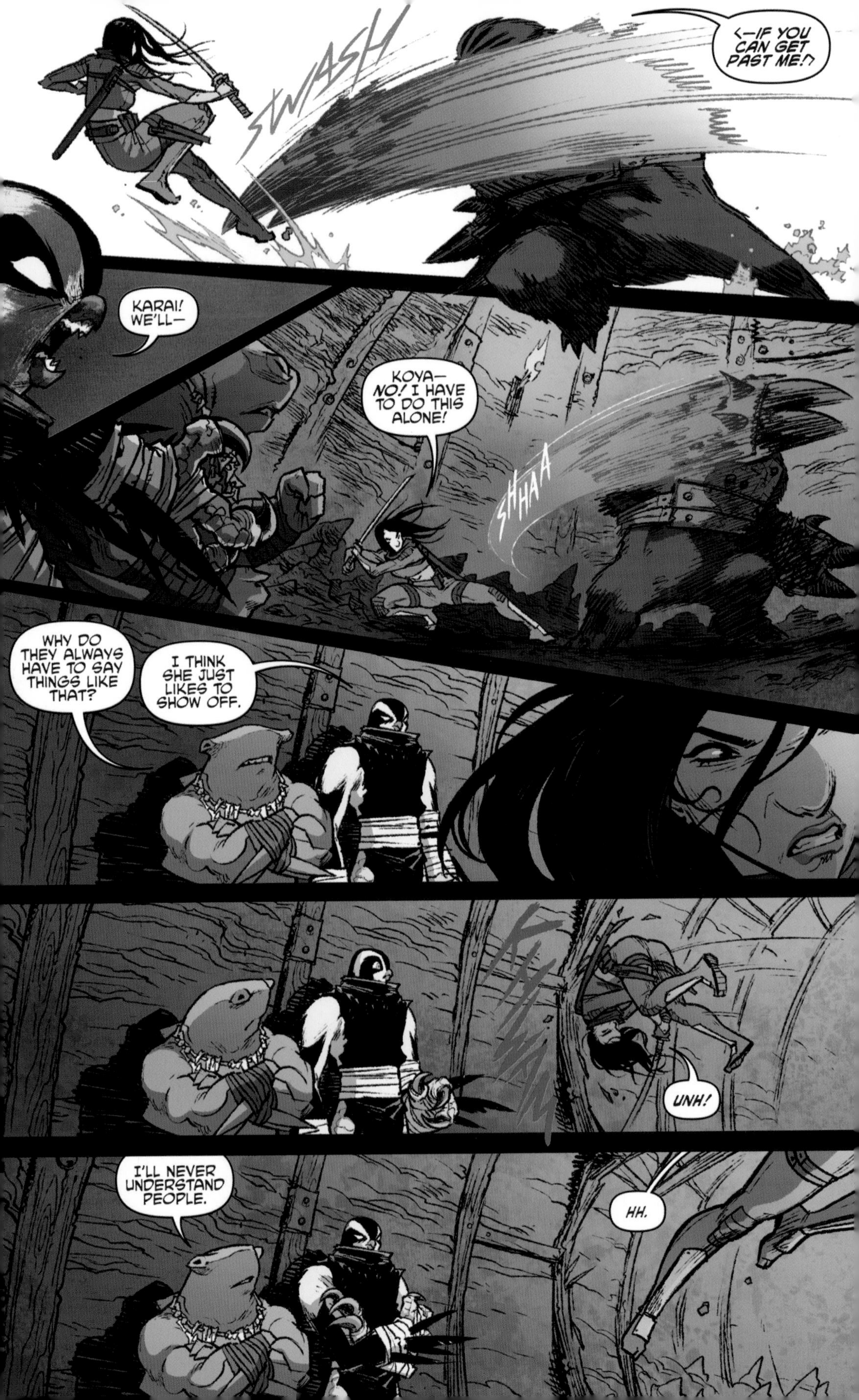
‹—IF YOU CAN GET PAST ME!›
SWASH
KARAI! WE'LL—
KOYA— NO! I HAVE TO DO THIS ALONE!
SHHAA
WHY DO THEY ALWAYS HAVE TO SAY THINGS LIKE THAT?
I THINK SHE JUST LIKES TO SHOW OFF.
UNH!
I'LL NEVER UNDERSTAND PEOPLE.
HH.

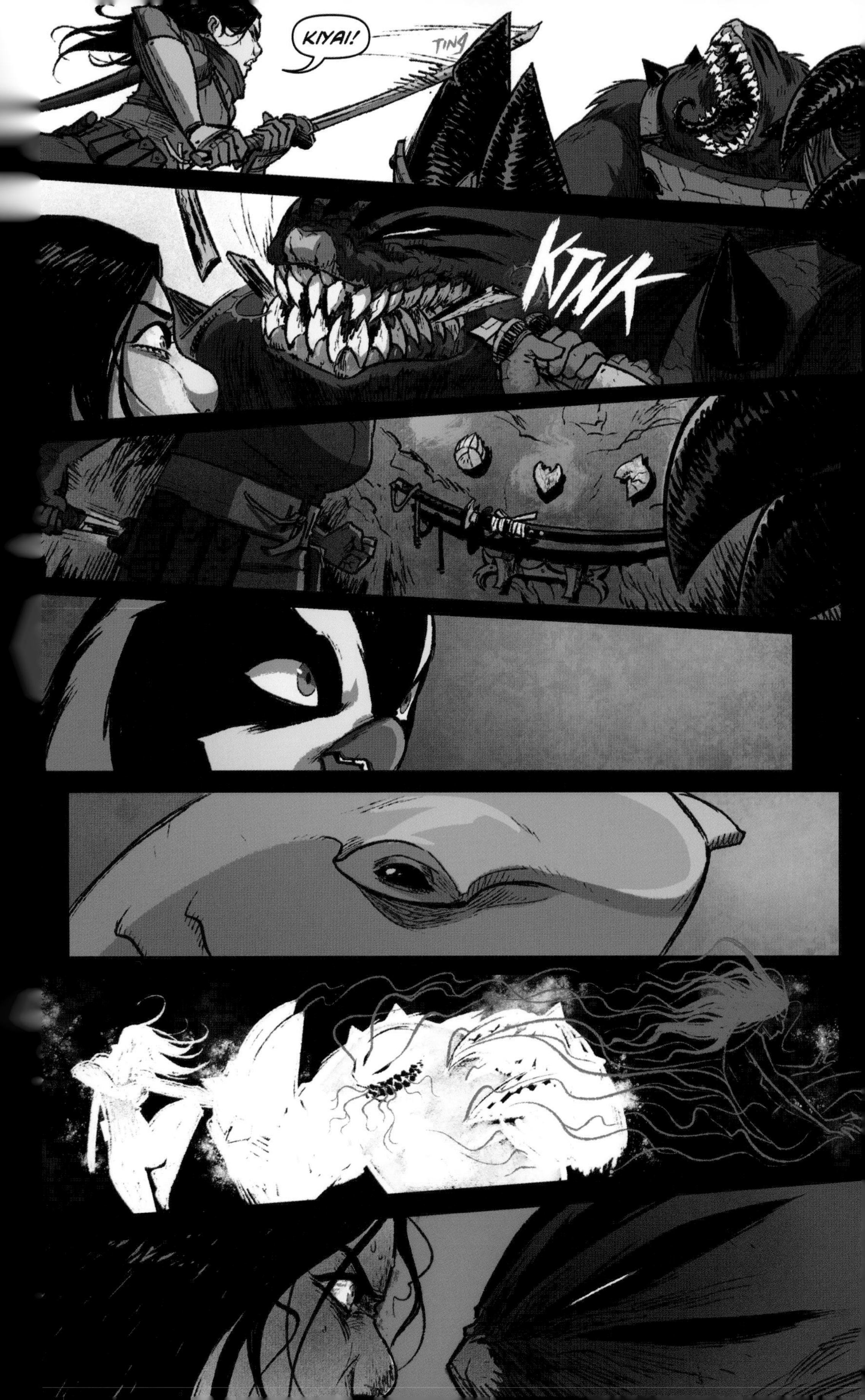
KIYAI!
TING
KTNK

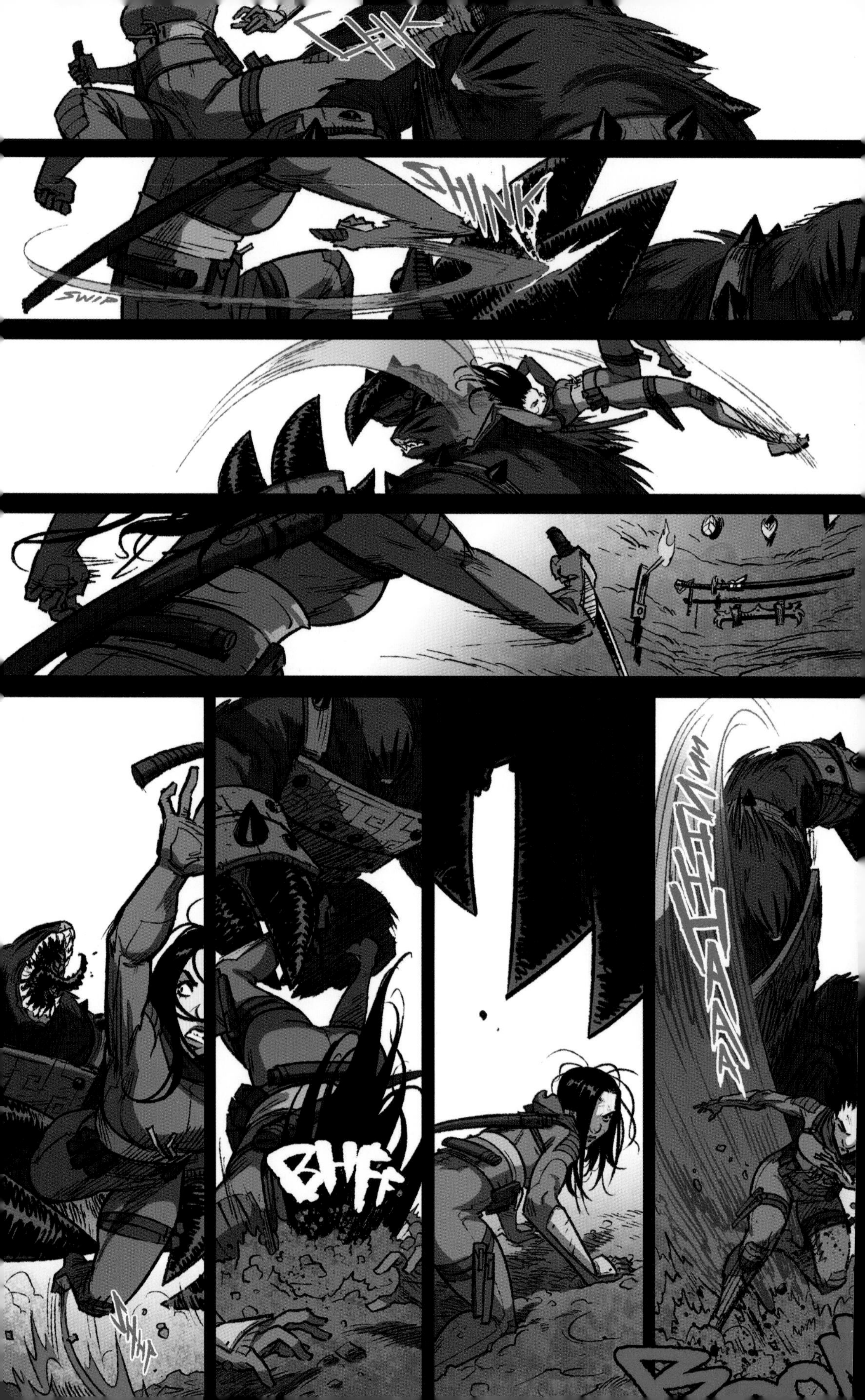
CHK
SHINK
SWIP
BHFF

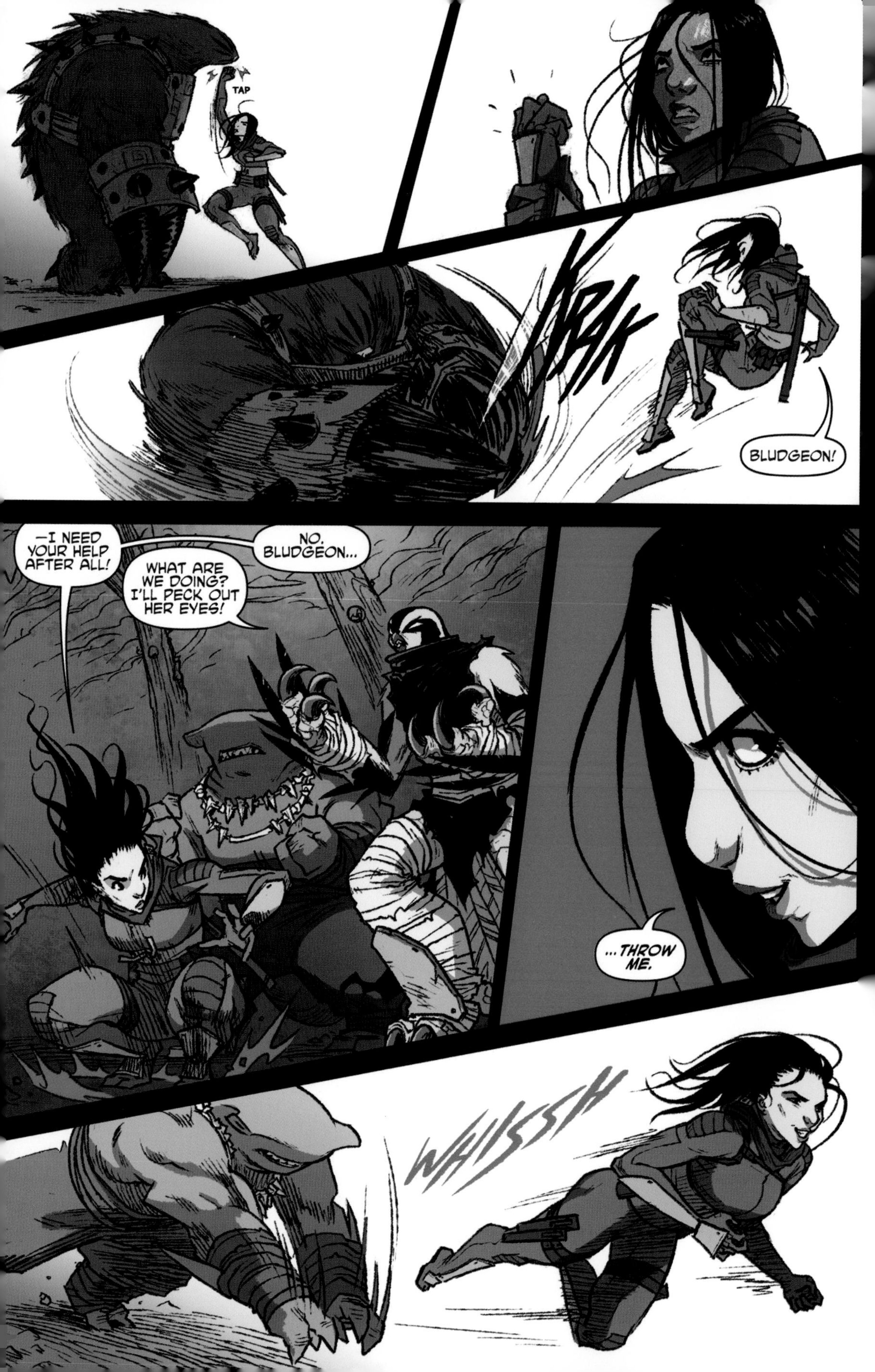
TAP
KRAK
BLUDGEON!
—I NEED YOUR HELP AFTER ALL!
NO. BLUDGEON...
WHAT ARE WE DOING? I'LL PECK OUT HER EYES!
...THROW ME.
WHISSH

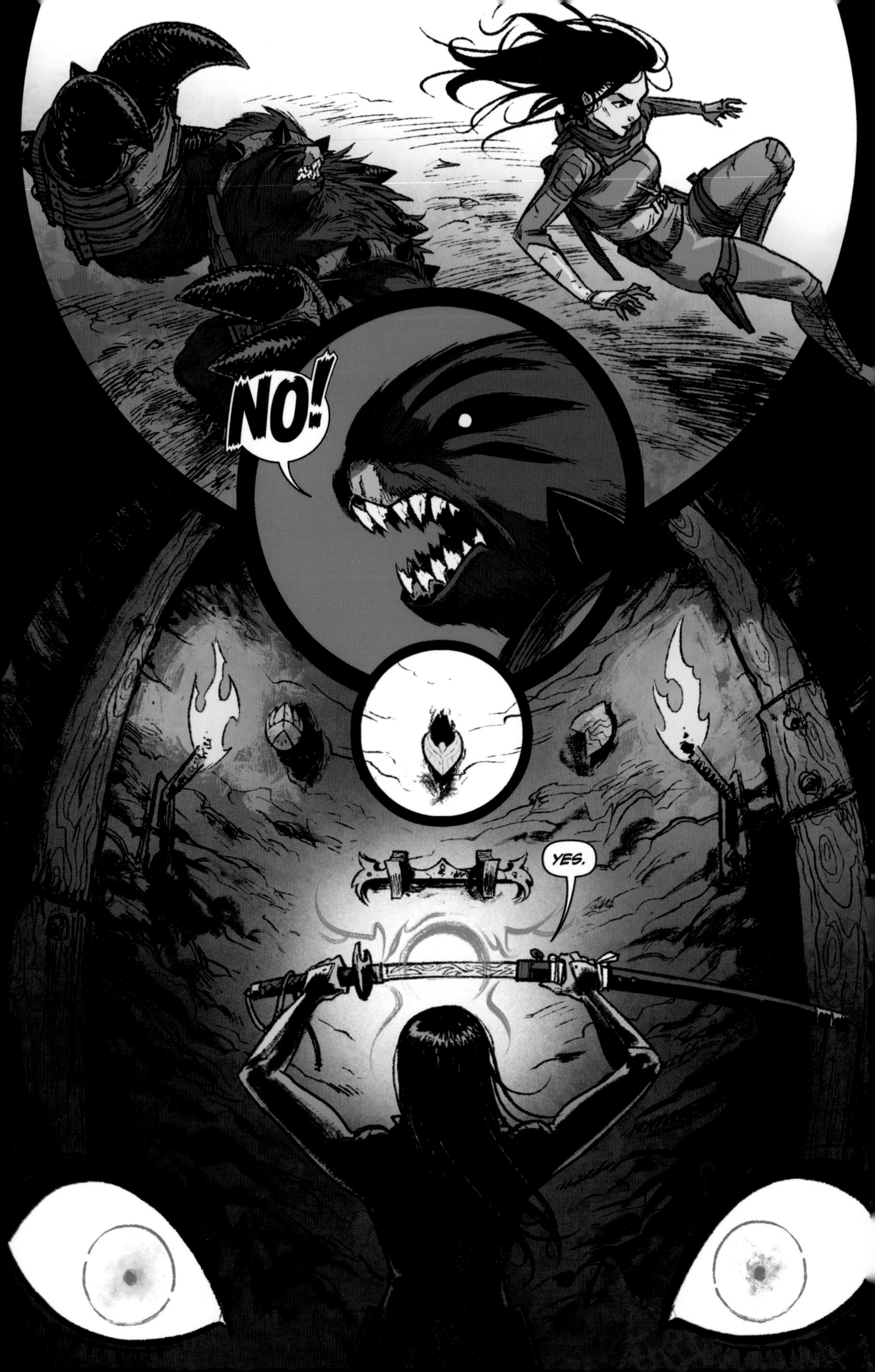
NO!
YES.

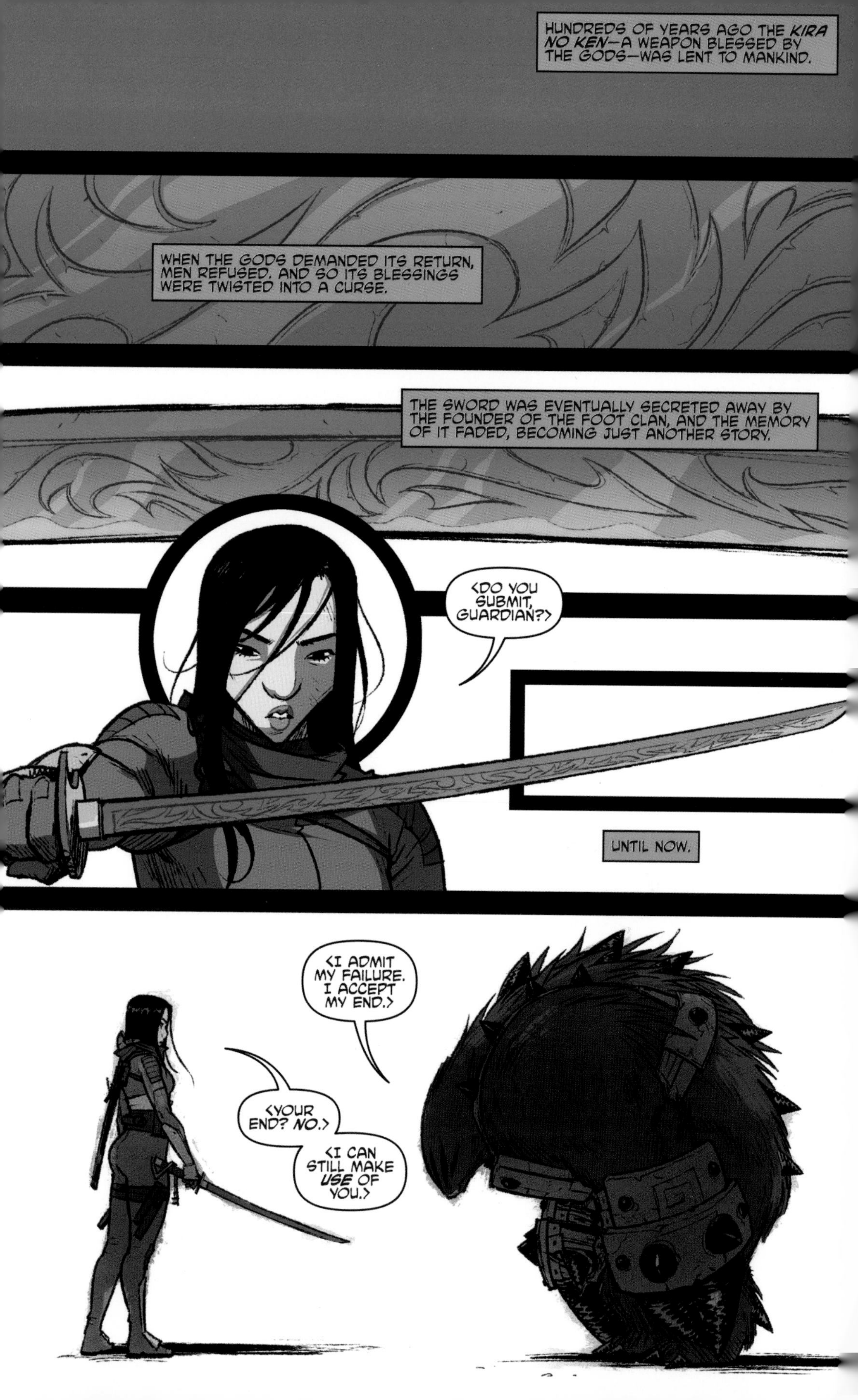

HUNDREDS OF YEARS AGO THE *KIRA NO KEN*—A WEAPON BLESSED BY THE GODS—WAS LENT TO MANKIND.
WHEN THE GODS DEMANDED ITS RETURN, MEN REFUSED. AND SO ITS BLESSINGS WERE TWISTED INTO A CURSE.
THE SWORD WAS EVENTUALLY SECRETED AWAY BY THE FOUNDER OF THE FOOT CLAN, AND THE MEMORY OF IT FADED, BECOMING JUST ANOTHER STORY.
<DO YOU SUBMIT, GUARDIAN?>
UNTIL NOW.
<I ADMIT MY FAILURE. I ACCEPT MY END.>
<YOUR END? *NO.*>
<I CAN STILL MAKE *USE* OF YOU.>

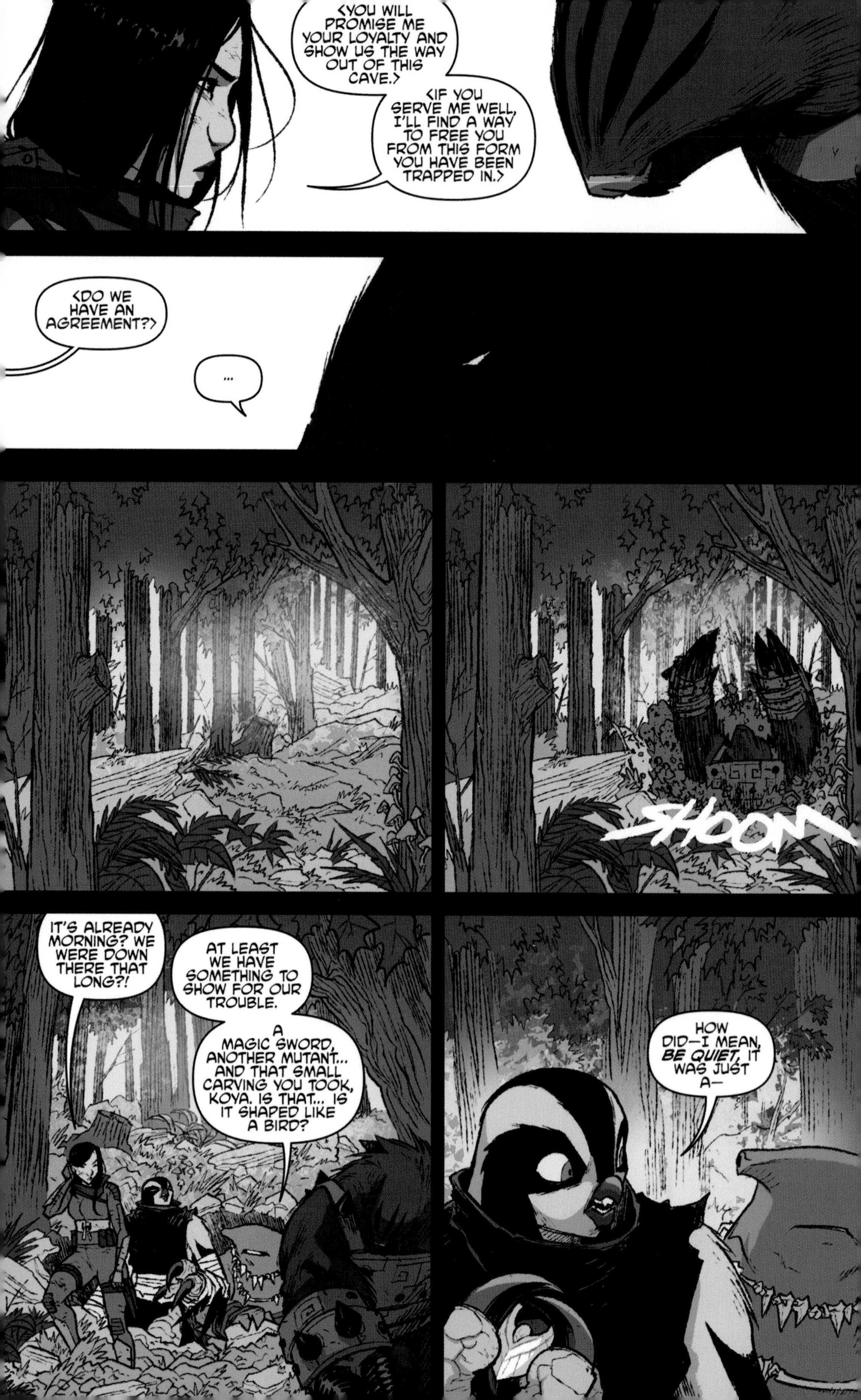
<YOU WILL PROMISE ME YOUR LOYALTY AND SHOW US THE WAY OUT OF THIS CAVE.>
<IF YOU SERVE ME WELL, I'LL FIND A WAY TO FREE YOU FROM THIS FORM YOU HAVE BEEN TRAPPED IN.>
<DO WE HAVE AN AGREEMENT?>
...
SHOOM
IT'S ALREADY MORNING? WE WERE DOWN THERE THAT LONG?!
AT LEAST WE HAVE SOMETHING TO SHOW FOR OUR TROUBLE.
A MAGIC SWORD, ANOTHER MUTANT... AND THAT SMALL CARVING YOU TOOK, KOYA. IS THAT... IS IT SHAPED LIKE A BIRD?
HOW DID—I MEAN, *BE QUIET*, IT WAS JUST A—

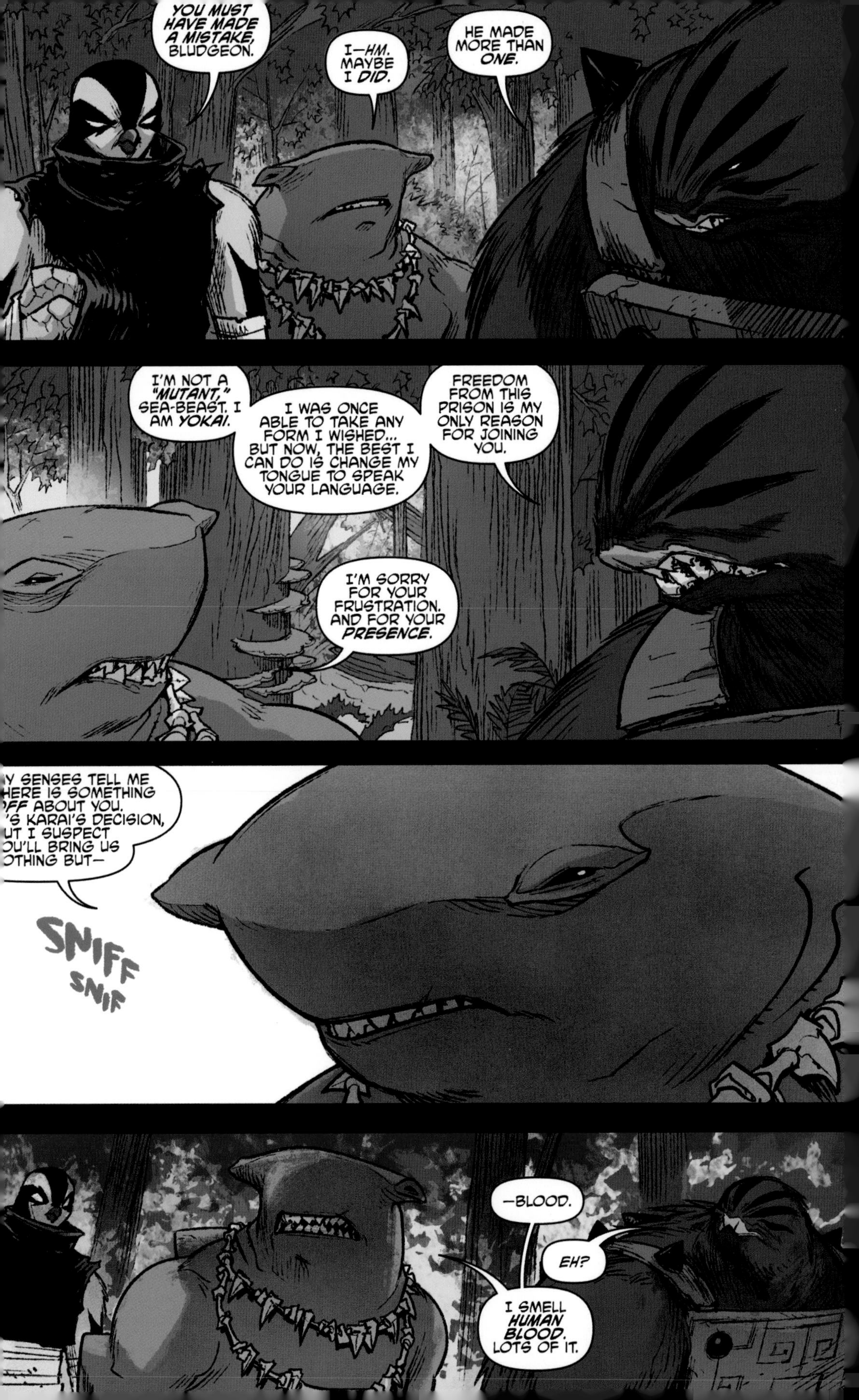
YOU MUST HAVE MADE A MISTAKE, BLUDGEON.
I—HM. MAYBE I DID.
HE MADE MORE THAN ONE.
I'M NOT A "MUTANT," SEA-BEAST. I AM YOKAI.
I WAS ONCE ABLE TO TAKE ANY FORM I WISHED... BUT NOW, THE BEST I CAN DO IS CHANGE MY TONGUE TO SPEAK YOUR LANGUAGE.
FREEDOM FROM THIS PRISON IS MY ONLY REASON FOR JOINING YOU.
I'M SORRY FOR YOUR FRUSTRATION. AND FOR YOUR PRESENCE.
Y SENSES TELL ME HERE IS SOMETHING FF ABOUT YOU. 'S KARAI'S DECISION, UT I SUSPECT OU'LL BRING US OTHING BUT—
SNIFF
SNIF
—BLOOD.
EH?
I SMELL HUMAN BLOOD. LOTS OF IT.

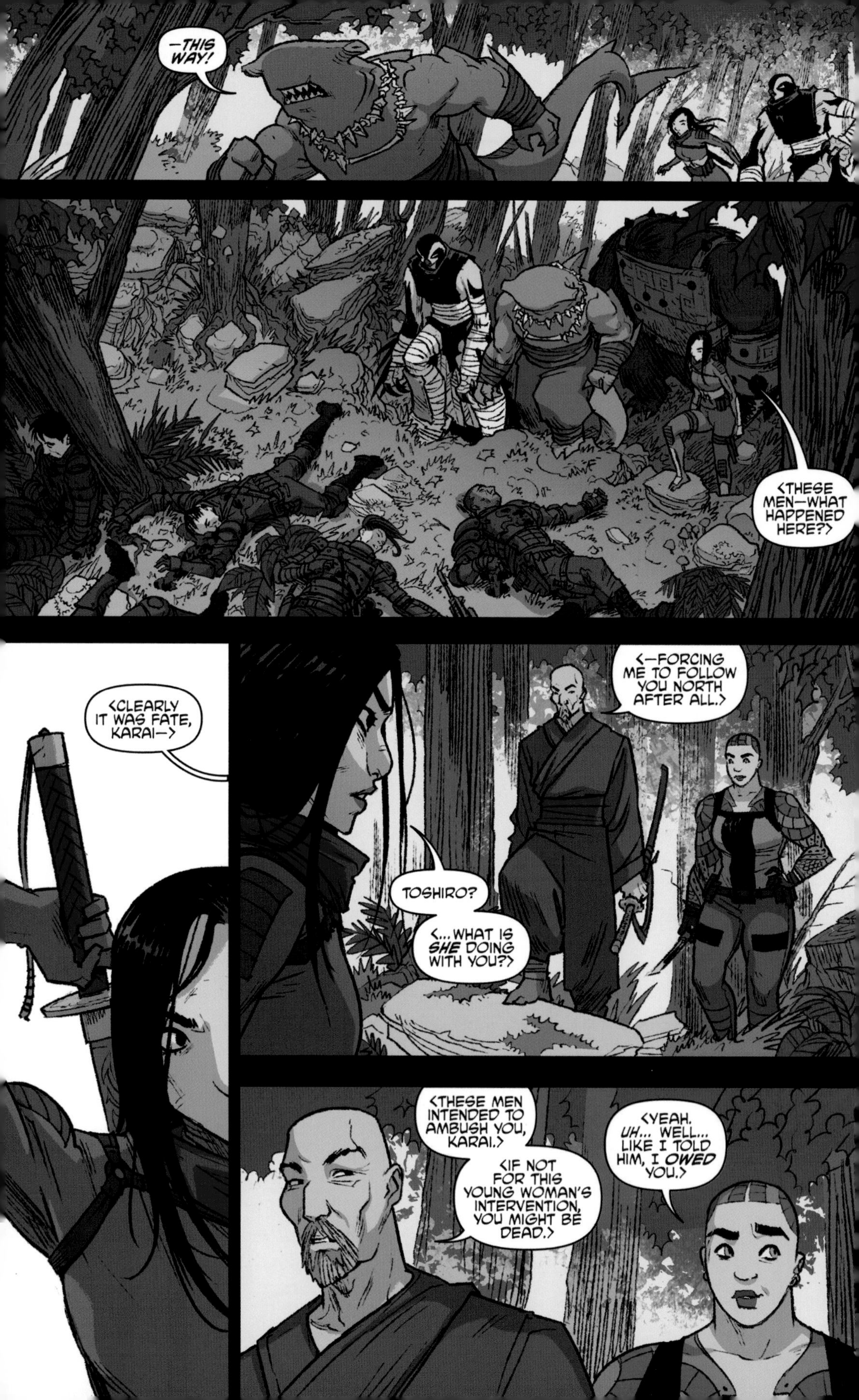
—THIS WAY!
<THESE MEN—WHAT HAPPENED HERE?>
<CLEARLY IT WAS FATE, KARAI—>
<—FORCING ME TO FOLLOW YOU NORTH AFTER ALL.>
TOSHIRO?
<...WHAT IS SHE DOING WITH YOU?>
<THESE MEN INTENDED TO AMBUSH YOU, KARAI.>
<IF NOT FOR THIS YOUNG WOMAN'S INTERVENTION, YOU MIGHT BE DEAD.>
<YEAH. UH... WELL... LIKE I TOLD HIM, I OWED YOU.>

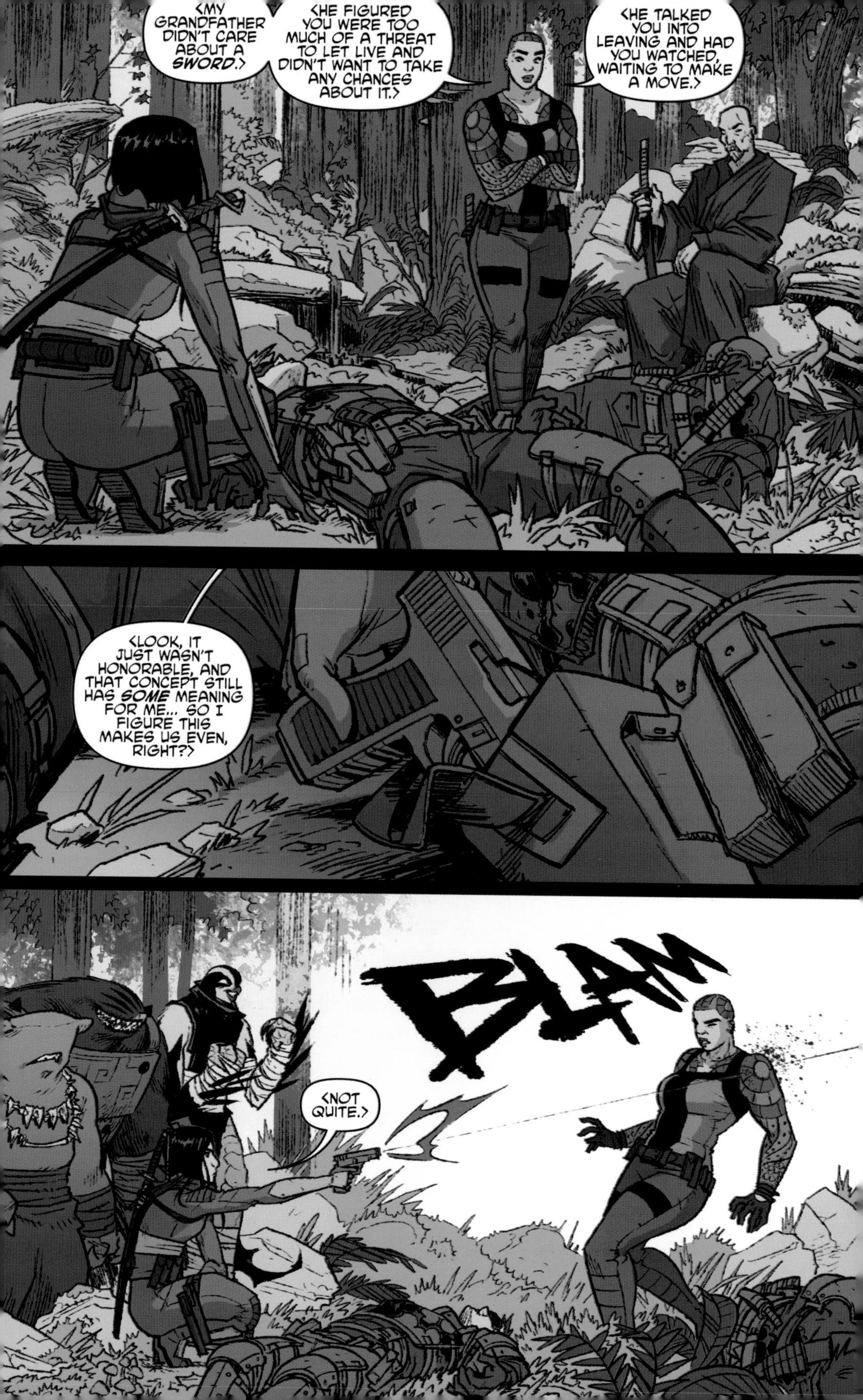
<MY GRANDFATHER DIDN'T CARE ABOUT A SWORD.>
<HE FIGURED YOU WERE TOO MUCH OF A THREAT TO LET LIVE AND DIDN'T WANT TO TAKE ANY CHANCES ABOUT IT.>
<HE TALKED YOU INTO LEAVING AND HAD YOU WATCHED, WAITING TO MAKE A MOVE.>
<LOOK, IT JUST WASN'T HONORABLE, AND THAT CONCEPT STILL HAS SOME MEANING FOR ME... SO I FIGURE THIS MAKES US EVEN, RIGHT?>
BLAM
<NOT QUITE.>

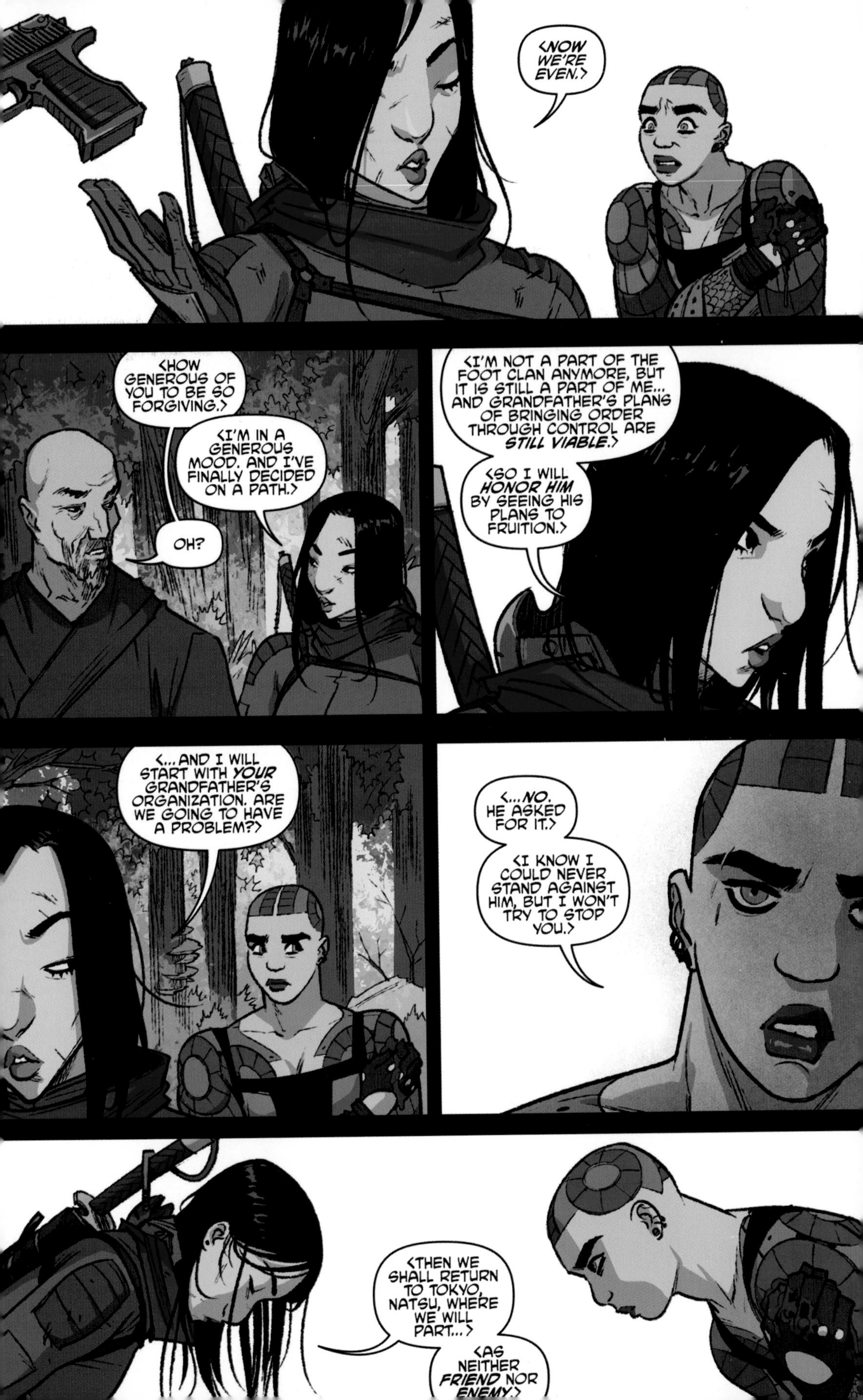
<NOW WE'RE EVEN.>
<HOW GENEROUS OF YOU TO BE SO FORGIVING.>
<I'M IN A GENEROUS MOOD. AND I'VE FINALLY DECIDED ON A PATH.>
OH?
<I'M NOT A PART OF THE FOOT CLAN ANYMORE, BUT IT IS STILL A PART OF ME... AND GRANDFATHER'S PLANS OF BRINGING ORDER THROUGH CONTROL ARE STILL VIABLE.>
<SO I WILL HONOR HIM BY SEEING HIS PLANS TO FRUITION.>
<...AND I WILL START WITH YOUR GRANDFATHER'S ORGANIZATION. ARE WE GOING TO HAVE A PROBLEM?>
<...NO. HE ASKED FOR IT.>
<I KNOW I COULD NEVER STAND AGAINST HIM, BUT I WON'T TRY TO STOP YOU.>
<THEN WE SHALL RETURN TO TOKYO, NATSU, WHERE WE WILL PART...>
<AS NEITHER FRIEND NOR ENEMY.>

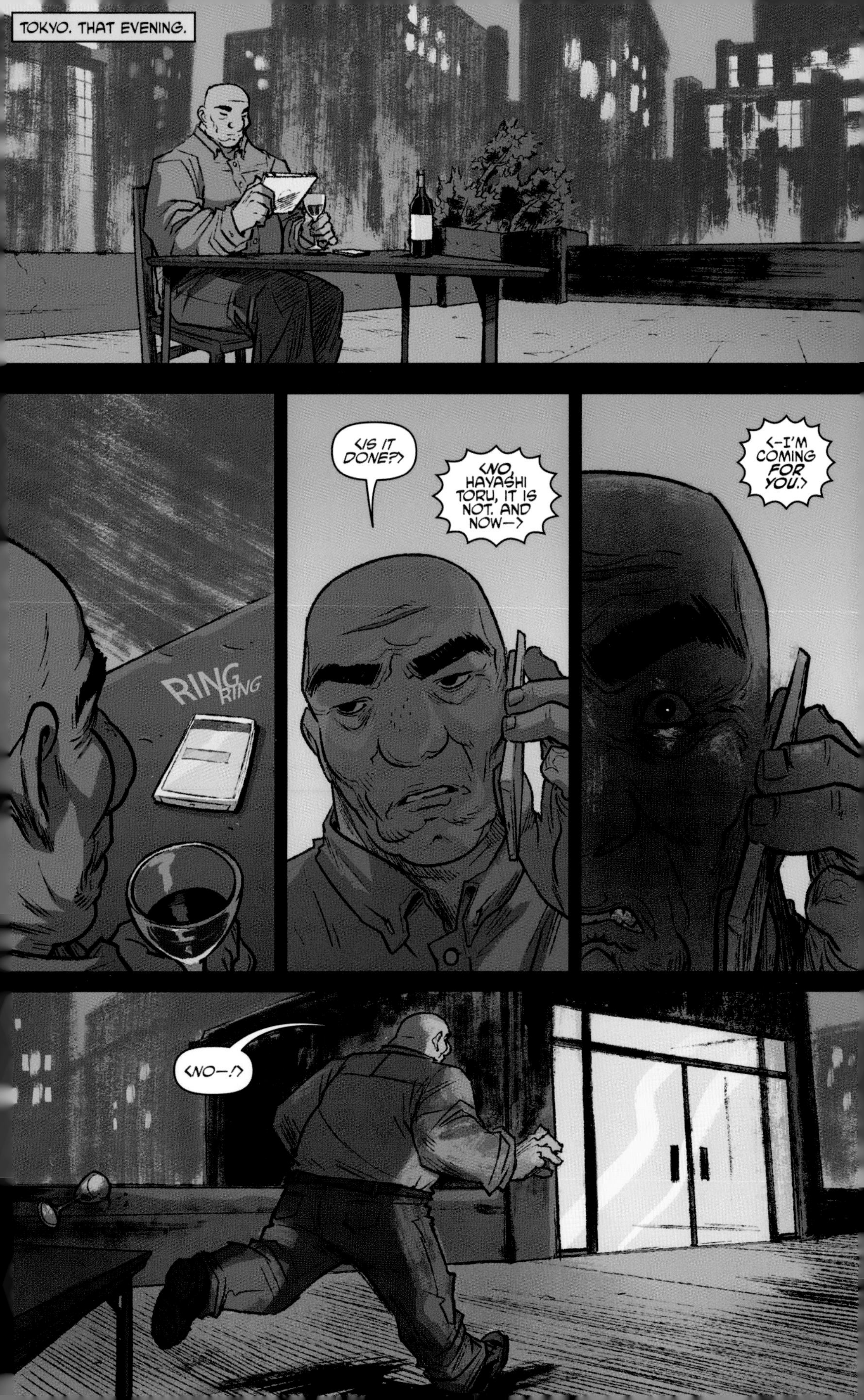
TOKYO. THAT EVENING.
RING RING
<IS IT DONE?>
<NO, HAYASHI TORU, IT IS NOT. AND NOW—>
<—I'M COMING FOR YOU.>
<NO—!>

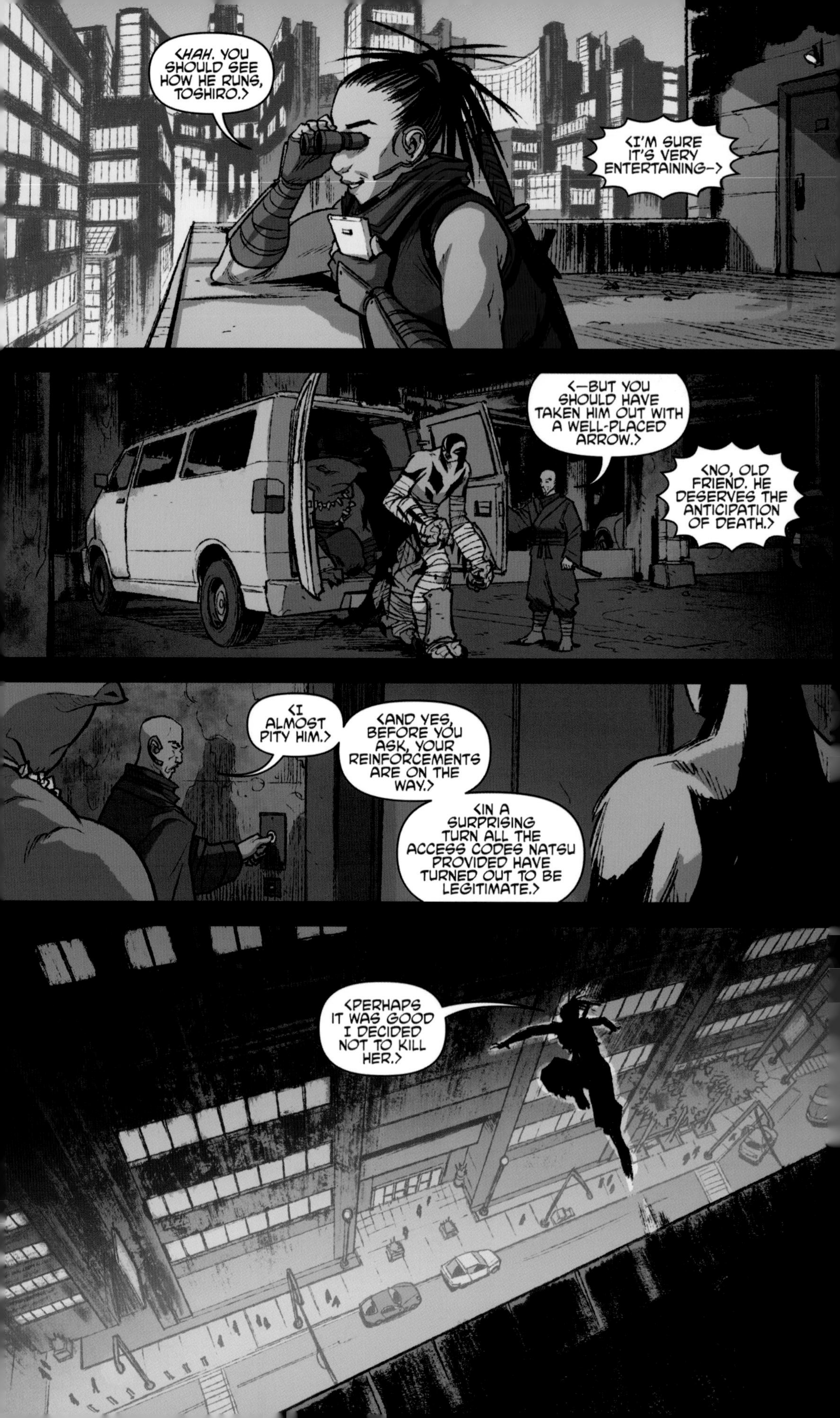
<*HAH*. YOU SHOULD SEE HOW HE RUNS, TOSHIRO.>
<I'M SURE IT'S VERY ENTERTAINING–>
<–BUT YOU SHOULD HAVE TAKEN HIM OUT WITH A WELL-PLACED ARROW.>
<NO, OLD FRIEND. HE DESERVES THE ANTICIPATION OF DEATH.>
<I ALMOST PITY HIM.>
<AND YES, BEFORE YOU ASK, YOUR REINFORCEMENTS ARE ON THE WAY.>
<IN A SURPRISING TURN ALL THE ACCESS CODES NATSU PROVIDED HAVE TURNED OUT TO BE LEGITIMATE.>
<PERHAPS IT WAS GOOD I DECIDED NOT TO KILL HER.>

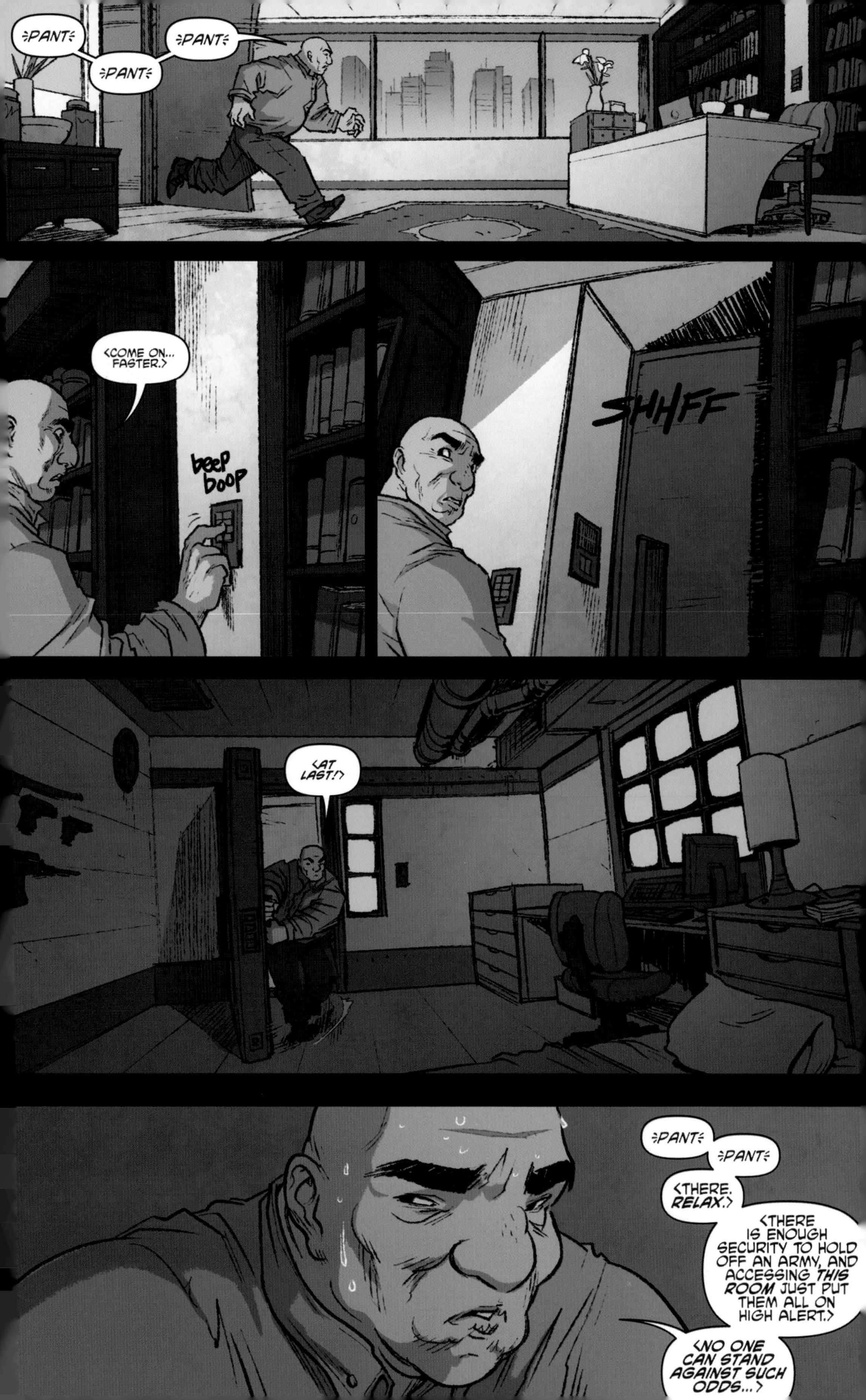
PANT
PANT
PANT
<COME ON... FASTER.>
beep boop
SHHFF
<AT LAST!>
PANT
PANT
<THERE. RELAX.>
<THERE IS ENOUGH SECURITY TO HOLD OFF AN ARMY, AND ACCESSING THIS ROOM JUST PUT THEM ALL ON HIGH ALERT.>
<NO ONE CAN STAND AGAINST SUCH ODDS...>

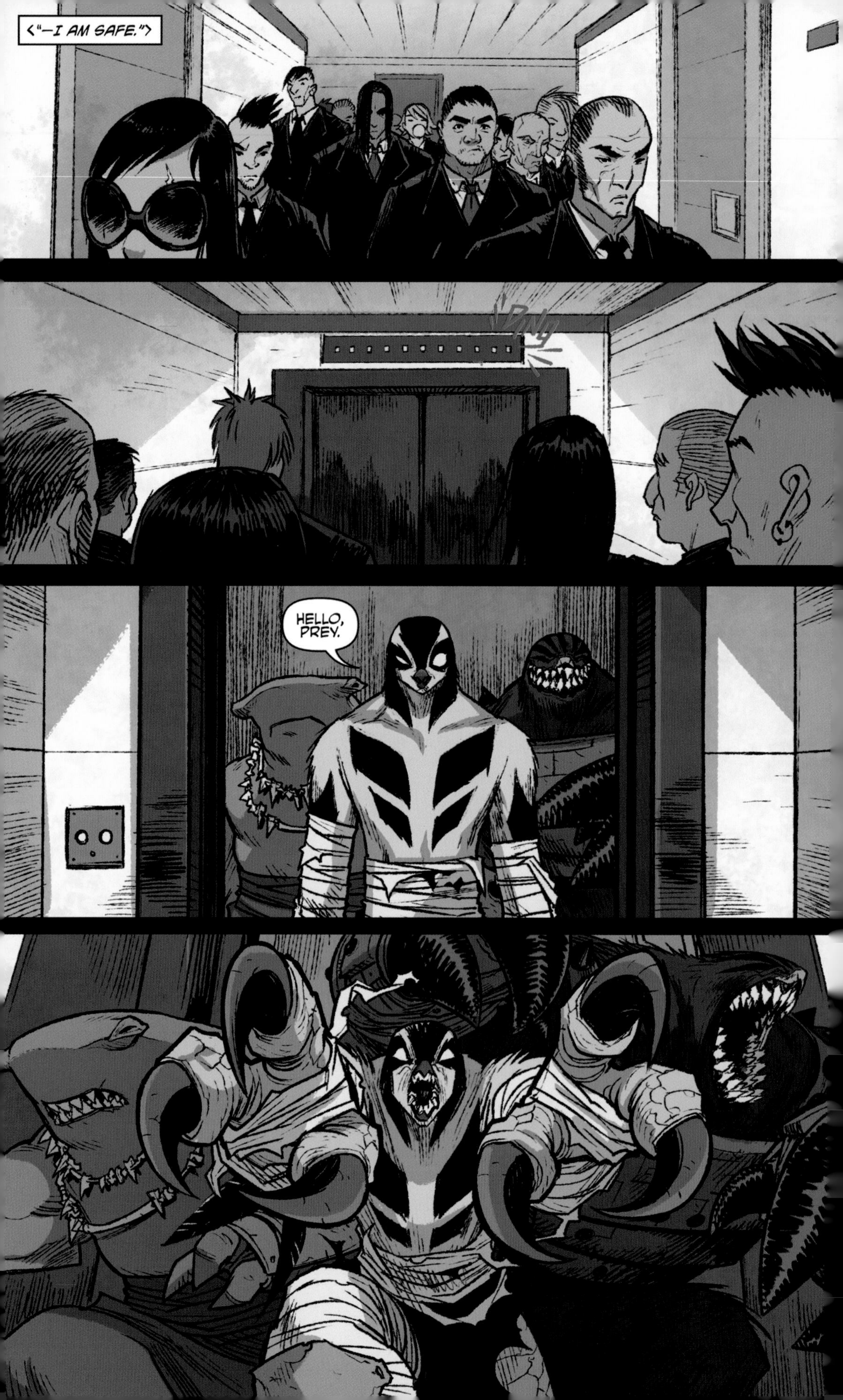
<"—I AM SAFE.">
DING
HELLO, PREY.

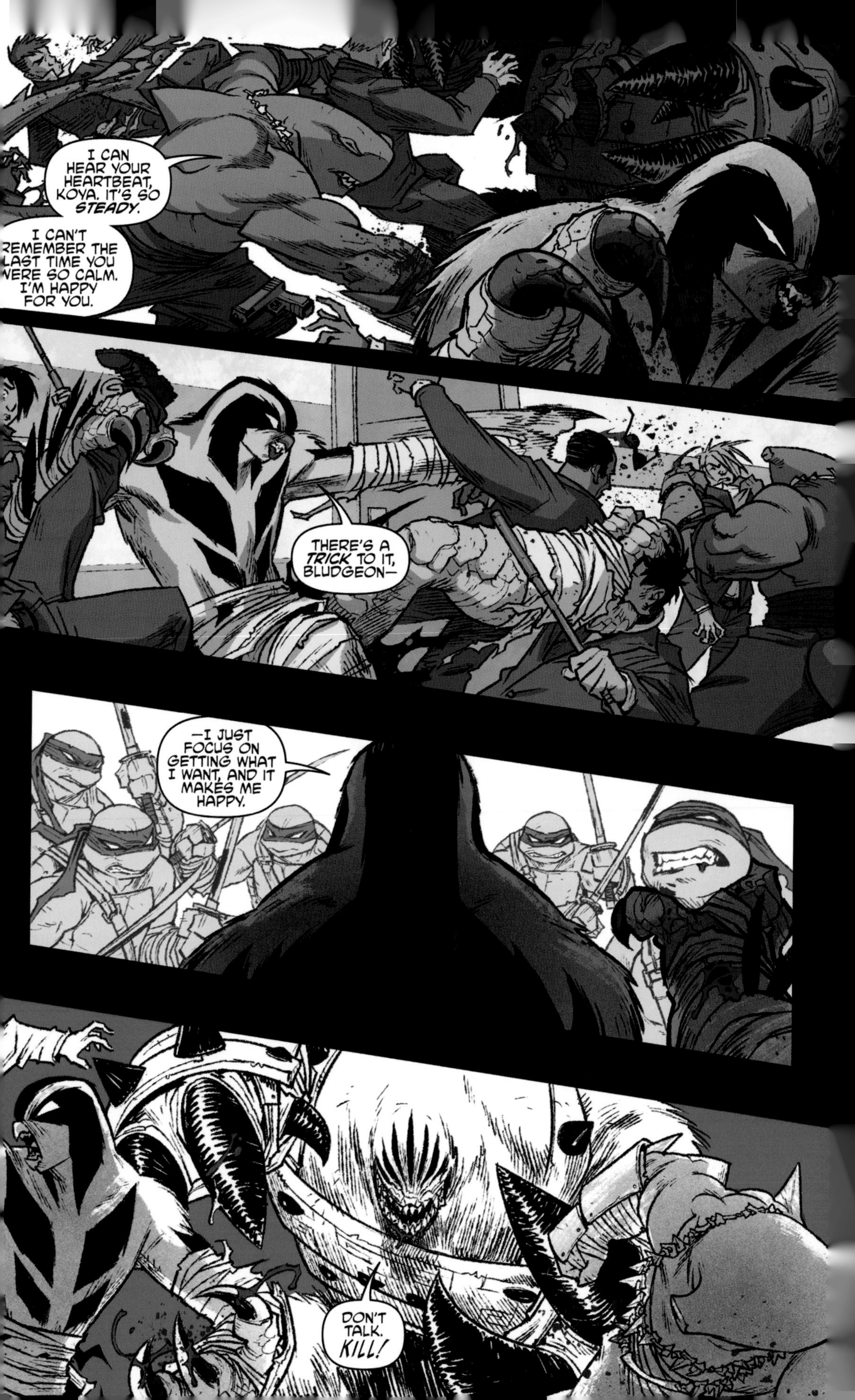
I CAN HEAR YOUR HEARTBEAT, KOYA. IT'S SO STEADY.
I CAN'T REMEMBER THE LAST TIME YOU WERE SO CALM. I'M HAPPY FOR YOU.
THERE'S A TRICK TO IT, BLUDGEON—
—I JUST FOCUS ON GETTING WHAT I WANT, AND IT MAKES ME HAPPY.
DON'T TALK. KILL!

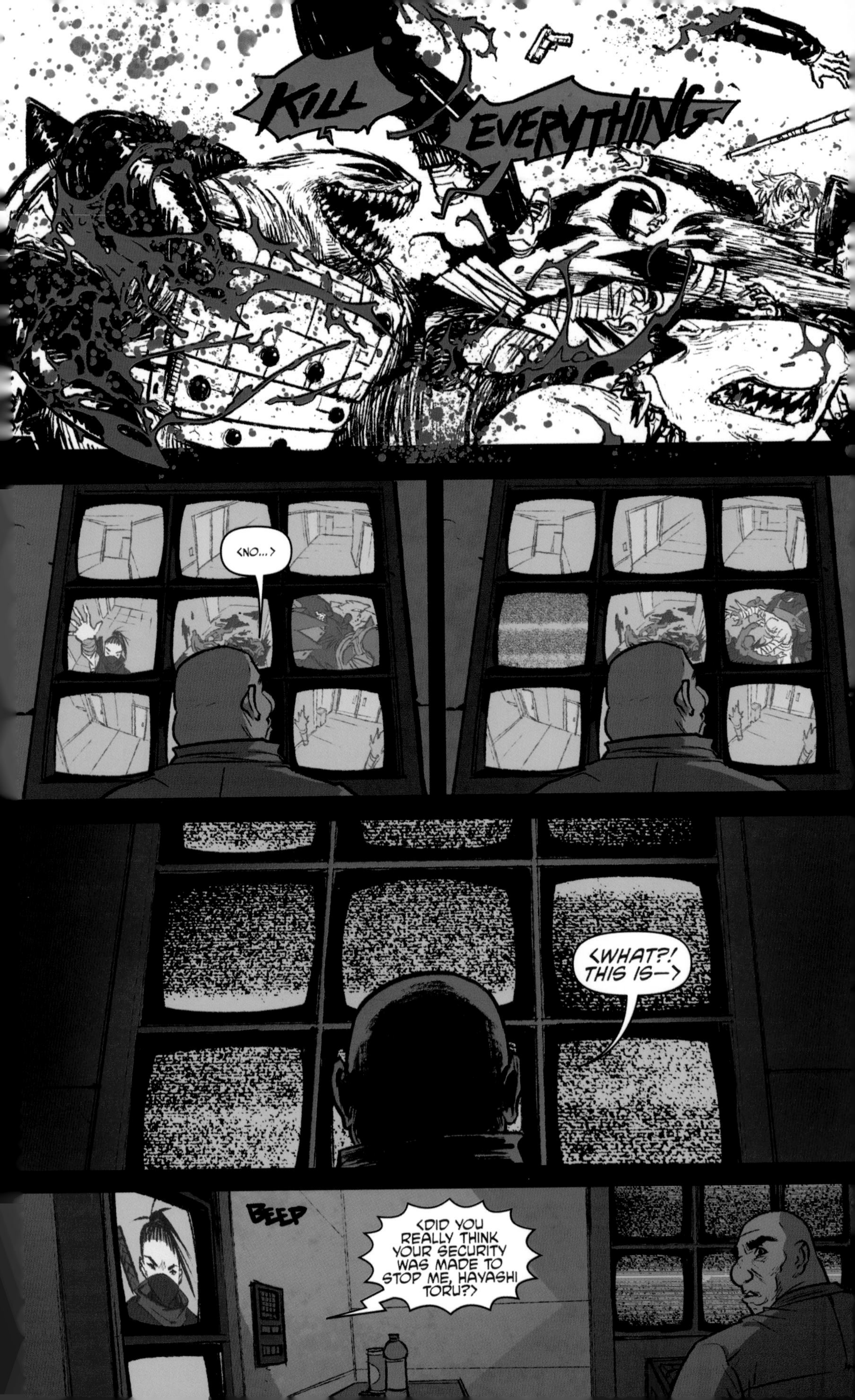
KILL EVERYTHING
<NO...>
<WHAT?! THIS IS—>
BEEP
<DID YOU REALLY THINK YOUR SECURITY WAS MADE TO STOP ME, HAYASHI TORU?>

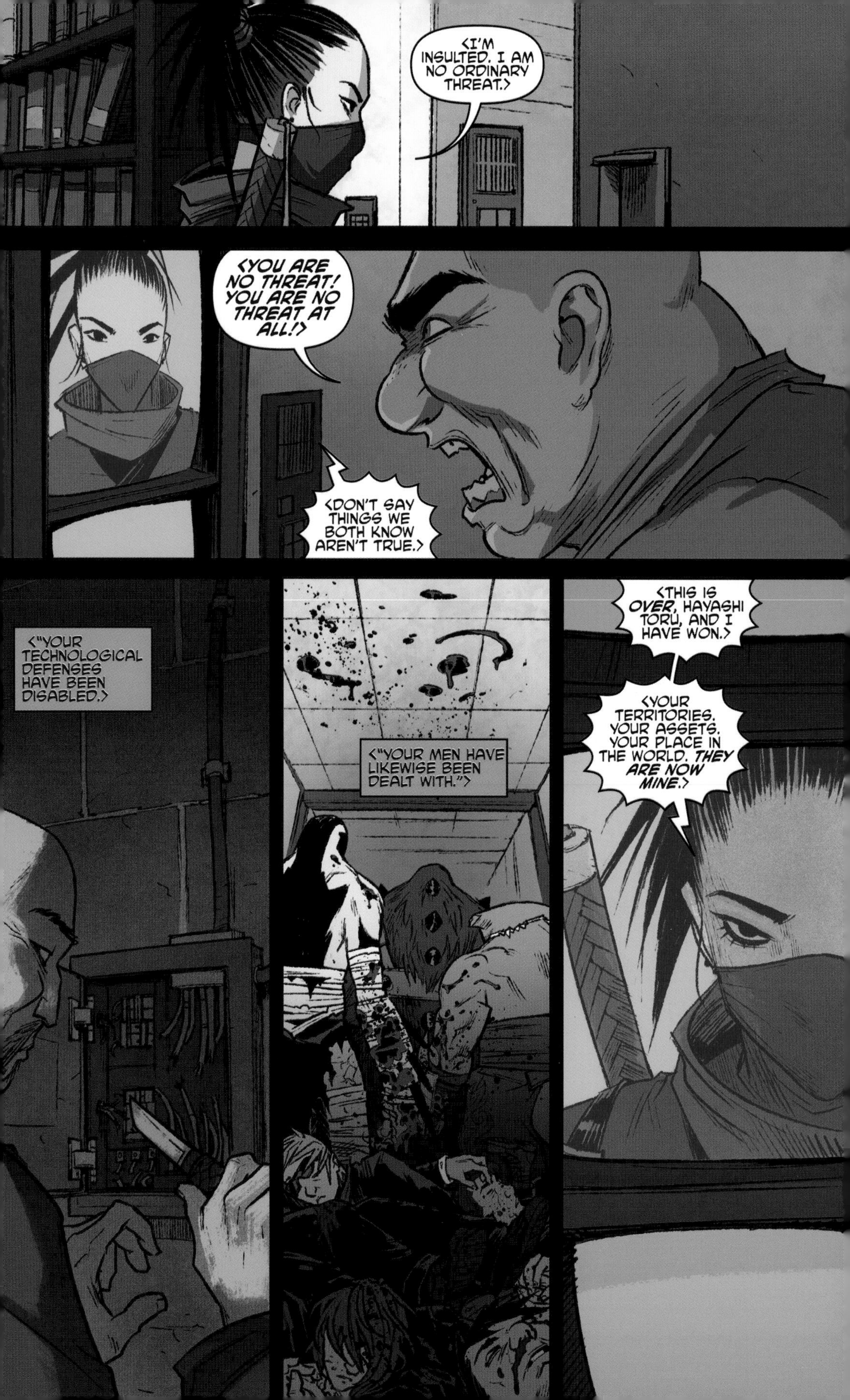

<I'M INSULTED. I AM NO ORDINARY THREAT.>
<YOU ARE NO THREAT! YOU ARE NO THREAT AT ALL!>
<DON'T SAY THINGS WE BOTH KNOW AREN'T TRUE.>
<"YOUR TECHNOLOGICAL DEFENSES HAVE BEEN DISABLED.>
<"YOUR MEN HAVE LIKEWISE BEEN DEALT WITH.">
<THIS IS *OVER*, HAYASHI TORU, AND I HAVE WON.>
<YOUR TERRITORIES. YOUR ASSETS. YOUR PLACE IN THE WORLD. *THEY ARE NOW MINE*.>

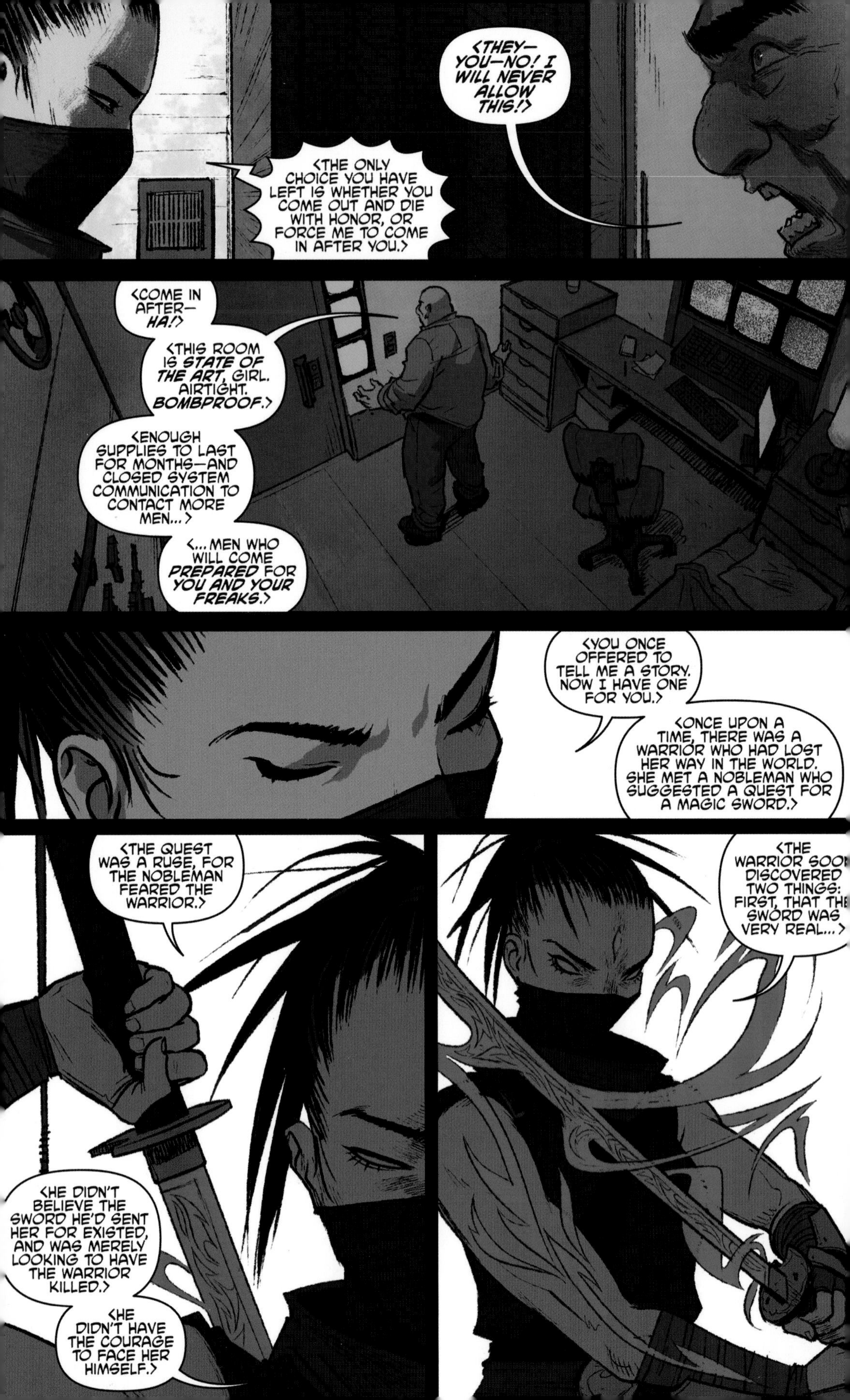

<THEY—YOU—NO! I WILL NEVER ALLOW THIS!>
<THE ONLY CHOICE YOU HAVE LEFT IS WHETHER YOU COME OUT AND DIE WITH HONOR, OR FORCE ME TO COME IN AFTER YOU.>
<COME IN AFTER— HA!>
<THIS ROOM IS STATE OF THE ART, GIRL. AIRTIGHT. BOMBPROOF.>
<ENOUGH SUPPLIES TO LAST FOR MONTHS—AND CLOSED SYSTEM COMMUNICATION TO CONTACT MORE MEN...>
<...MEN WHO WILL COME PREPARED FOR YOU AND YOUR FREAKS.>
<YOU ONCE OFFERED TO TELL ME A STORY. NOW I HAVE ONE FOR YOU.>
<ONCE UPON A TIME, THERE WAS A WARRIOR WHO HAD LOST HER WAY IN THE WORLD. SHE MET A NOBLEMAN WHO SUGGESTED A QUEST FOR A MAGIC SWORD.>
<THE QUEST WAS A RUSE, FOR THE NOBLEMAN FEARED THE WARRIOR.>
<HE DIDN'T BELIEVE THE SWORD HE'D SENT HER FOR EXISTED, AND WAS MERELY LOOKING TO HAVE THE WARRIOR KILLED.>
<HE DIDN'T HAVE THE COURAGE TO FACE HER HIMSELF.>
<THE WARRIOR SOO DISCOVERED TWO THINGS: FIRST, THAT THE SWORD WAS VERY REAL...>

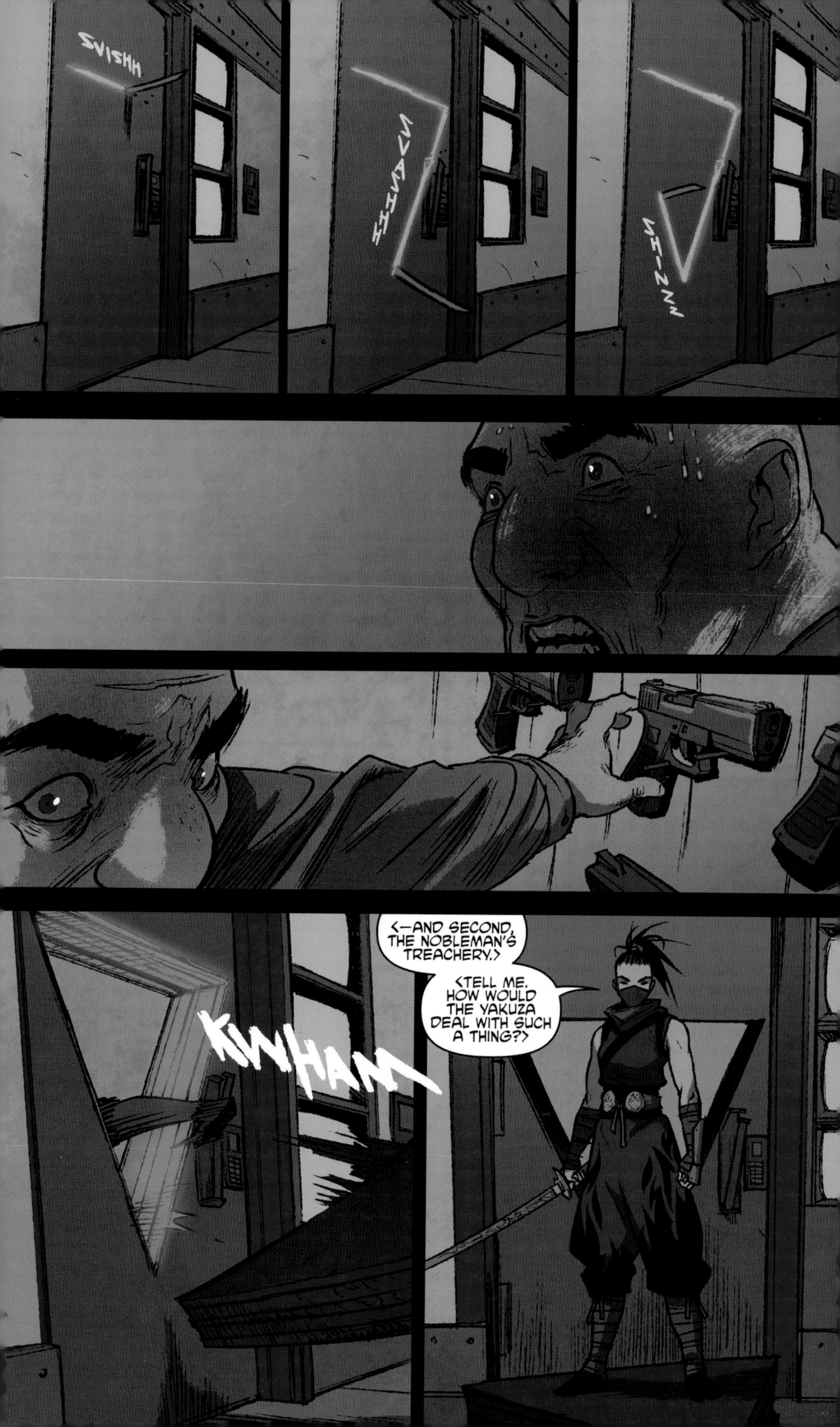
SVISHH
SVASHHH
SHINNN
KWHAM
<—AND SECOND, THE NOBLEMAN'S TREACHERY.>
<TELL ME. HOW WOULD THE YAKUZA DEAL WITH SUCH A THING?>

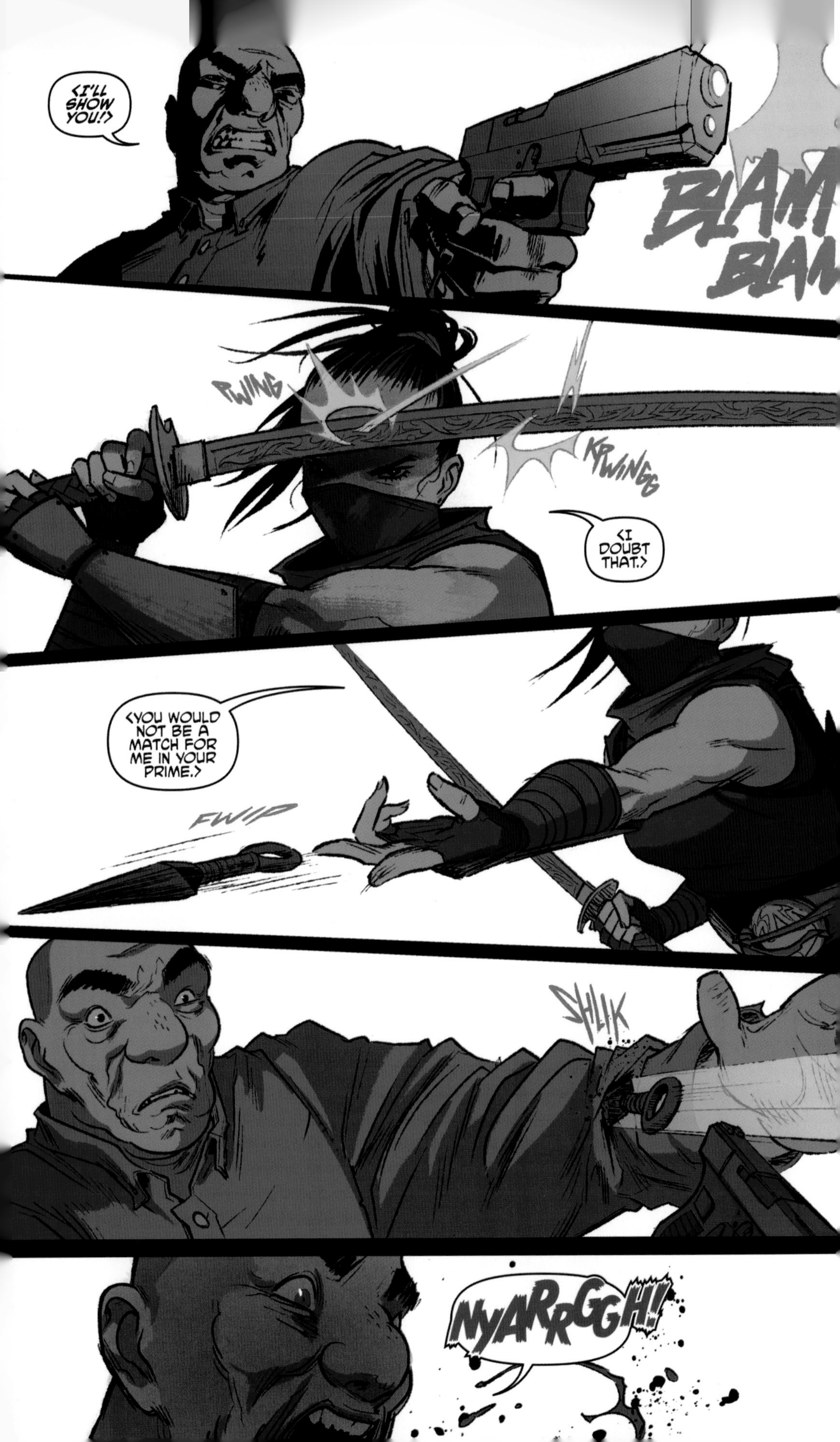
<I'LL SHOW YOU!>
BLAM
BLAM
PWING
KRWINGG
<I DOUBT THAT.>
<YOU WOULD NOT BE A MATCH FOR ME IN YOUR PRIME.>
FWIP
SHLIK
NYARRGGH!

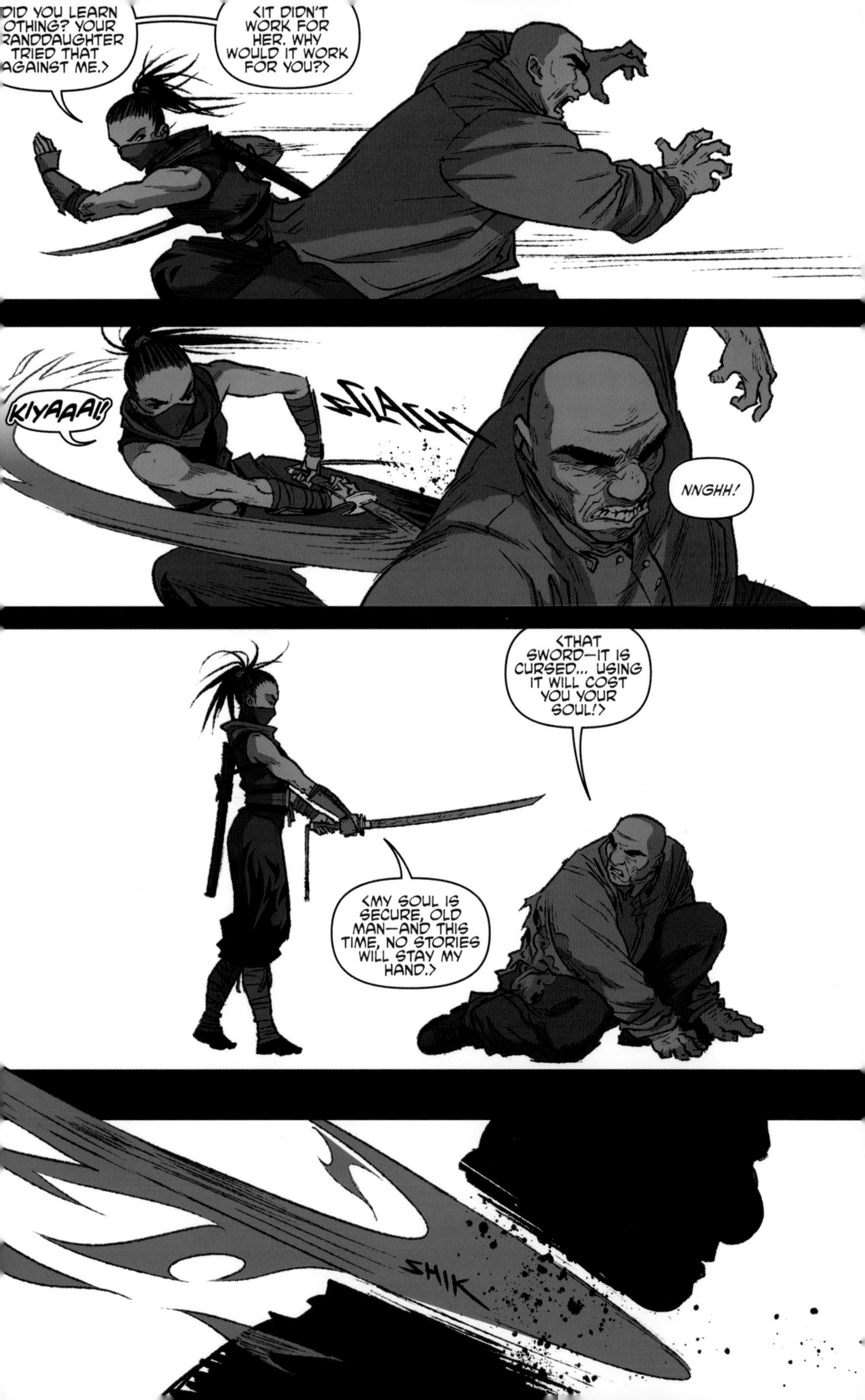
DID YOU LEARN OTHING? YOUR RANDDAUGHTER TRIED THAT AGAINST ME.>
<IT DIDN'T WORK FOR HER. WHY WOULD IT WORK FOR YOU?>
KIYAAAI!
NNGHH!
<THAT SWORD—IT IS CURSED... USING IT WILL COST YOU YOUR SOUL!>
<MY SOUL IS SECURE, OLD MAN—AND THIS TIME, NO STORIES WILL STAY MY HAND.>
SHIK

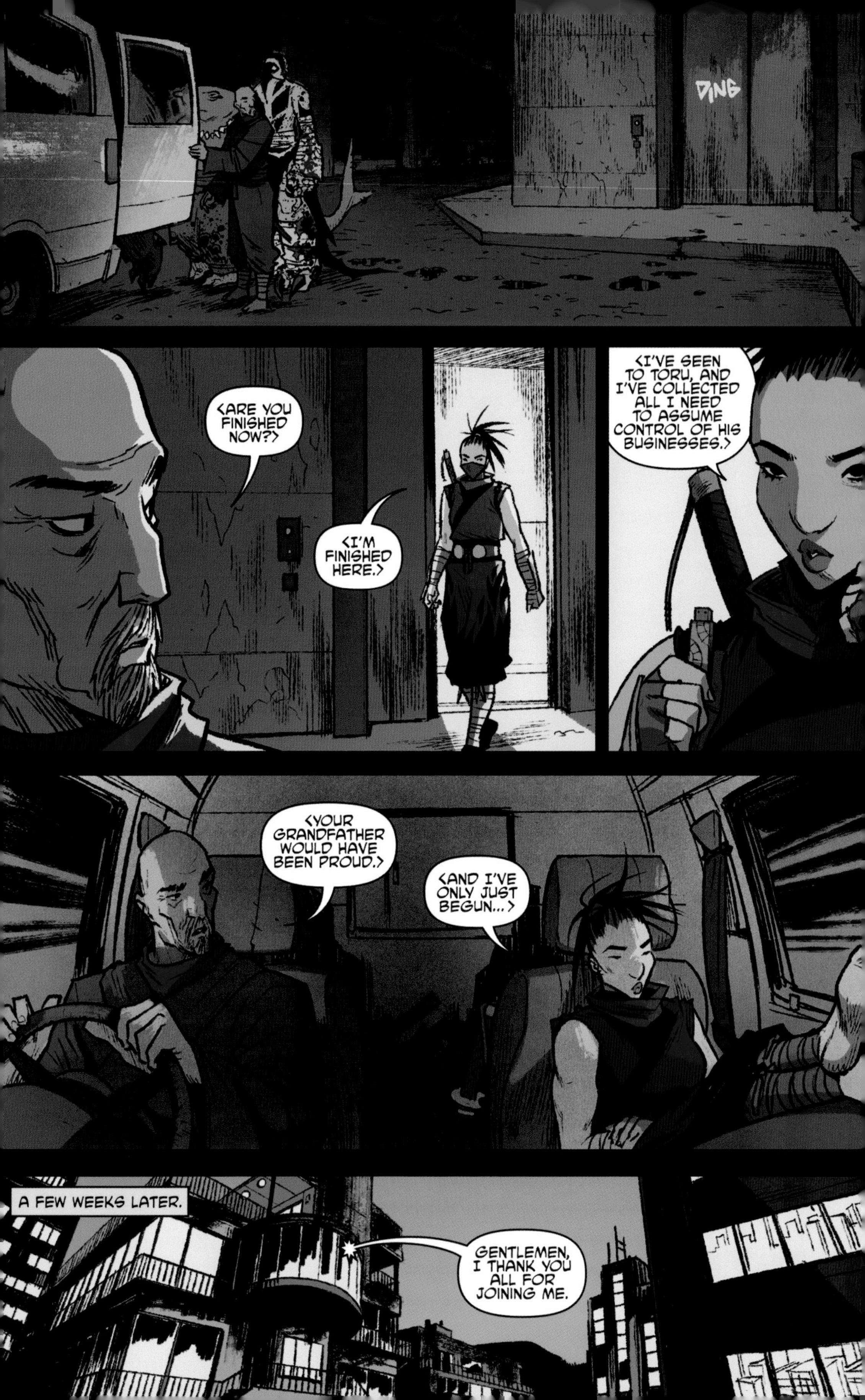
DING
<ARE YOU FINISHED NOW?>
<I'M FINISHED HERE.>
<I'VE SEEN TO TORU, AND I'VE COLLECTED ALL I NEED TO ASSUME CONTROL OF HIS BUSINESSES.>
<YOUR GRANDFATHER WOULD HAVE BEEN PROUD.>
<AND I'VE ONLY JUST BEGUN...>
A FEW WEEKS LATER.
GENTLEMEN, I THANK YOU ALL FOR JOINING ME.

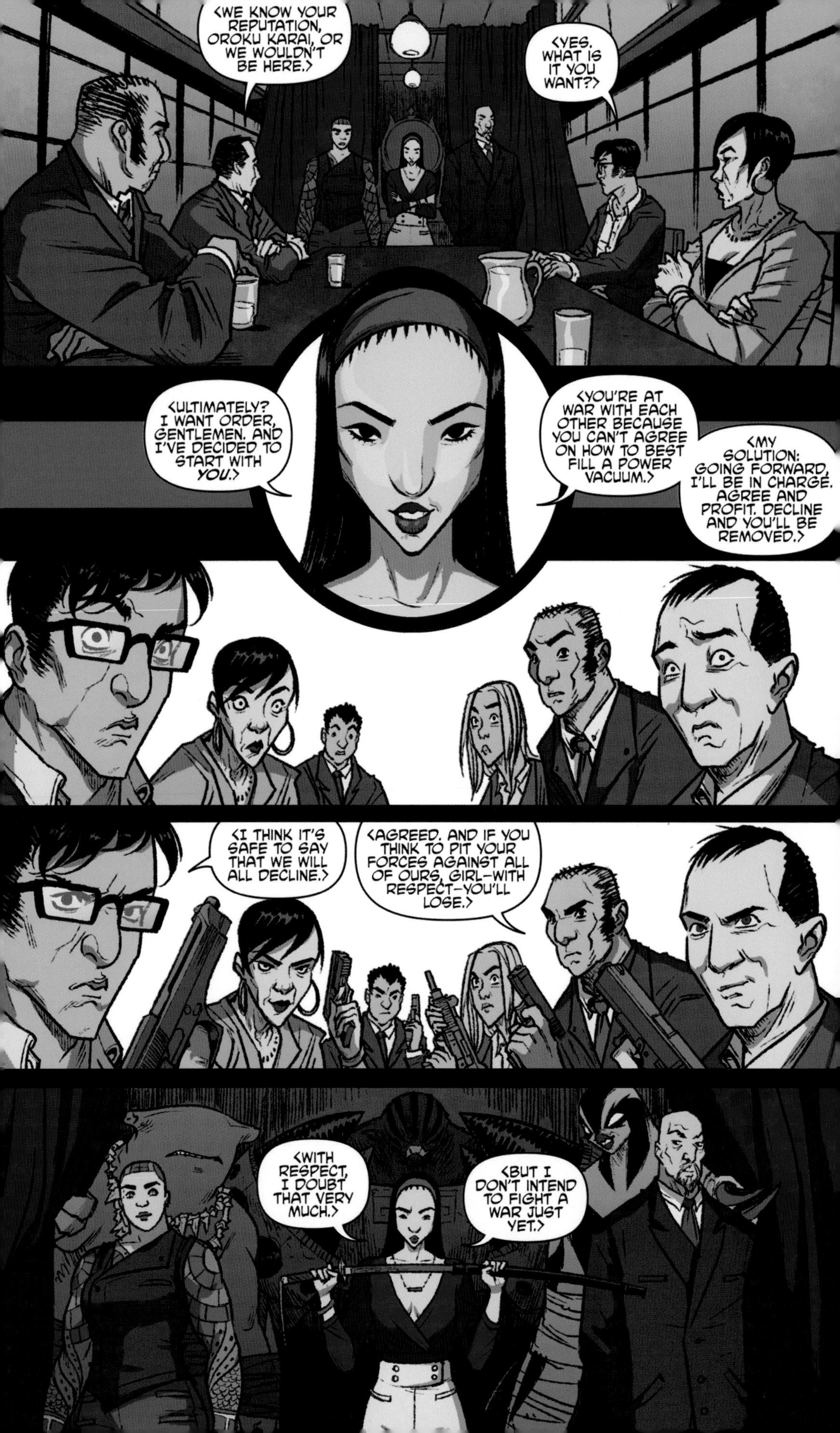
<WE KNOW YOUR REPUTATION, OROKU KARAI, OR WE WOULDN'T BE HERE.>
<YES. WHAT IS IT YOU WANT?>
<ULTIMATELY? I WANT ORDER, GENTLEMEN. AND I'VE DECIDED TO START WITH *YOU*.>
<YOU'RE AT WAR WITH EACH OTHER BECAUSE YOU CAN'T AGREE ON HOW TO BEST FILL A POWER VACUUM.>
<MY SOLUTION: GOING FORWARD, I'LL BE IN CHARGE. AGREE AND PROFIT. DECLINE AND YOU'LL BE REMOVED.>
<I THINK IT'S SAFE TO SAY THAT WE WILL ALL DECLINE.>
<AGREED. AND IF YOU THINK TO PIT YOUR FORCES AGAINST ALL OF OURS, GIRL—WITH RESPECT—YOU'LL LOSE.>
<WITH RESPECT, I DOUBT THAT VERY MUCH.>
<BUT I DON'T INTEND TO FIGHT A WAR JUST YET.>

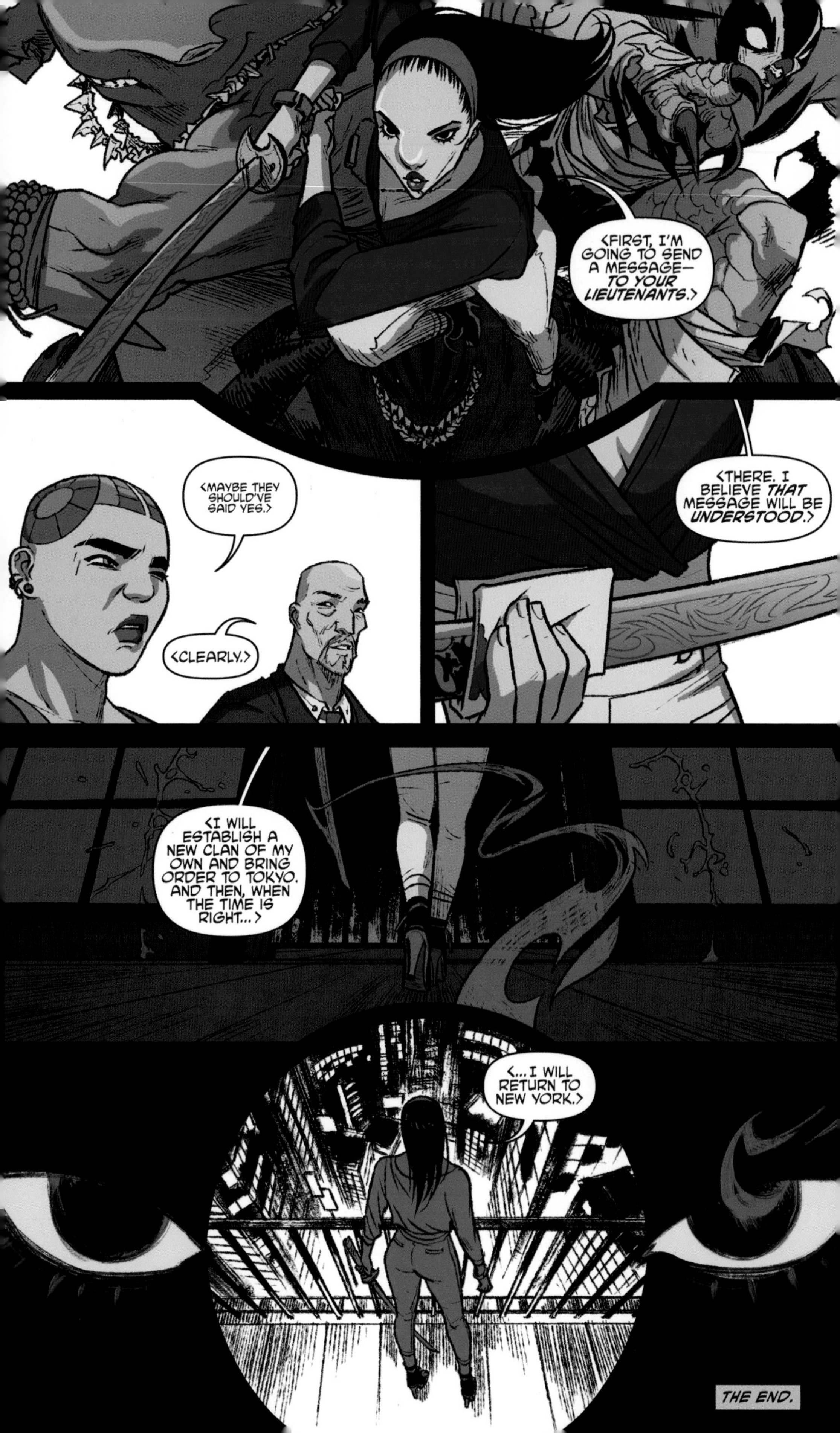
<FIRST, I'M GOING TO SEND A MESSAGE— TO YOUR LIEUTENANTS.>
<MAYBE THEY SHOULD'VE SAID YES.>
<CLEARLY.>
<THERE. I BELIEVE THAT MESSAGE WILL BE UNDERSTOOD.>
<I WILL ESTABLISH A NEW CLAN OF MY OWN AND BRING ORDER TO TOKYO. AND THEN, WHEN THE TIME IS RIGHT...>
<...I WILL RETURN TO NEW YORK.>
THE END.

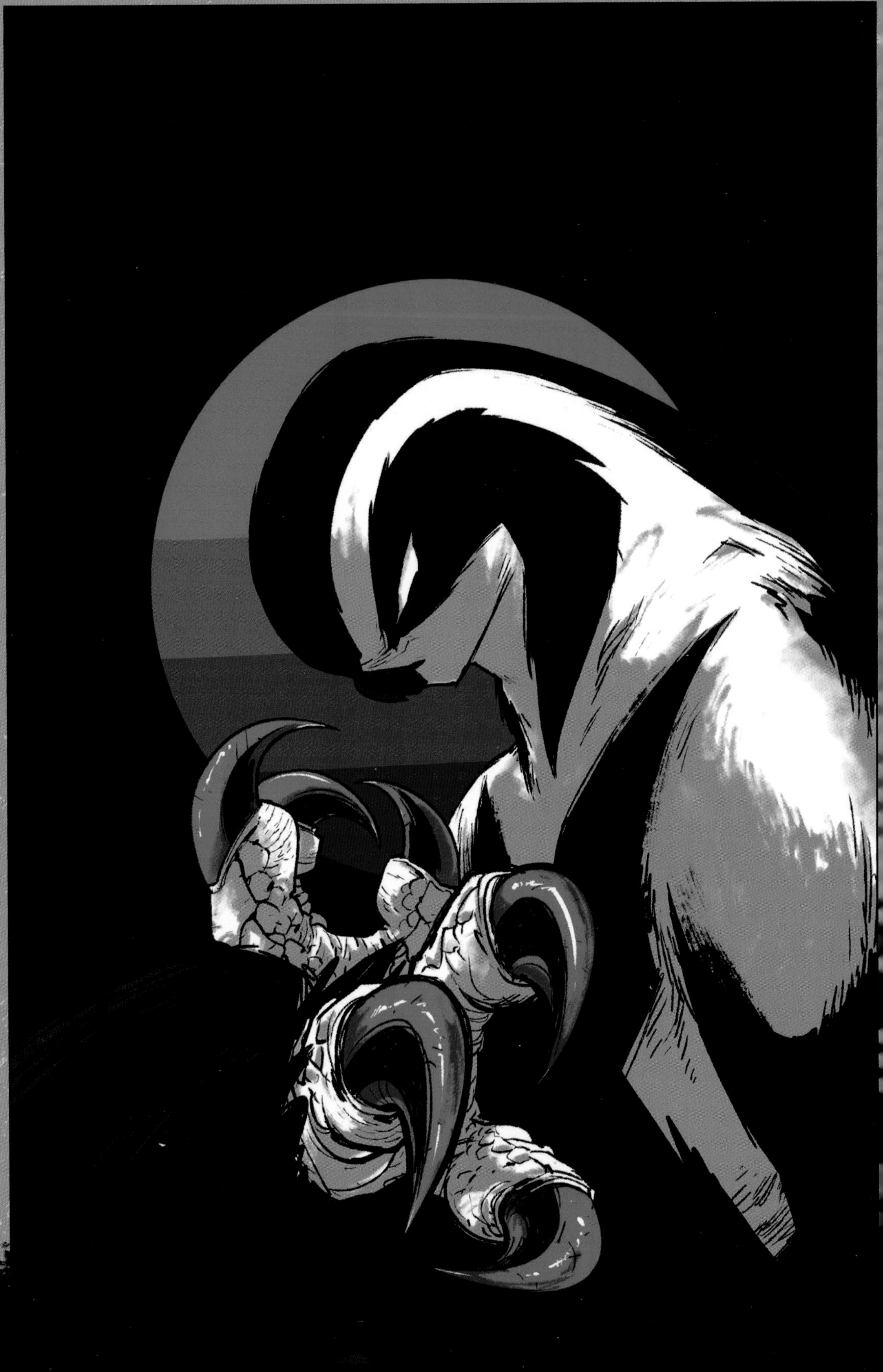

ART BY SOPHIE CAMPBELL

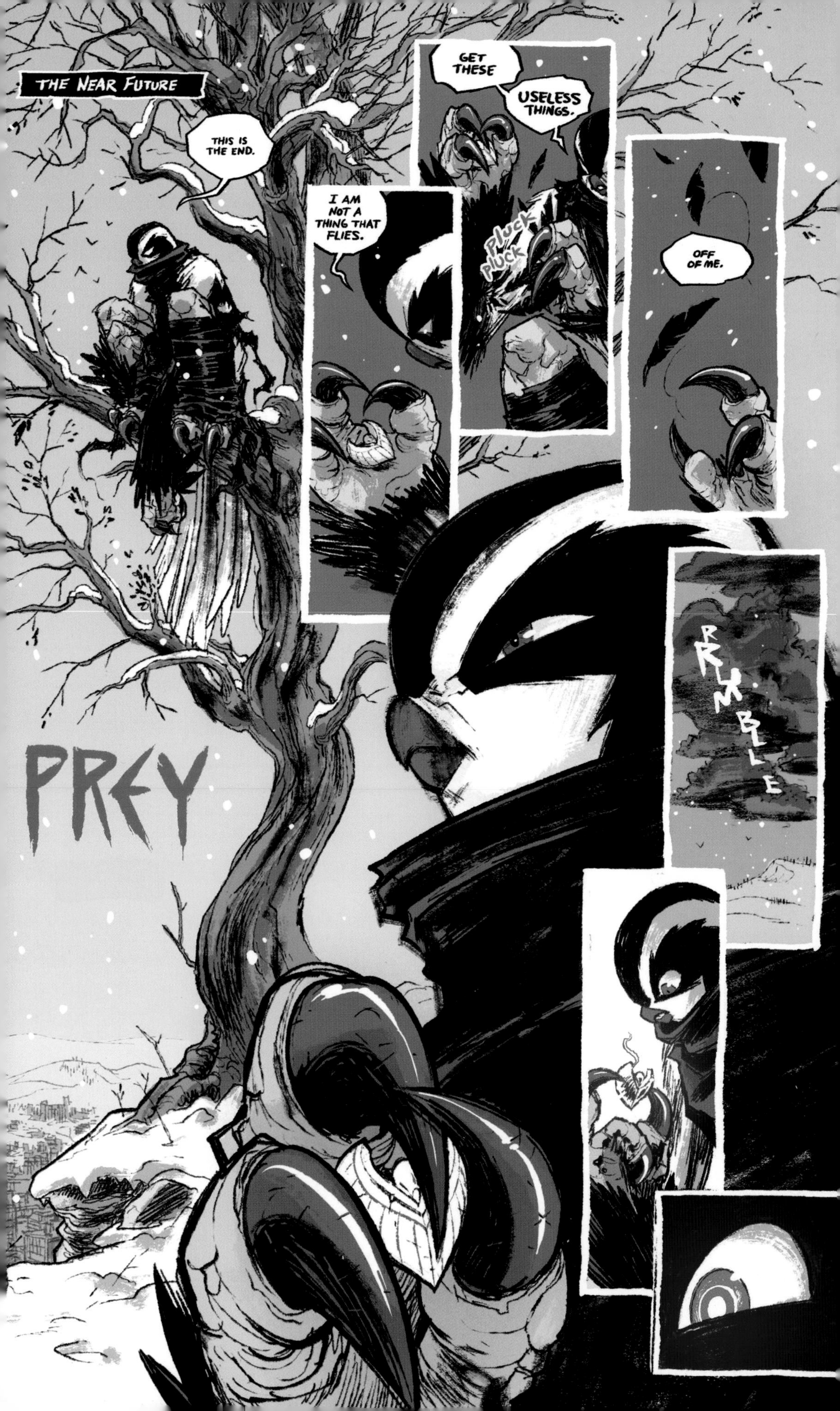
THE NEAR FUTURE
THIS IS THE END.
PREY
I AM NOT A THING THAT FLIES.
GET THESE
USELESS THINGS.
PLUCK
PLUCK
OFF OF ME.
RRUMBLE

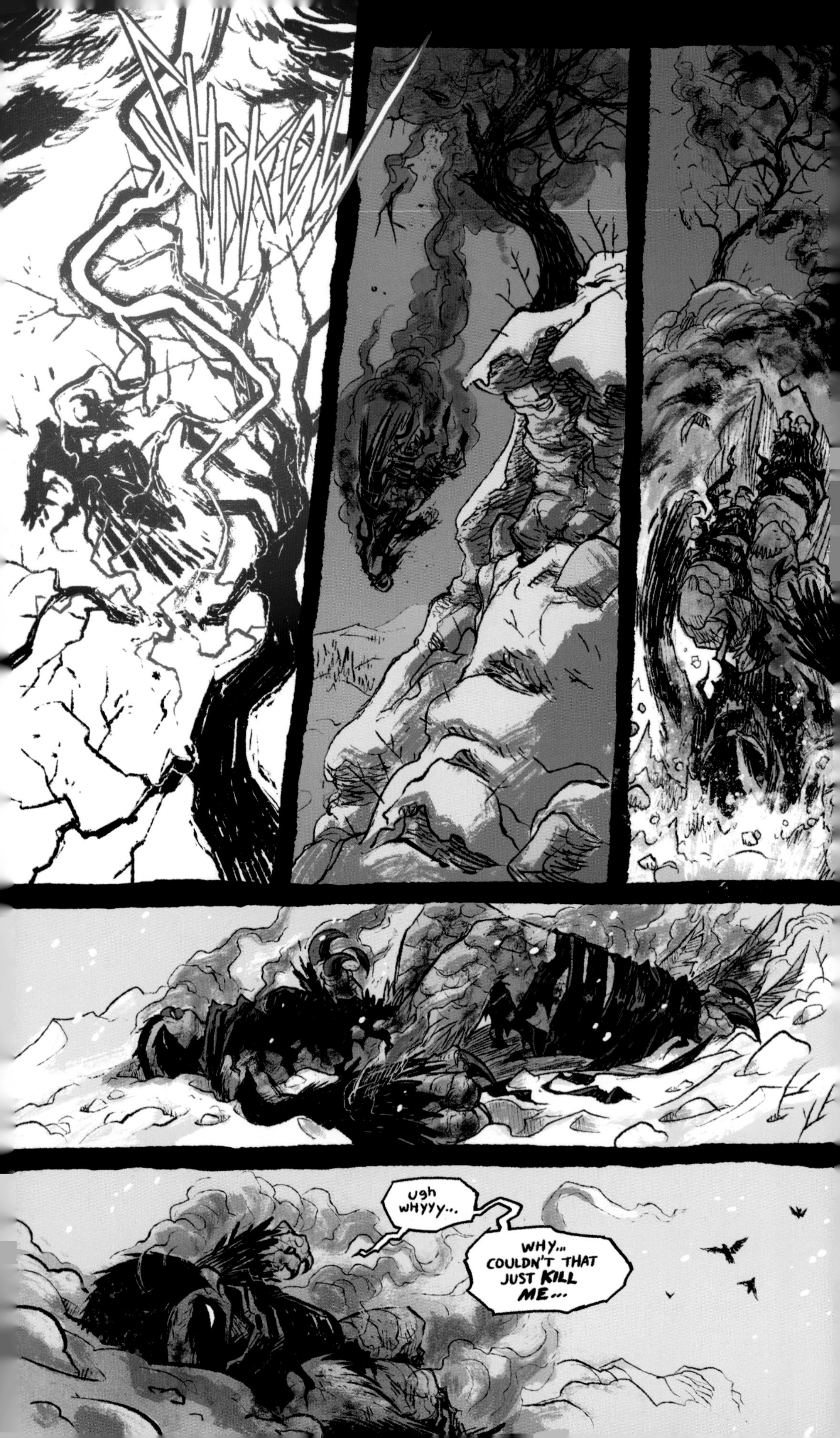

ugh WHYYY...
WHY... COULDN'T THAT JUST KILL ME...

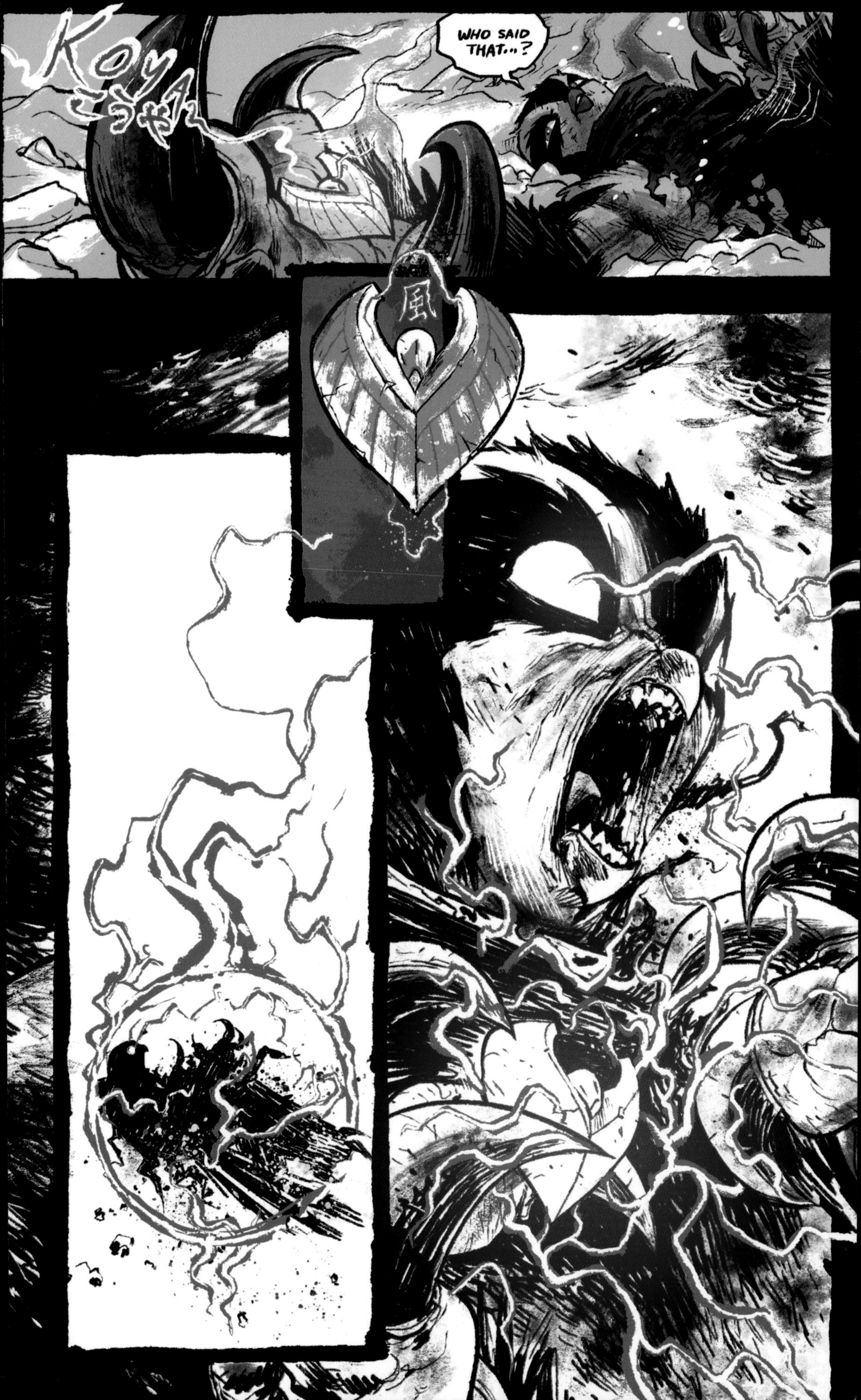
KOYA
こうや
WHO SAID THAT...?

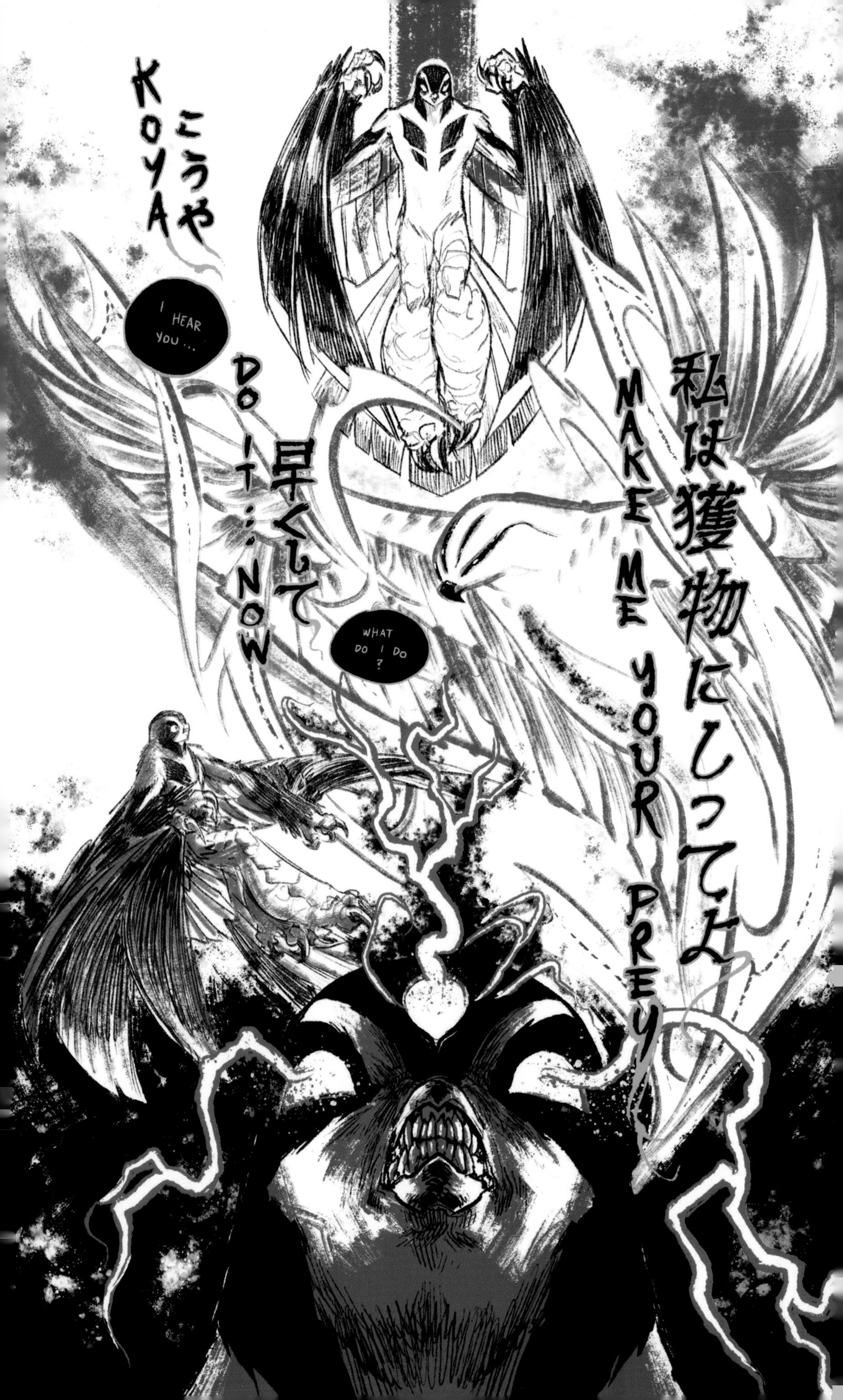

私は獲物にしってよ
MAKE ME YOUR PREY
WHAT DO I DO?
早くして
DO IT... NOW
I HEAR YOU...
こうや
KOYA

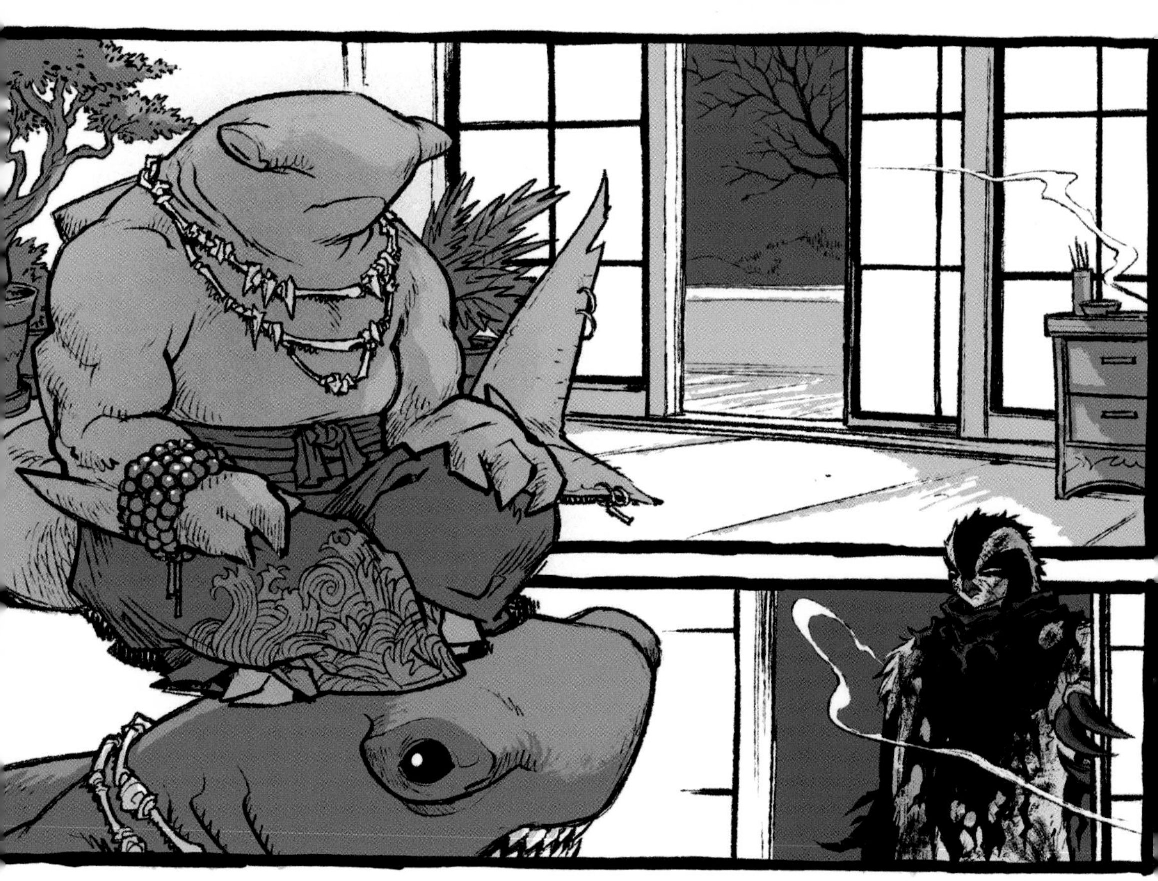

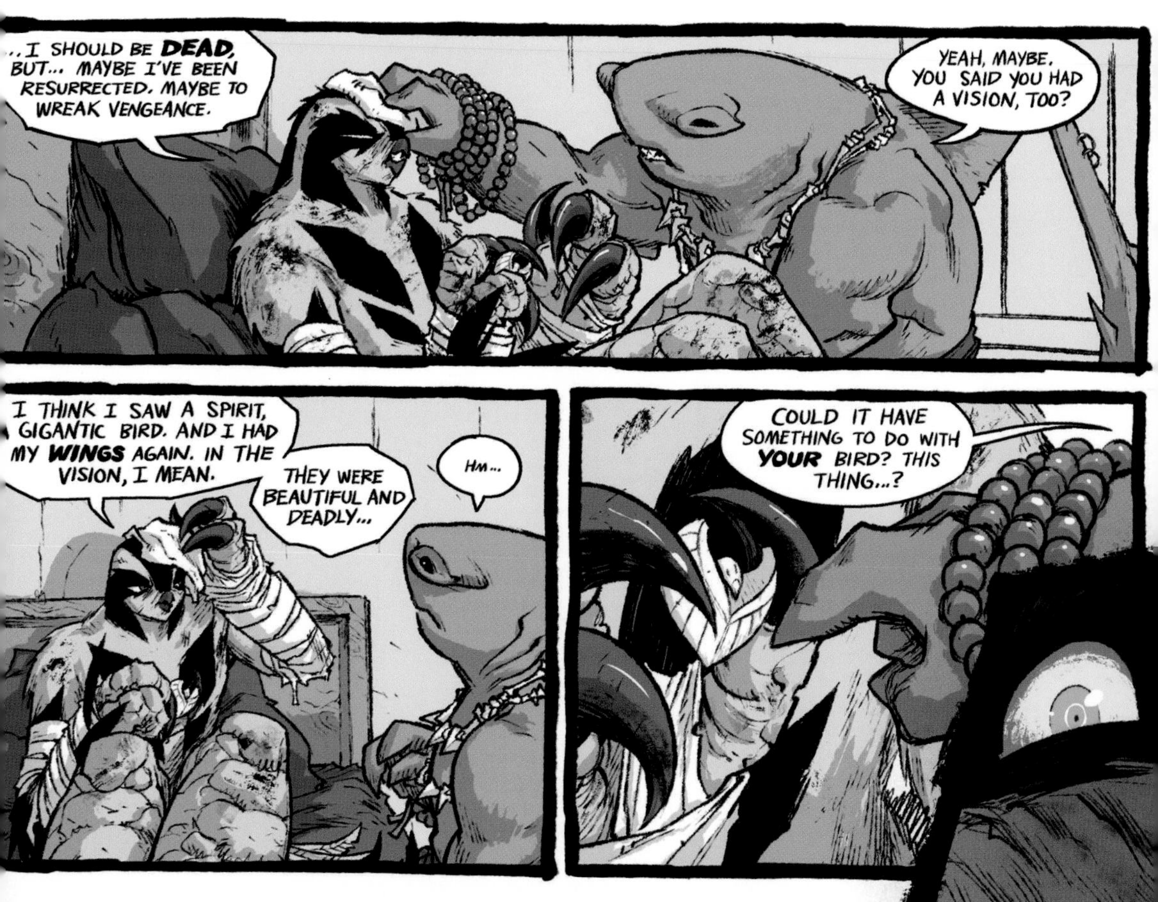
..I SHOULD BE DEAD, BUT... MAYBE I'VE BEEN RESURRECTED. MAYBE TO WREAK VENGEANCE.
YEAH, MAYBE. YOU SAID YOU HAD A VISION, TOO?
I THINK I SAW A SPIRIT, GIGANTIC BIRD. AND I HAD MY WINGS AGAIN. IN THE VISION, I MEAN.
THEY WERE BEAUTIFUL AND DEADLY...
HM...
COULD IT HAVE SOMETHING TO DO WITH YOUR BIRD? THIS THING...?

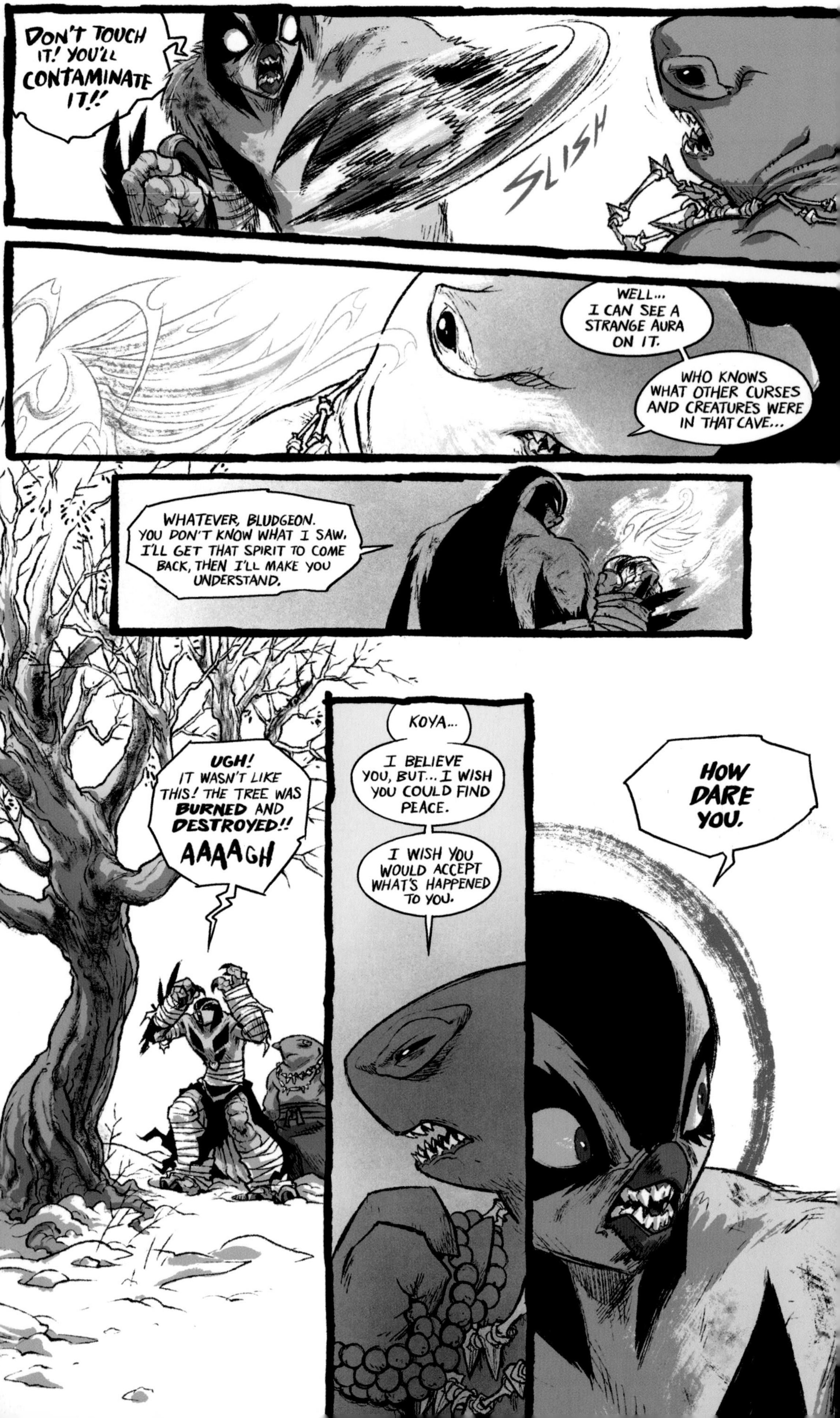

DON'T TOUCH IT! YOU'LL CONTAMINATE IT!!
SLISH
WELL... I CAN SEE A STRANGE AURA ON IT.
WHO KNOWS WHAT OTHER CURSES AND CREATURES WERE IN THAT CAVE...
WHATEVER, BLUDGEON. YOU DON'T KNOW WHAT I SAW. I'LL GET THAT SPIRIT TO COME BACK, THEN I'LL MAKE YOU UNDERSTAND.
UGH! IT WASN'T LIKE THIS! THE TREE WAS BURNED AND DESTROYED!! AAAAGH
KOYA...
I BELIEVE YOU, BUT... I WISH YOU COULD FIND PEACE.
I WISH YOU WOULD ACCEPT WHAT'S HAPPENED TO YOU.
HOW DARE YOU.

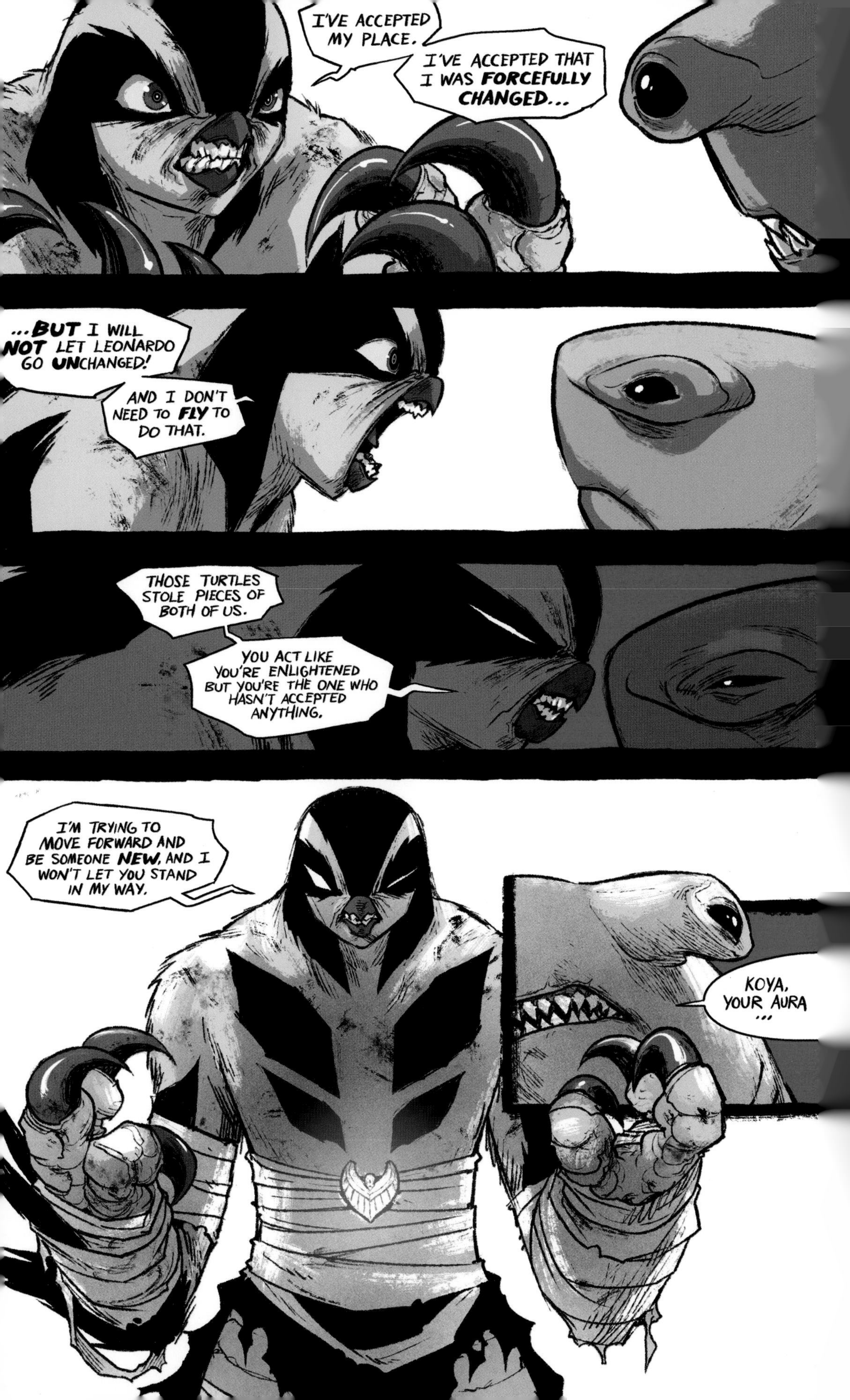
I'VE ACCEPTED MY PLACE.
I'VE ACCEPTED THAT I WAS FORCEFULLY CHANGED...
...BUT I WILL NOT LET LEONARDO GO UNCHANGED!
AND I DON'T NEED TO FLY TO DO THAT.
THOSE TURTLES STOLE PIECES OF BOTH OF US.
YOU ACT LIKE YOU'RE ENLIGHTENED BUT YOU'RE THE ONE WHO HASN'T ACCEPTED ANYTHING.
I'M TRYING TO MOVE FORWARD AND BE SOMEONE NEW, AND I WON'T LET YOU STAND IN MY WAY.
KOYA, YOUR AURA ...

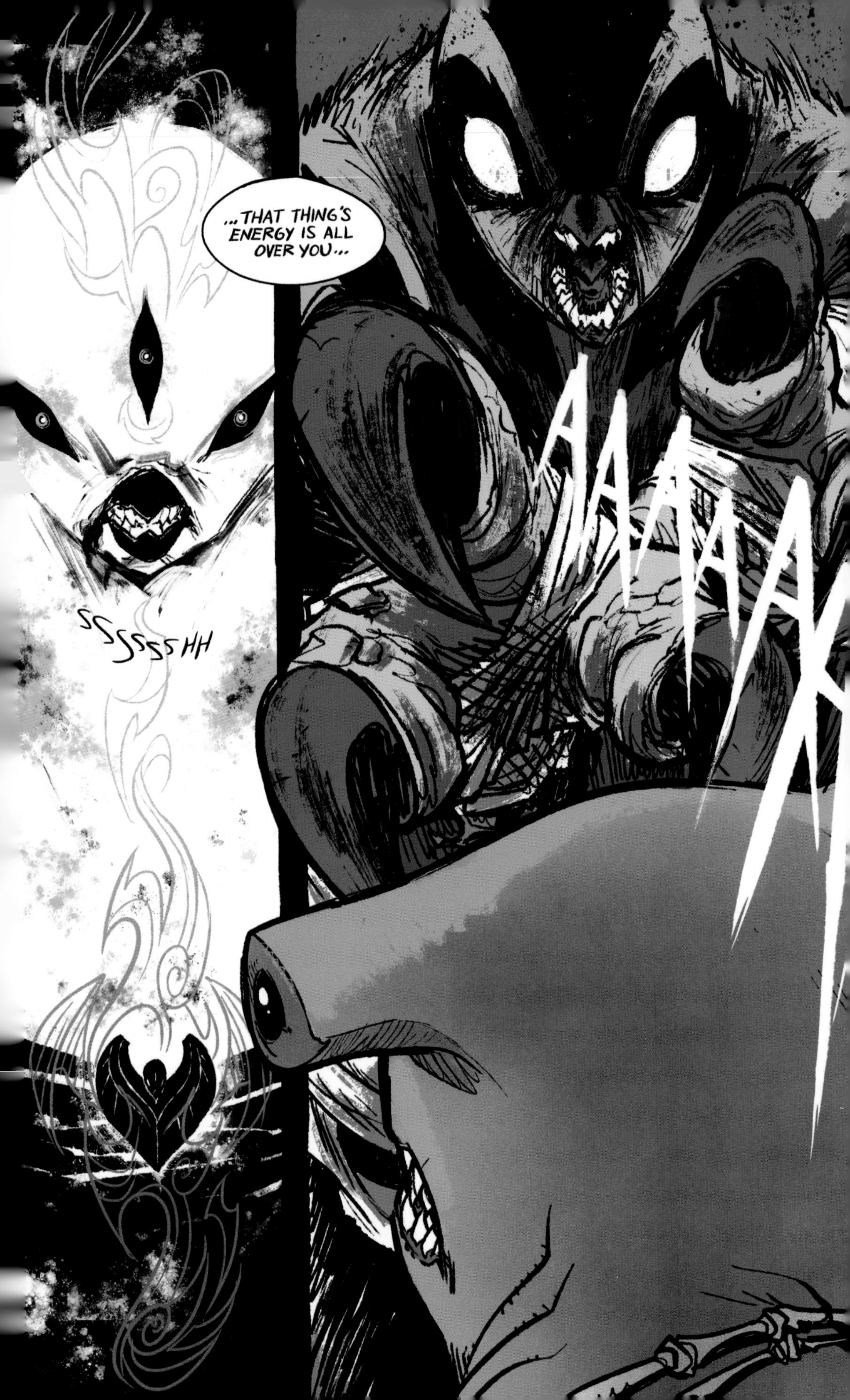
...THAT THING'S ENERGY IS ALL OVER YOU...
SSSSSSHH
AAAAAA

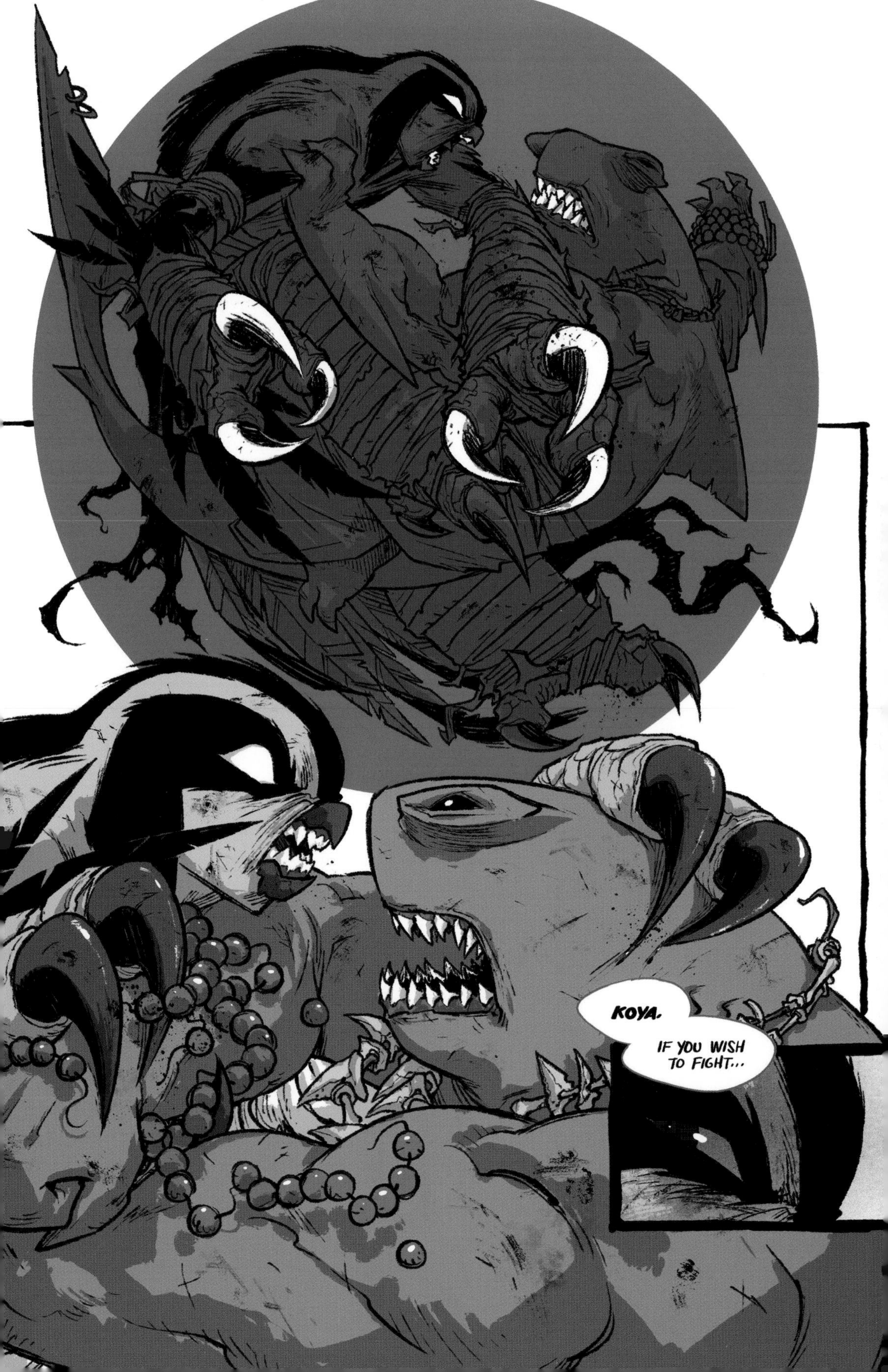
KOYA.
IF YOU WISH TO FIGHT...

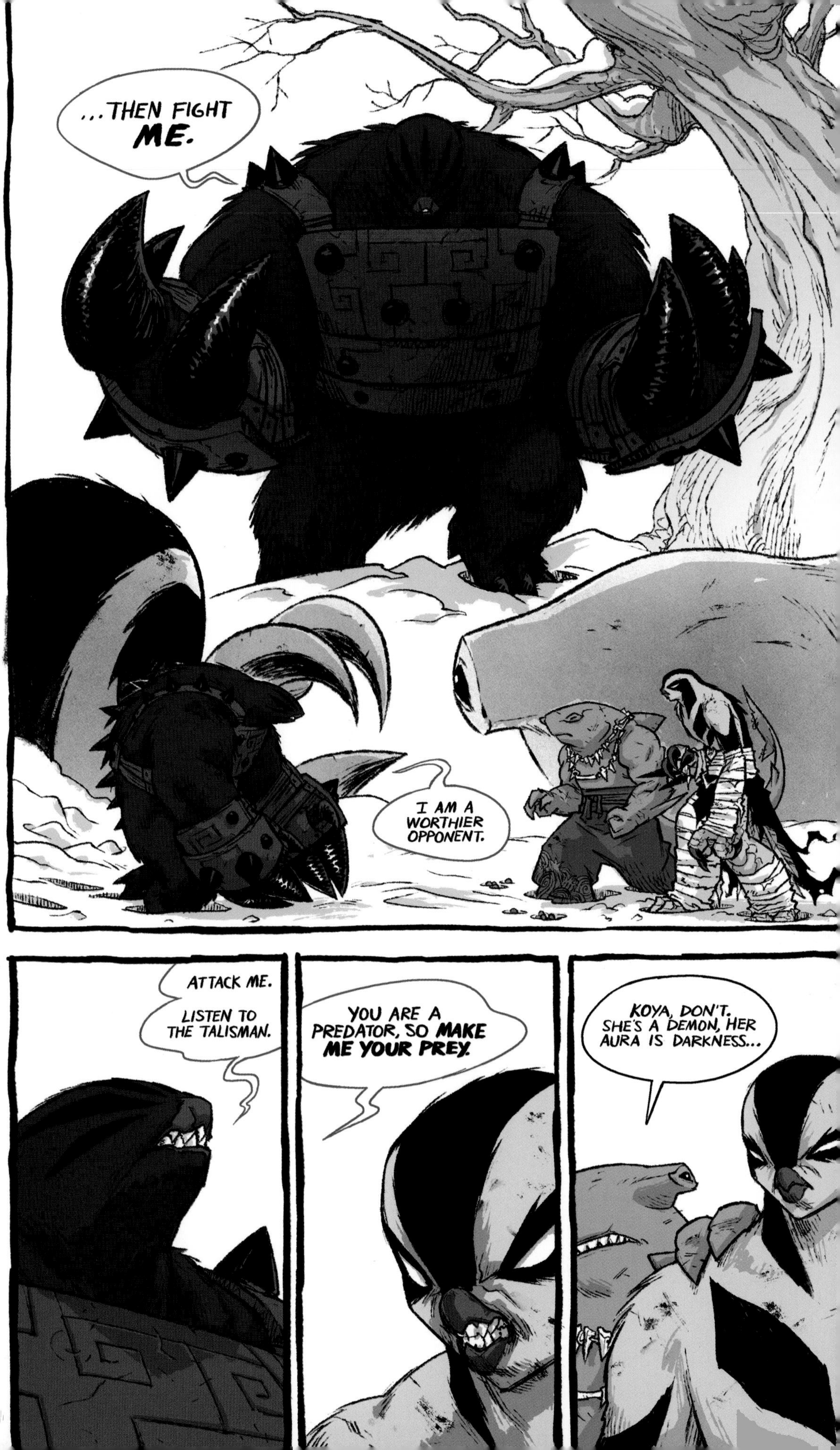
...THEN FIGHT ME.
I AM A WORTHIER OPPONENT.
ATTACK ME.
LISTEN TO THE TALISMAN.
YOU ARE A PREDATOR, SO MAKE ME YOUR PREY.
KOYA, DON'T. SHE'S A DEMON, HER AURA IS DARKNESS...

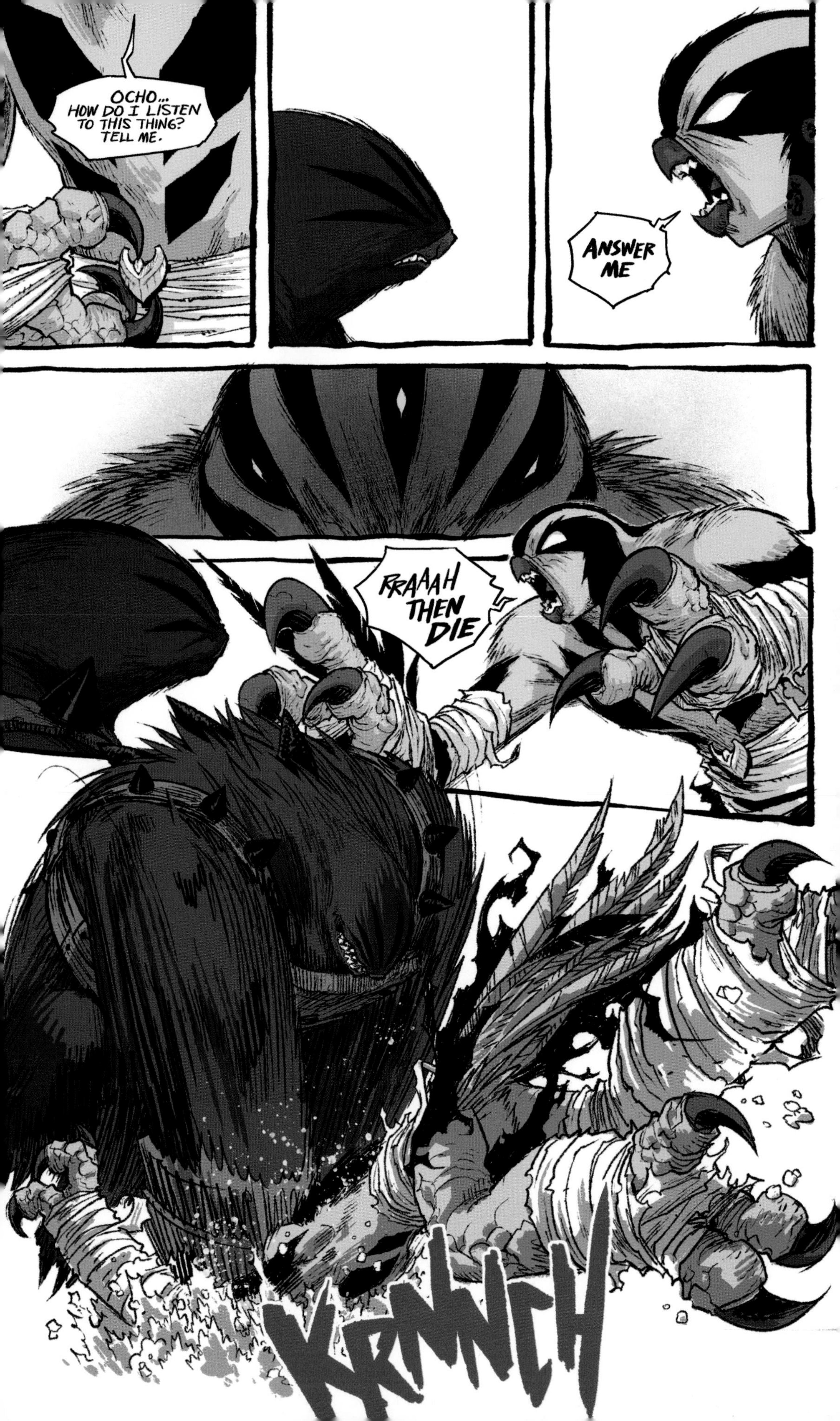
OCHO... HOW DO I LISTEN TO THIS THING? TELL ME.
ANSWER ME
RRAAAH THEN DIE
KRNNCH

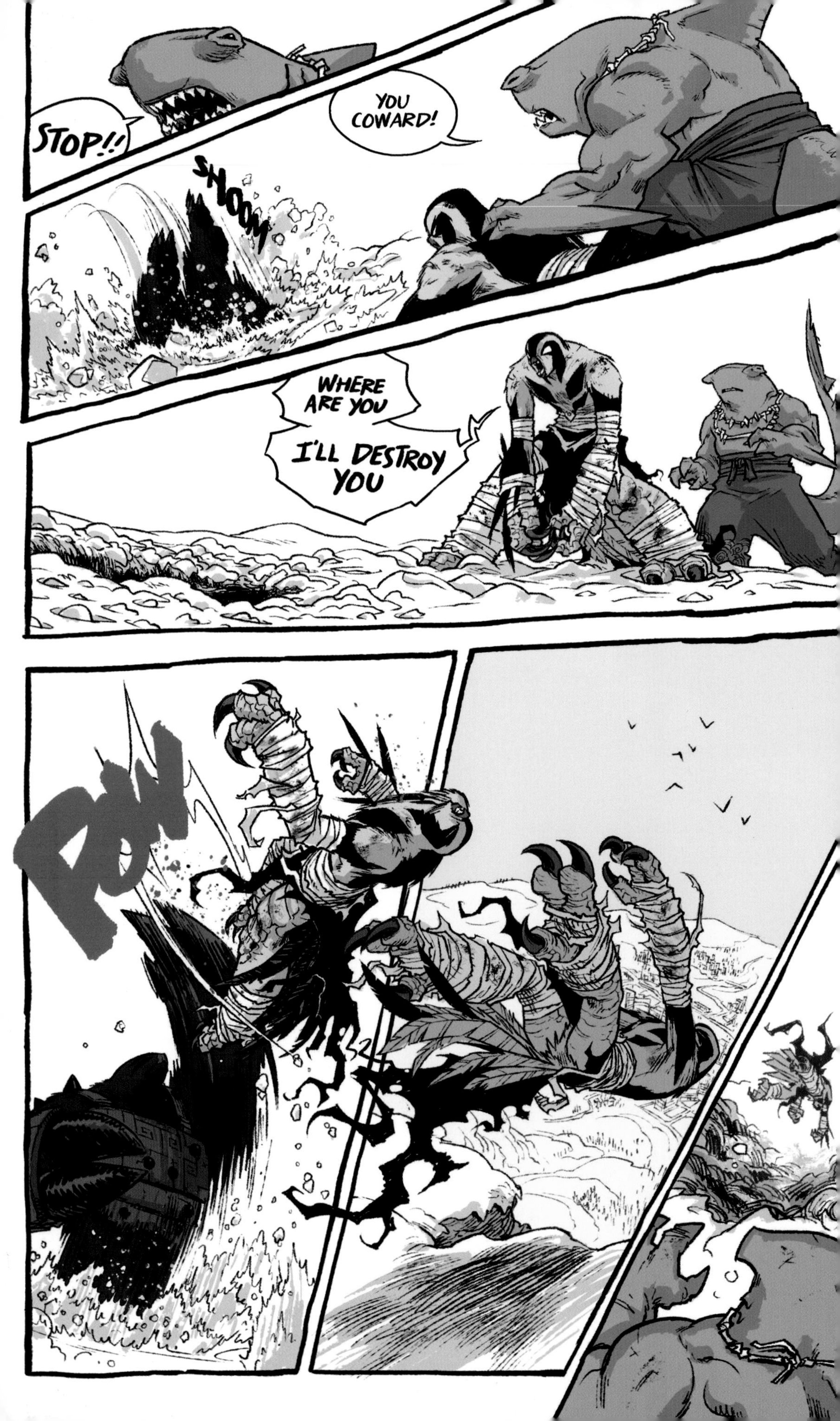
STOP!!
YOU COWARD!
SHOOM
WHERE ARE YOU
I'LL DESTROY YOU
POW

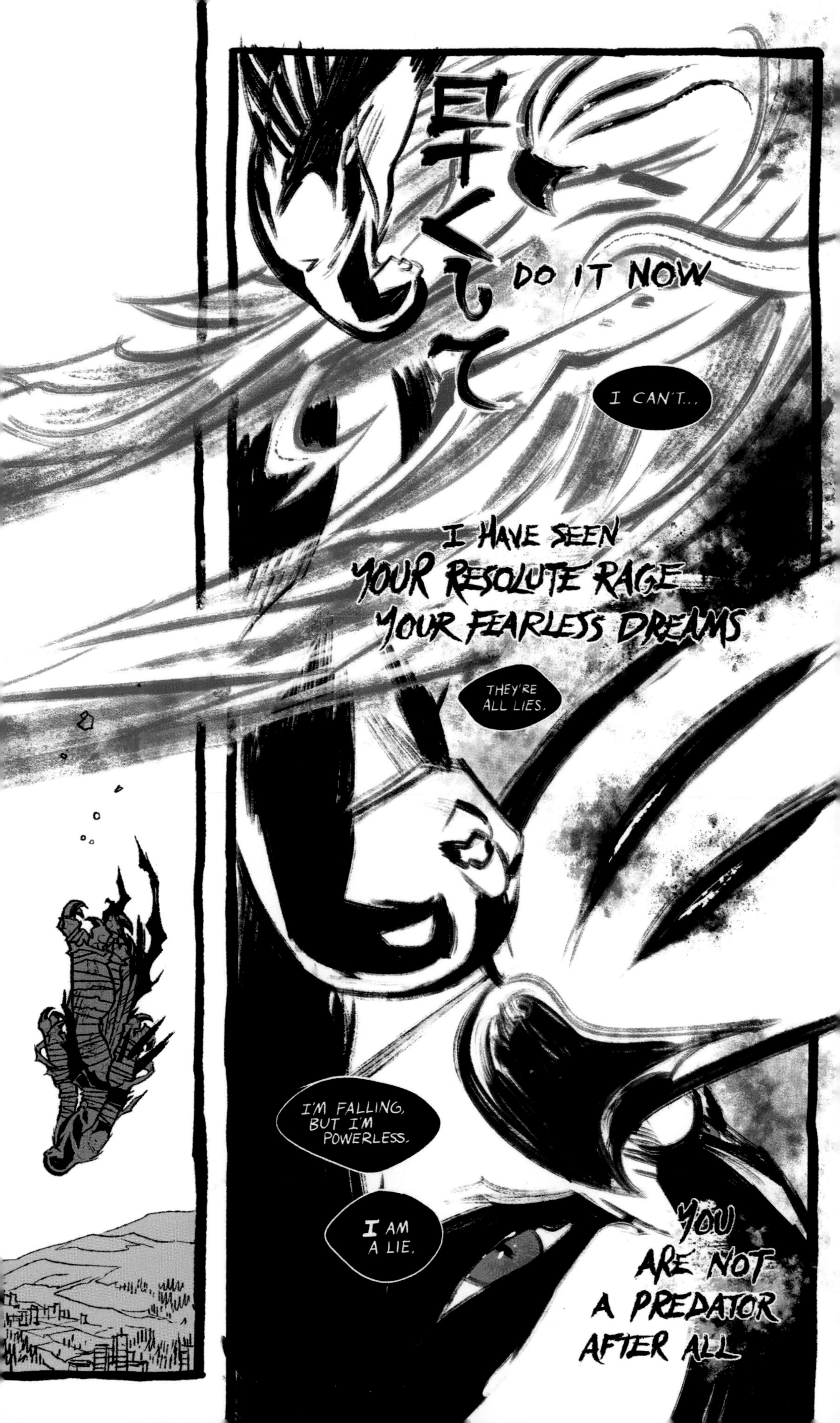

早くして
DO IT NOW
I CAN'T...
I HAVE SEEN
YOUR RESOLUTE RAGE
YOUR FEARLESS DREAMS
THEY'RE ALL LIES.
I'M FALLING, BUT I'M POWERLESS.
I AM A LIE.
YOU ARE NOT A PREDATOR AFTER ALL

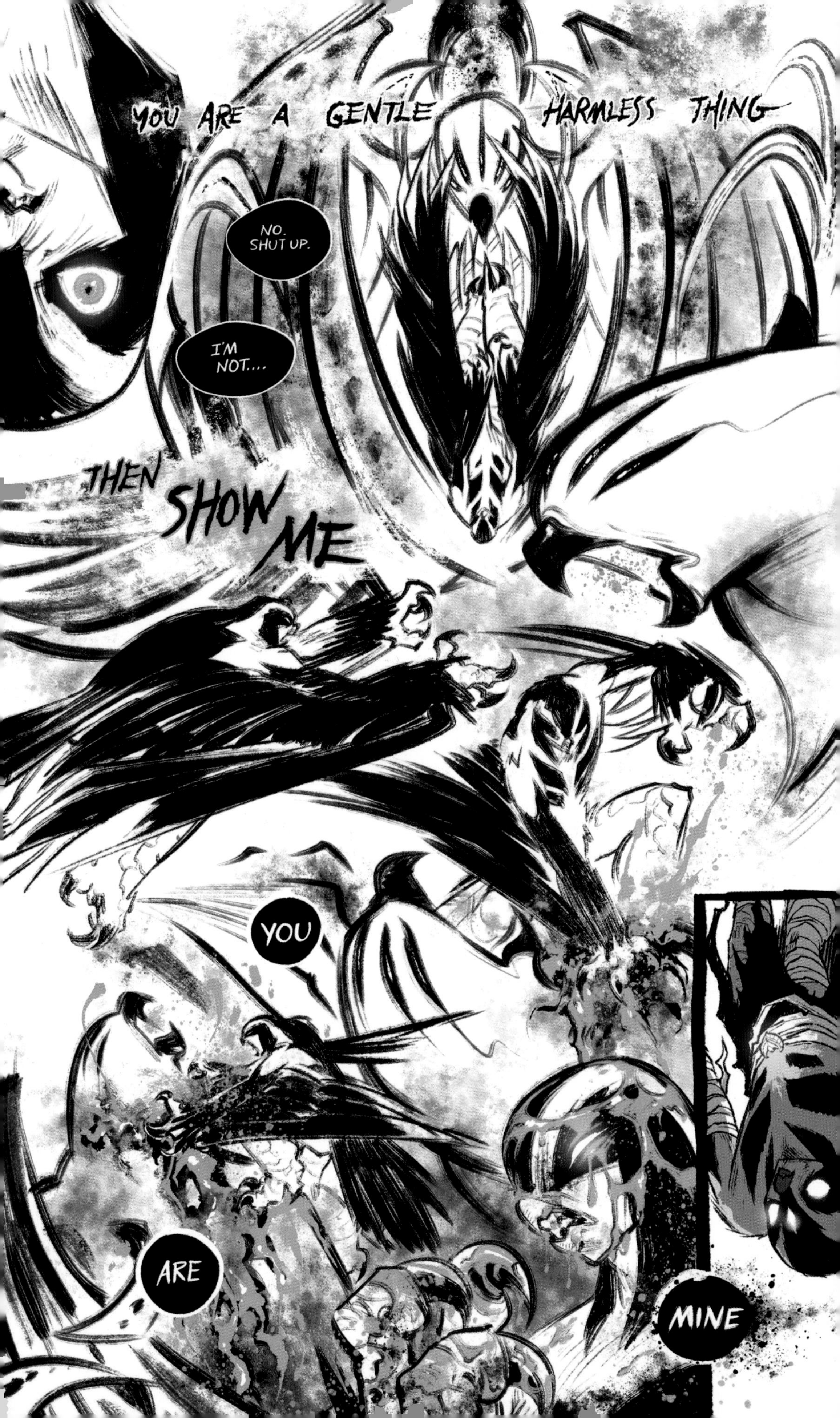
YOU ARE A GENTLE HARMLESS THING
NO. SHUT UP.
I'M NOT....
THEN SHOW ME
YOU
ARE
MINE

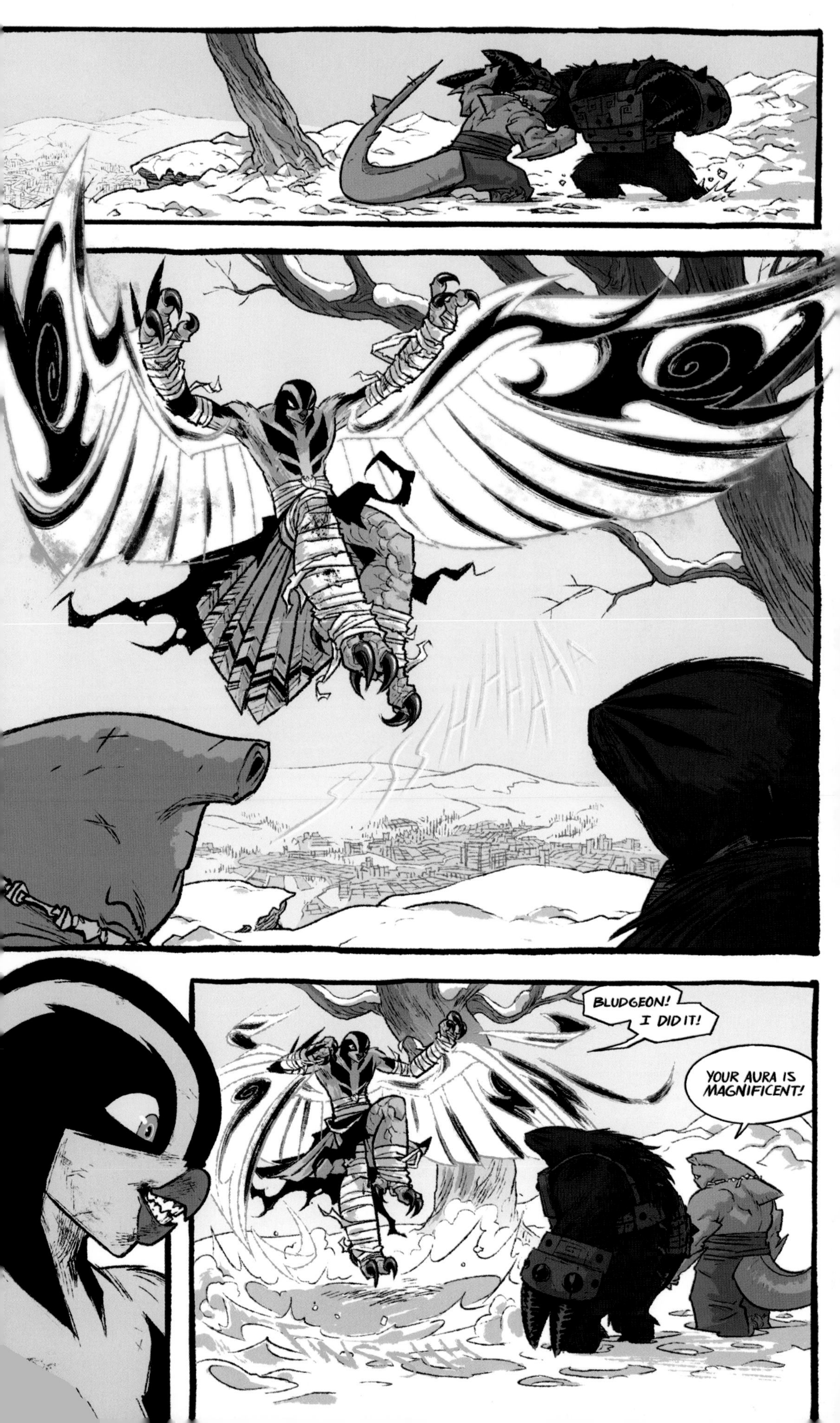
BLUDGEON! I DID IT!
YOUR AURA IS MAGNIFICENT!

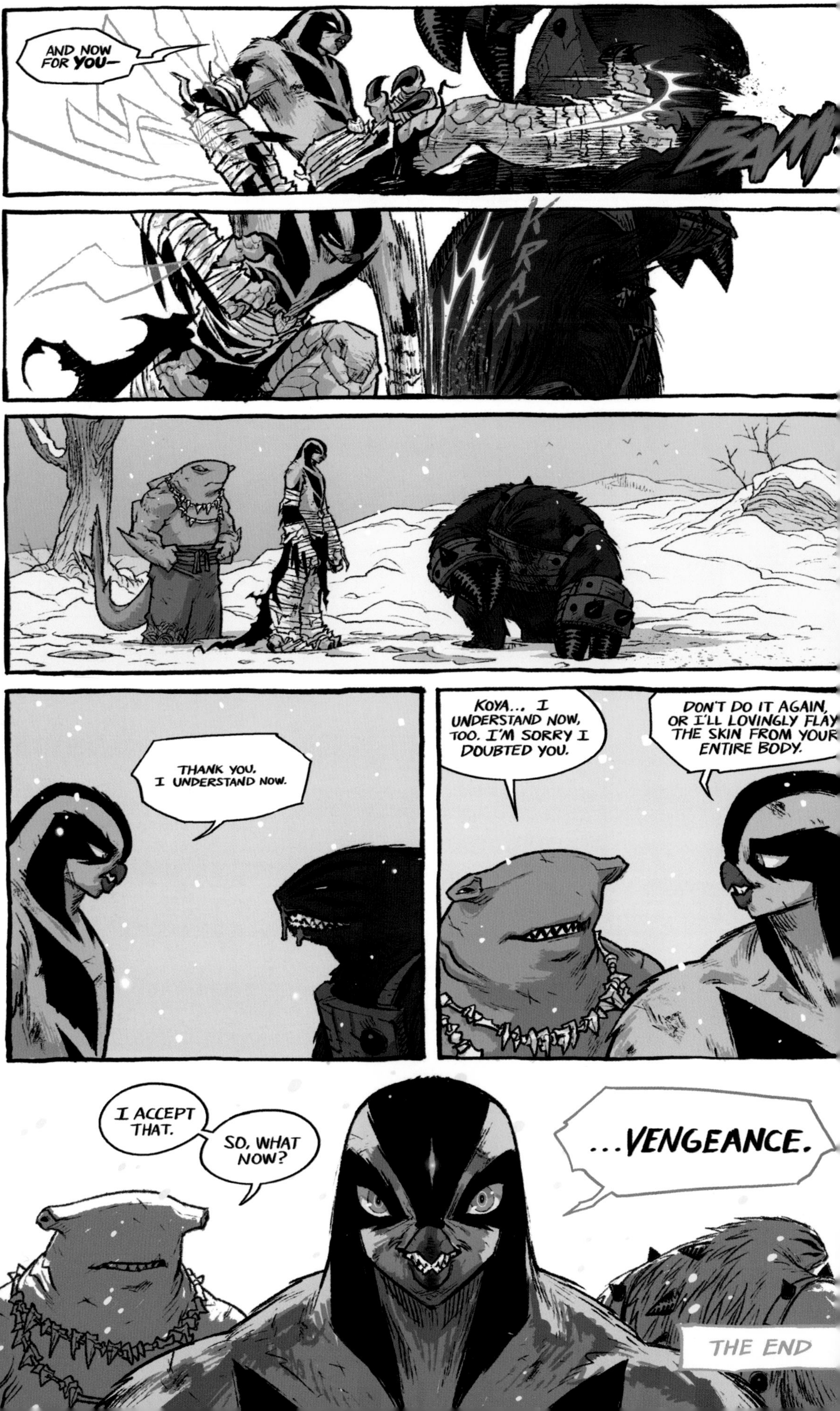
AND NOW FOR YOU—
BAMM
KRAK
THANK YOU, I UNDERSTAND NOW.
KOYA... I UNDERSTAND NOW, TOO. I'M SORRY I DOUBTED YOU.
DON'T DO IT AGAIN, OR I'LL LOVINGLY FLAY THE SKIN FROM YOUR ENTIRE BODY.
I ACCEPT THAT.
SO, WHAT NOW?
...VENGEANCE.
THE END

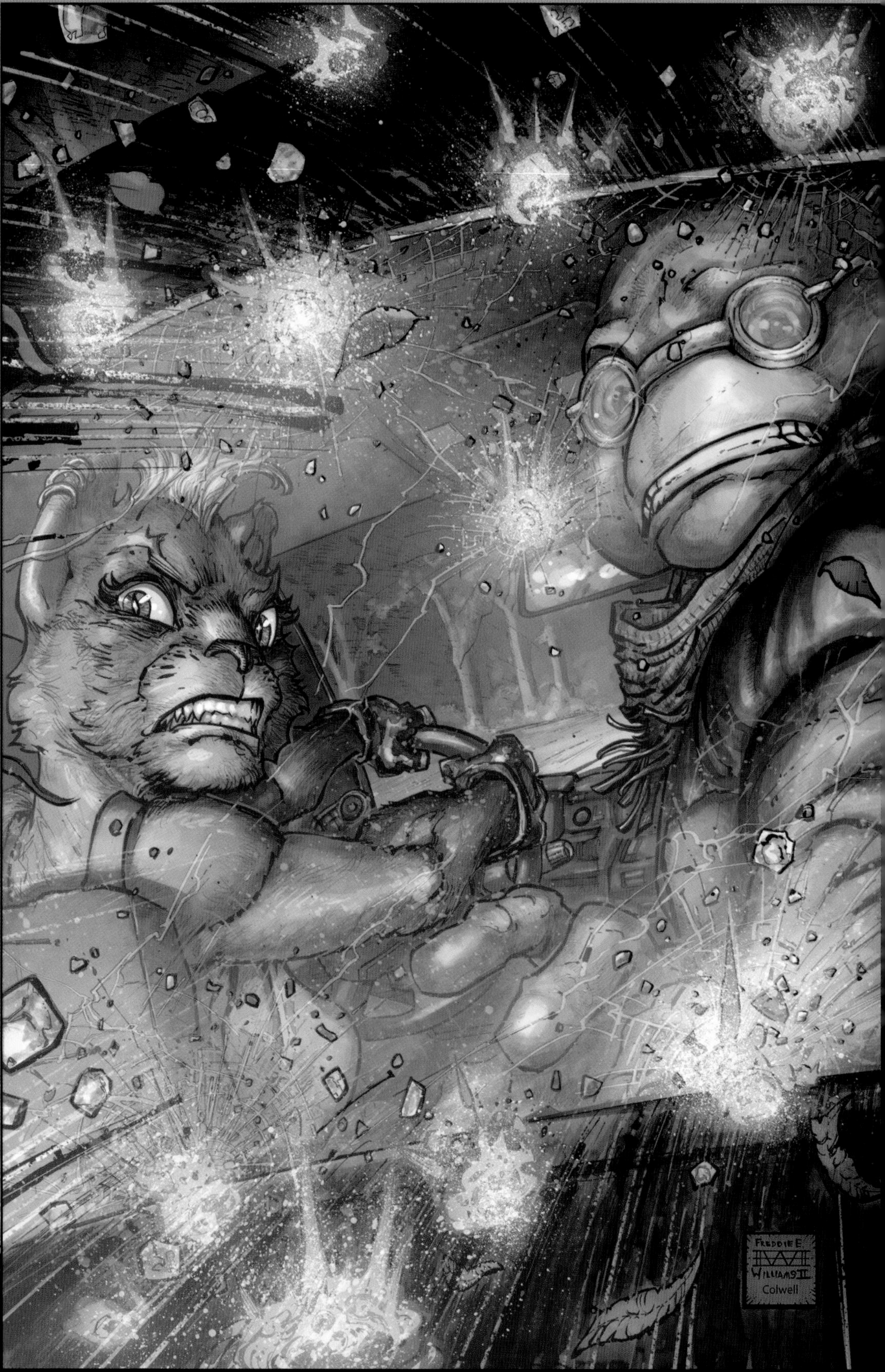
FREDDIE E.
WILLIAMS II
Colwell

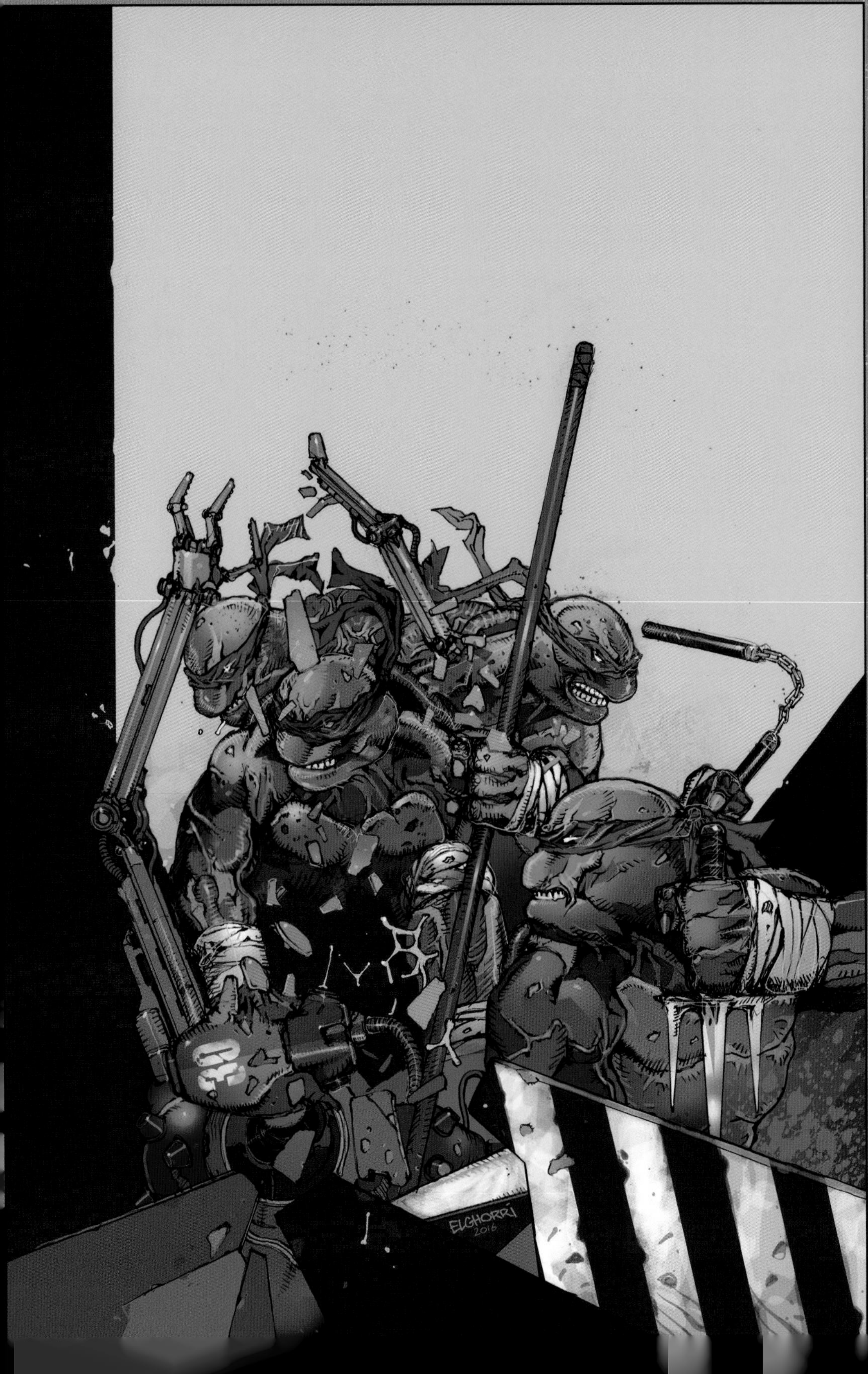
30
ELGHORRI
2016

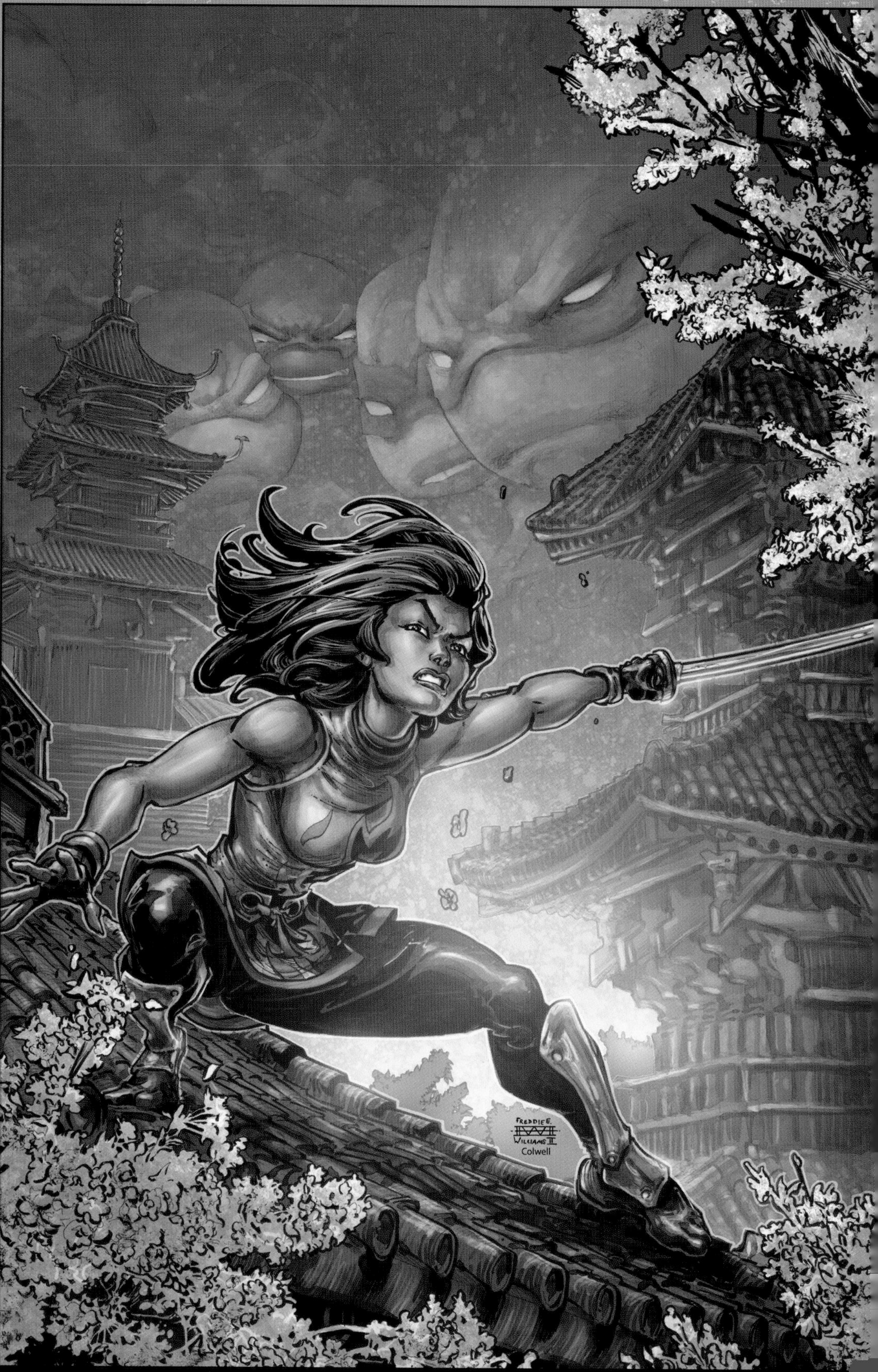
FREDDIE E WILLIAMS II
Colwell

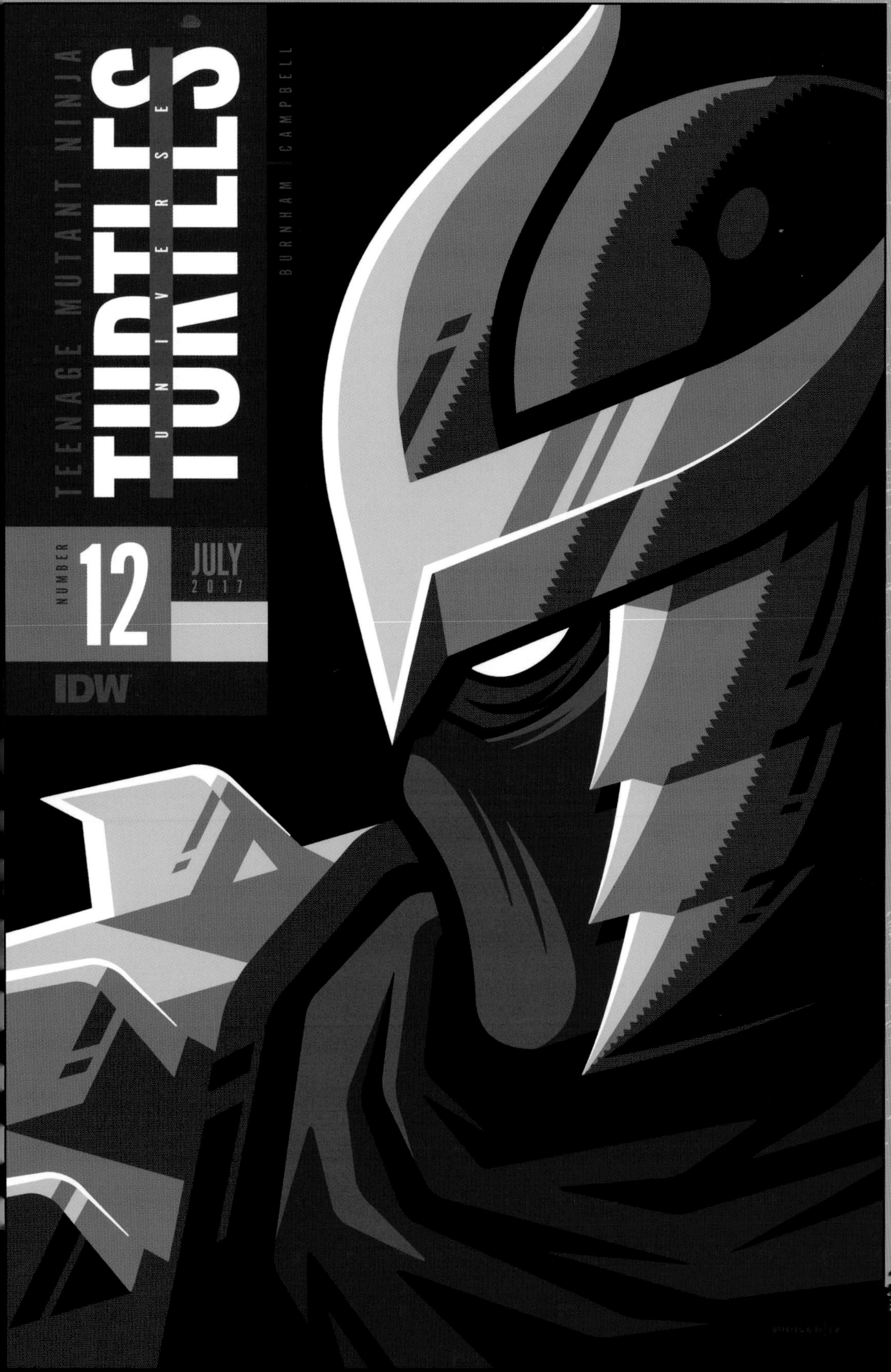
TEENAGE MUTANT NINJA
TURTLES
UNIVERSE
BURNHAM | CAMPBELL
NUMBER 12
JULY 2017
IDW

ART BY **TOM WHALEN**

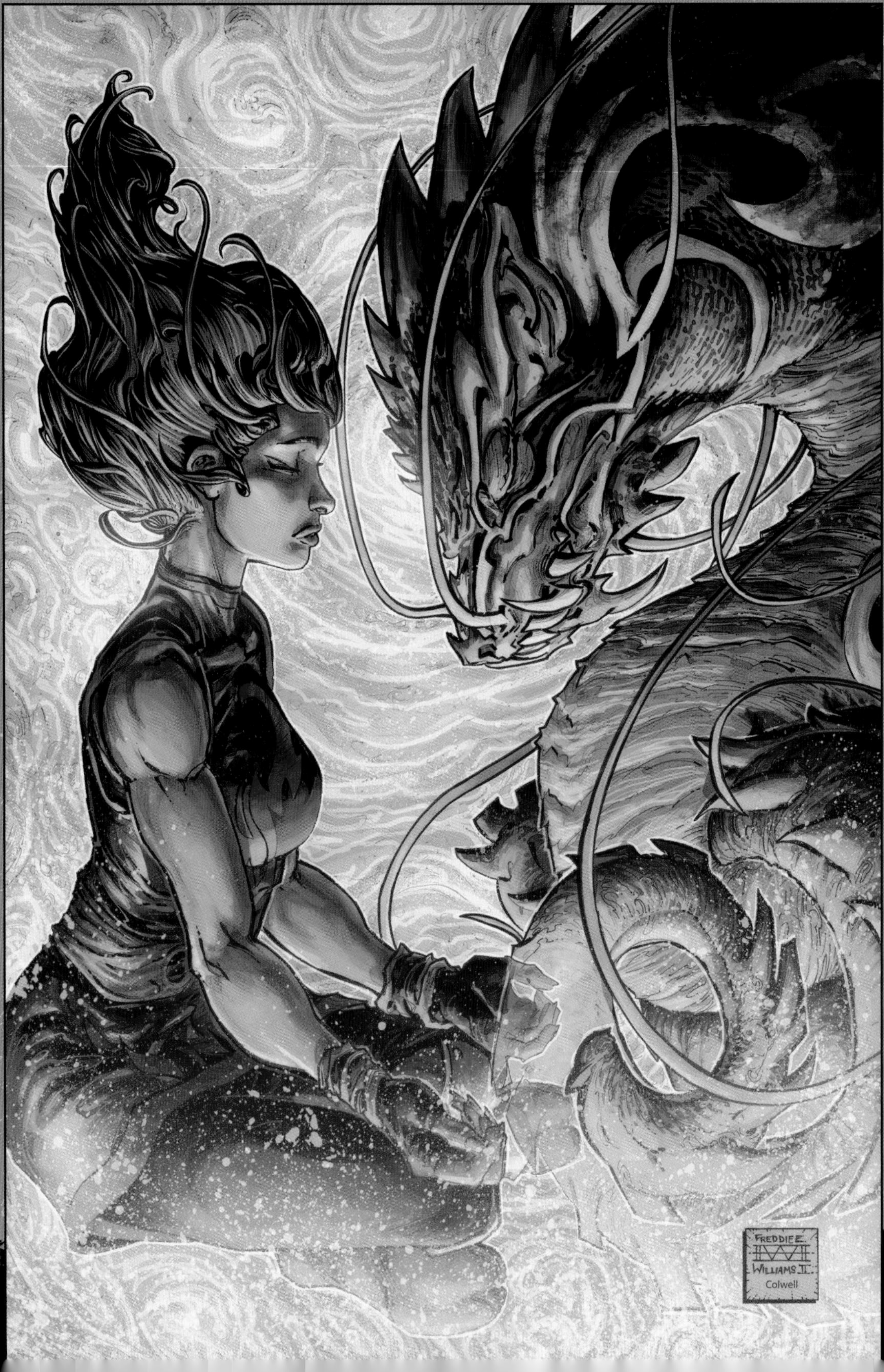
FREDDIE E.
WILLIAMS II
Colwell

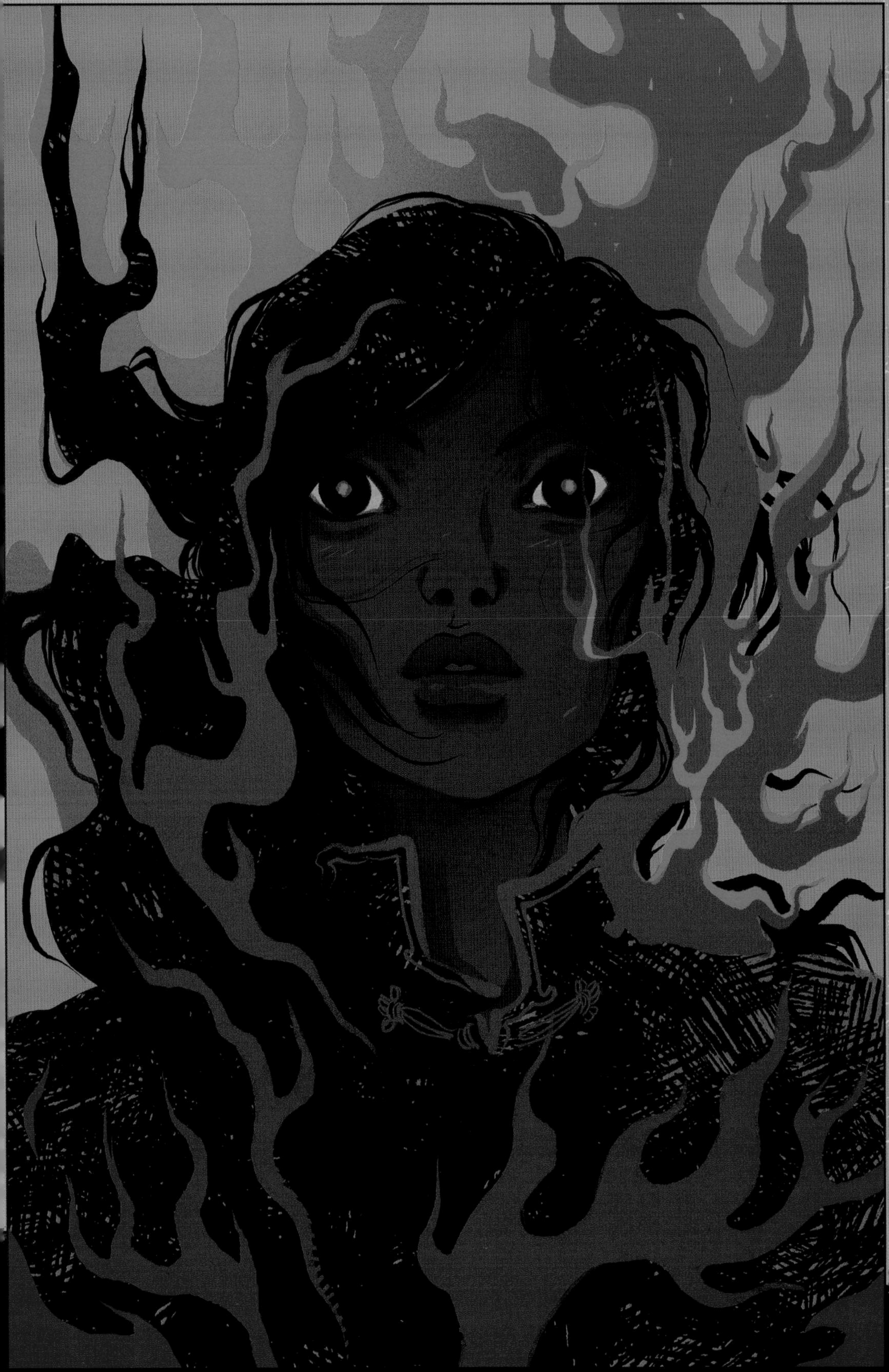

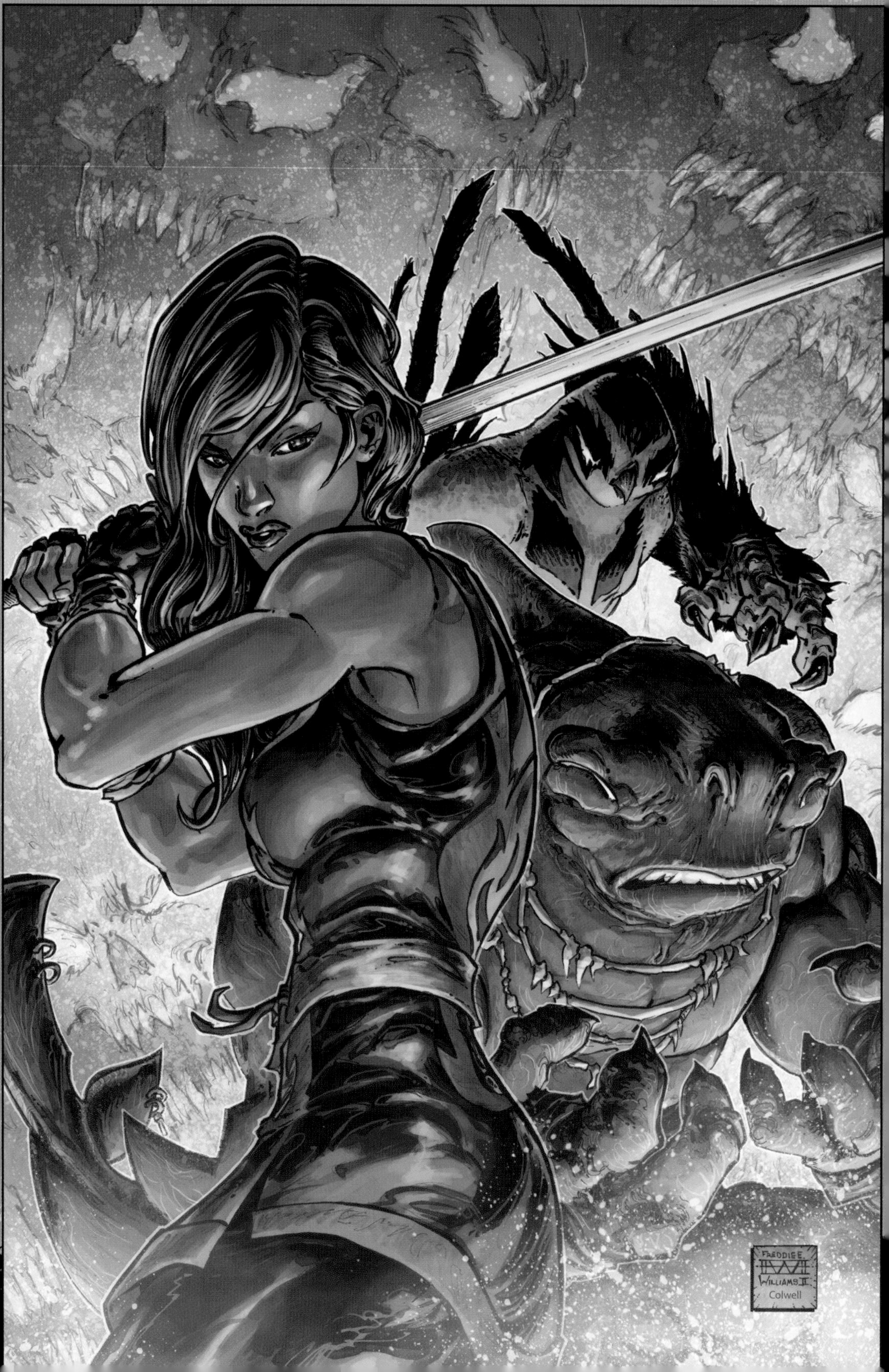
FREDDIE E.
WILLIAMS II
Colwell

ART BY **ERNIE CAMPBELL**

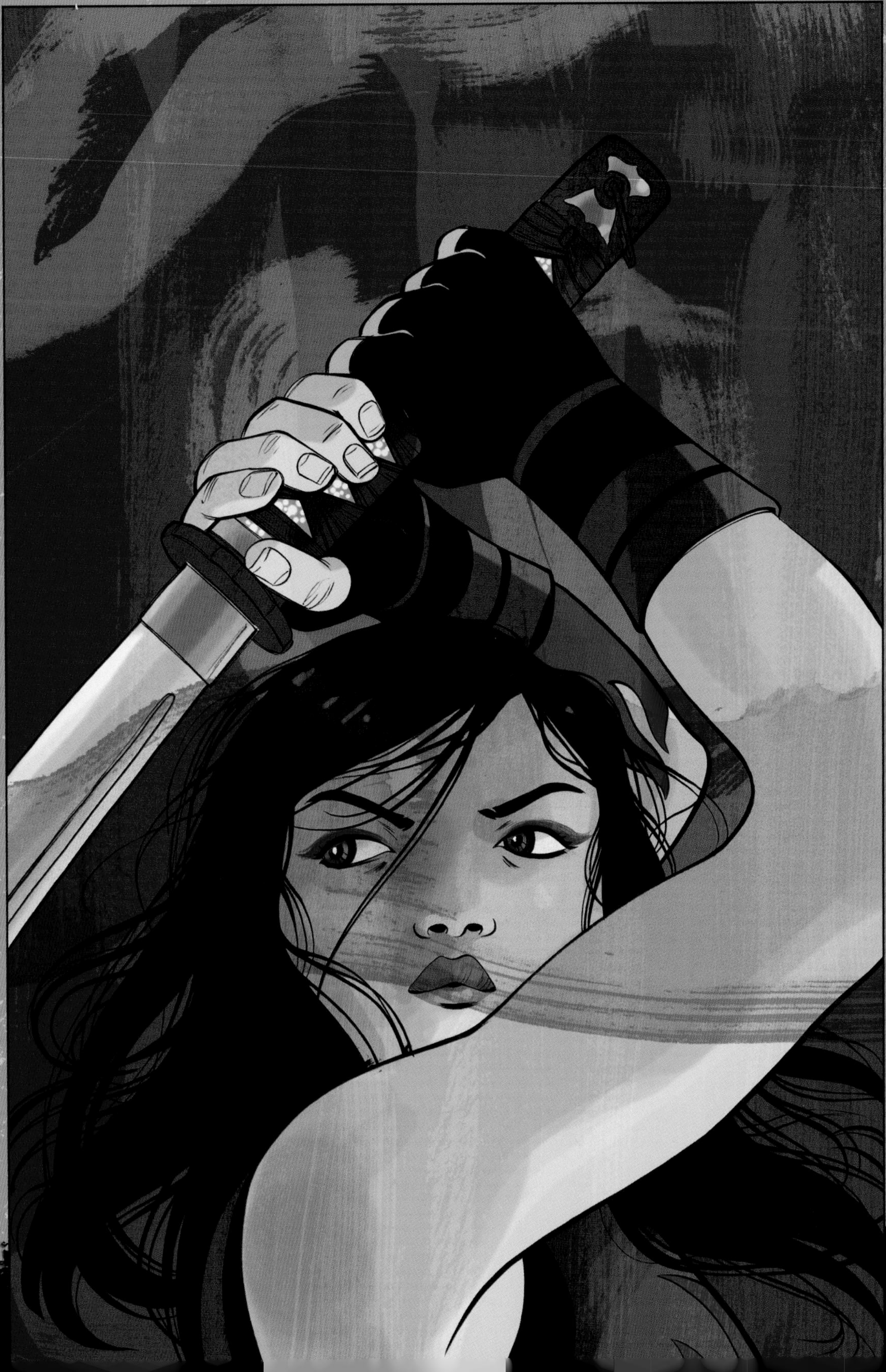

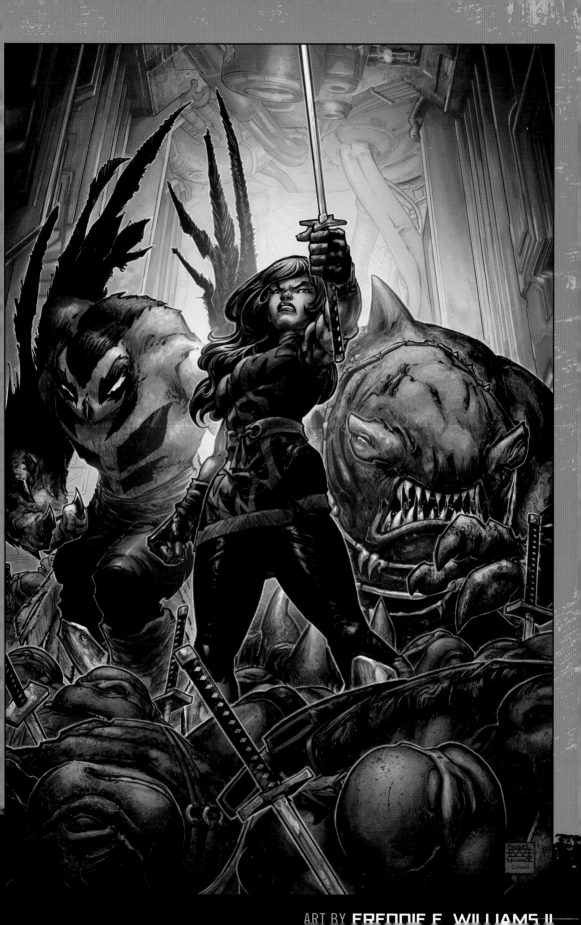

ART BY FREDDIE E. WILLIAMS II

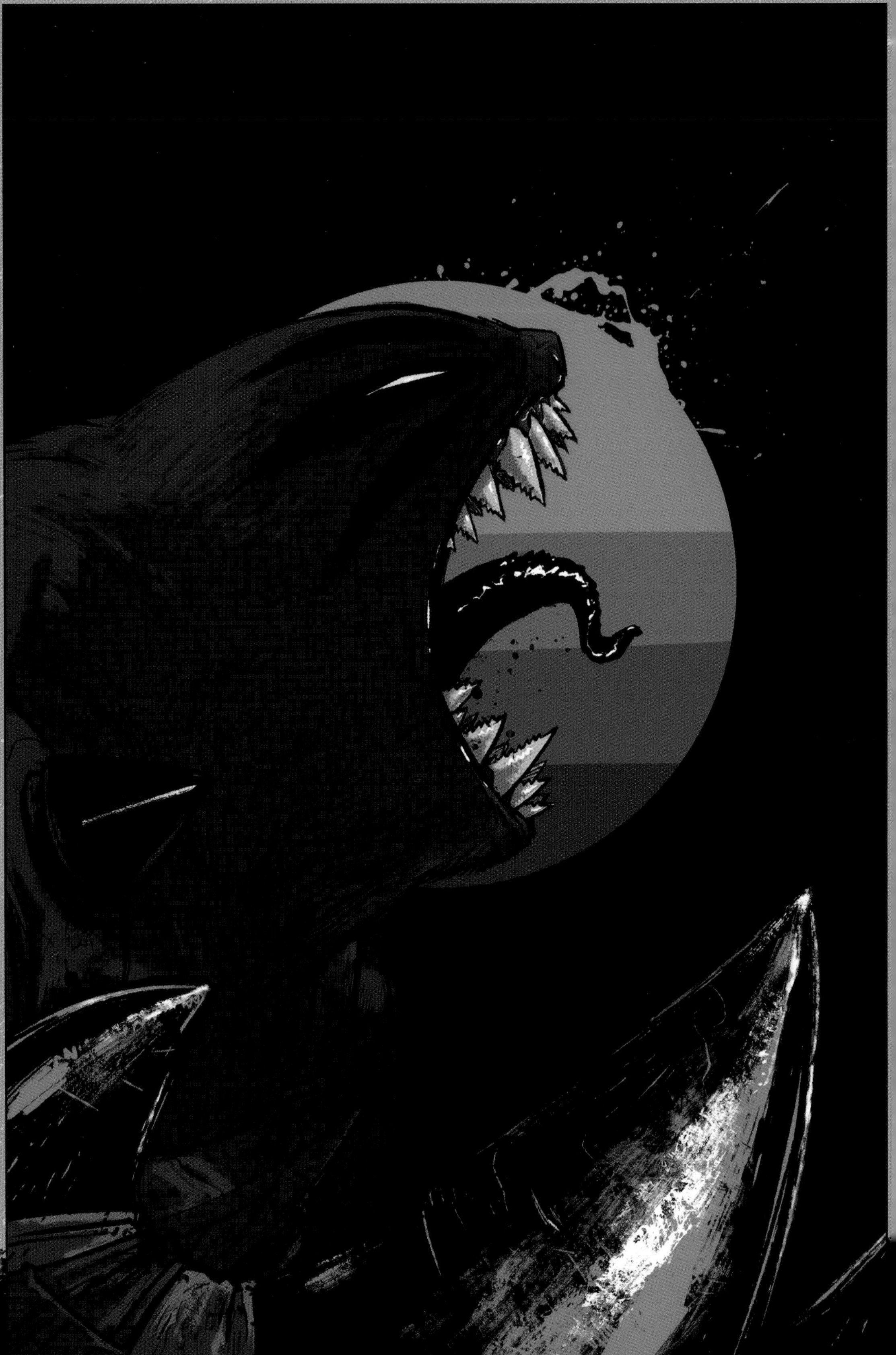